# SINNERS IN THE HANDS
# OF AN ANGRY GOD
## AND OTHER PURITAN SERMONS

# SINNERS IN THE HANDS OF AN ANGRY GOD
## AND OTHER PURITAN SERMONS

DOVER THRIFT EDITIONS

## Jonathan Edwards
### and Others

DOVER PUBLICATIONS, INC.
MINEOLA, NEW YORK

# DOVER THRIFT EDITIONS

GENERAL EDITOR: MARY CAROLYN WALDREP
EDITOR OF THIS VOLUME: DAVID DUTKANICZ

*Bibliographical Note*

This Dover edition, first published in 2005, is an original collection of sermons gathered from standard texts.

*International Standard Book Number*

*ISBN-13: 978-0-486-44601-1*
*ISBN-10: 0-486-44601-8*

Manufactured in the United States by LSC Communications
44601808     2020
www.doverpublications.com

# Contents

iii

# Publisher's Note

The God that holds you over the pit of Hell, much as one holds a spider, or some loathsome insect over the fire, abhors you, and is dreadfully provoked . . .*

Delivered in a stunning and severe monotone, this sermon brought Edwards' congregation to tears and convulsions. It's since come to be known as one of the first and finest expressions of American Puritan thought and a testament to the intense religious revivals of the Great Awakening. Painting an image of sinful mankind against a canvas of a vengeful God, Edwards and other preachers of New England rained down fire and brimstone sermons on their congregations. Some of the finest have been selected for the collection presented here. Looking beyond the severe imagery, the reader can find examples of classical rhetoric and argumentative structures used up to the present day. These sermons also chronicle early American life, as they evolve from the idealistic notions of a religious community sailing towards a New Jerusalem, to the neo-Inquisition of the witch trials, and ending with calls to a new pragmatism and unity as the Revolution approached. They are windows into the minds of the founding fathers that can shed light onto their forgotten humanity and American society as a whole.

---

*From Jonathan Edwards' *Sinners in the Hands of an Angry God* (p. 178)

# Biographies

**Peter Bulkeley,** the son of Rev. Edward Bulkeley, was born in Odell, Bedfordshire, on January 31, 1583 and educated at Cambridge University. Bulkeley succeeded his father as rector of the Church of All Saints in 1610. Adopting Puritan beliefs, he opposed the religious policies of the Archbishop of Canterbury, William Laud, and in 1634 was suspended from duty. The following year he emigrated to the United States on the *Susan & Ellin* and settled in the Boston area. In 1635 Bulkeley purchased land at Musketaquid, which eventually became the Concord settlement. He died there on March 9, 1659 and contributed a large part of his own valuable collection to establish the library of Harvard College.

**John Cotton** was born in Derby, England in 1584. After being educated at Trinity College in Cambridge, he became vicar of St. Botolph's Church in Boston, Lincolnshire [England] in 1612. Over the next 21 years Cotton became increasingly critical of the Anglican Church and adopted Puritan views. When legal action was taken against Cotton in 1632 he decided to escape to North America and settled in the Massachusetts Colony where he became pastor of the First Church of Boston. Cotton died in the colony on December 23, 1652.

**Thomas Hooker** was born in Leicester, England, in 1586. He became a fellow of Emmanuel College, Cambridge and for three years was a Puritan lecturer in Chelmsford. After living in Holland for three years, he emigrated to America in 1633, settled in Massachusetts Bay and became a minister in Newtown (Cambridge). In 1636 he moved with his congregation to Connecticut, where he founded the town of Hartford. Thomas Hooker died there in 1647.

**John Winthrop** was born in Groton, Suffolk, England in 1588. Educated at Cambridge University, he practiced law in London but was persecuted for his Puritan religious views. Winthrop was adamant in removing the last vestiges of Roman Catholicism (such as vestments, hierarchs, altars and kneeling) from the Church of England. He also wanted sinners to be more severely punished by law for such trespasses as adultery and breaching the Sabbath. Eventually Winthrop was granted a charter for the Massachusetts Bay Colony and arrived with 700 settlers in 1630. He served as governor of Massachusetts for 12 terms and became the first president of the Confederation of New England in 1645. His monumental *History of New England* was published posthumously after his death in 1649.

Known as the "soul-melting preacher of New England," **Thomas Shepard** was born on November 5, 1605 in Towcester, England. His college years were marred by what he described as "loose company" and it was after an intense drinking binge that he experienced his conversion, henceforth devoting his life to studying and meditating upon scripture. By 1630 he was a practising minister; however, for his Puritanical views he was forbidden by Archbishop Laud to preach or maintain any priestly office. After his first attempt failed, Shepard arrived in New England in 1635. The following year Shepard's church was formed in Cambridge (then New Town). In 1637 he married Joanna Hooker, daughter of the renowned preacher, Thomas Hooker, and was to marry once more before his death in 1649.

**Increase Mather** was born in Dorchester, Suffolk County, Massachusetts on June 21, 1639. The youngest son of the Rev. Richard Mather and Catherine Hoult, Increase entered Harvard University in 1651, and graduated in 1656. In 1657 he enrolled at Trinity College in Dublin, Ireland and graduated the following year with an MA. He became chaplain to the English garrison at Guernsey from April through to December of 1659 and then again in 1661. During his second tenure as chaplain, his Puritan ideals were tested by way of a material bribe. Refusing to "conform", he was forced to return to the Colonies and embarked for Boston, Massachusetts where he was the pastor of North Church till the end of his life in 1723. He also served as president of Harvard on more than one occasion.

**Samuel Willard** was born on Jan. 31, 1640 in Concord, Massachusetts to one of the town founders, Simon Willard. Samuel graduated from Harvard in 1659 and earned an MA in the early 1660s. In the summer of 1663 he became pastor to the frontier community of Groton. It was here in 1671 that he became involved in one of the colonies first cases of demonic possession. His expertise was called upon during the colonial witchcraft crisis and he was amongst a handful of preachers critical of the legal use of spectral evidence. Refugees after Groton was destroyed in 1675 during King Philip's War, Willard and his family settled in Boston, where he eventually became head pastor of Old South Church in 1678. Upon the insistence of Increase Mather, Willard was made a fellow at Harvard and later vice president of the university in 1700. Willard's long legacy is highlighted by his role in the Massachusetts Reforming Synod of 1679, his proposal of a "Half-Way Covenant" easing church membership, criticism of Quaker reforms, and his posthumously published texts on witchcraft. He died in 1707 in Boston and was laid to rest in the Old Granary Burial Ground.

**Cotton Mather** was born Feb. 12, 1663 in Boston, Massachusetts where he would spend all of his life until his death on Feb. 13, 1728. The son of the well-known preacher and academic Increase Mather, Cotton exhibited unusual intellectual gifts. At 12 he entered Harvard, receiving his MA at the age of 18 from the hands of his father, who was president of the college at the time. He preached his first sermon in his father's church in August 1680 and was formally ordained in 1685 becoming his father's colleague. While believing in witchcraft, he sided with Samuel Willard on trying to bar the legality of spectral evidence. His championship of smallpox inoculations for the colonies was an unprecedented public health policy in colonial times. Cotton published over 400 works in his lifetime, the magnum opus being an account of American ecclesiastical history entitled *Magnalia Christi Americana*.

**Jonathan Edwards** was born on Oct. 5, 1703 in East Windsor, Connecticut where his father was the local pastor. The only son of eleven children, he demonstrated intellectual gifts entering Yale at the age of 12 and graduating at the top of his class four years later. He soon was preaching from a Presbyterian pulpit in New York and returned to Yale as tutor in 1724, effectively serving as rector for a year while the position was vacant. In 1728 he succeeded his maternal grandfather as pastor in Northampton, Massachusetts. It was during this tenure that he preached his famous sermon *Sinners in the Hands of an Angry God* while visiting Enfield, Ct. in 1741. After 20 years of serving the community, he created a schism by refusing to administer communion to those who did not demonstrate satisfactory evidence of being truly converted. He was dismissed in 1750 and moved to Stockbridge where he served a small parish and began missionary work with the Housatonic tribes. Seven years later he was elected as third president of Princeton University upon the repose of the second, his son-in-law Aaron Burr. He died one year later on March 22, 1758 from a fever following smallpox inoculation.

Born in Boston on New Years Day, 1705, **Charles Chauncy** was the namesake of his minister great-grandfather who came to Plymouth in 1638 and served as Harvard's second president. Charles graduated from Harvard in 1721 and received his MA in 1724. In 1727 he was ordained as minister to the First Church in Boston and held the position for 60 years, till his death on Feb 10, 1787. During these years Chauncy would become a stern and stoic critic of the emotionalism of the Great Awakening, opposing the revivalism and religious enthusiasm preached by Jonathan Edwards. He was politically active, championing the American Revolution and fighting against the establishment of an Anglican bishopric and *cathedra* in the colonies. His teachings firmly defended universalist doctrines, and he is regarded as a key founder of Unitarianism.

**Jonathan Mayhew** was born at Martha's Vineyard on the October 8, 1720, a fifth descent of Thomas Mayhew, an early settler and the grantee (in 1641) of Martha's Vineyard. The Mayhew family was very active in missionary work among the Indians of the coastal towns. Jonathan graduated from Harvard in 1744. He earned a very liberal reputation while in school as was ordained to the West Church of Boston in 1747, a parish that was under scrutiny by its more conservative peers. Under Mayhew, his church became the first Unitarian Congregational church in New England, although it never adopted that moniker. He preached the strict unity of God, salvation by character, and was amongst the earliest to teach an anti-Trinitarian understanding of Christ. Also politically active, Mayhew preached against the Stamp Act and called for a pragmatic communion of all colonists to secure their rights. A year before his death in 1766 he held the position of Dudleian Lecturer at Harvard.

# PETER BULKELEY
## (1583–1659)

# THE LESSON OF THE COVENANT, FOR ENGLAND AND NEW ENGLAND

THIS MAY serve to be a warning to all such people to whom the Gospel of Christ is come: let them in the fear of God take heed lest they neglect so great salvation, and let them with thankfulness and love entertain the grace which is brought unto them by the revelation of Jesus Christ. If you become despisers, God will work such things among you as whoso heareth them, his ears shall tingle, and your hearts shall ache in the suffering of them much more; for if every transgression and disobedience committed against the law, or against the dim light of nature, do receive a just recompense of reward—if those which are without the law perished in those sins which they committed without the law, and if those which are without the Gospel perish in their ignorance because they know it not—how then shall those escape which have law of grace and Gospel of grace revealed unto them, and do neglect those great things? ...

And here, O England, my dear native country (whose womb bare me, whose breasts nourished me, and in whose arms I should desire to die), give ear to one of thy children which dearly loveth thee. Be thou exhorted thankfully to accept the grace which is now ready to be revealed unto thee. The way is now preparing: the high mountains, which with their shadows caused darkness, are now alaying low, and the low valleys ready to be exalted, the crooked things to be made straight, that all flesh (that lives within thy borders) may see the salvation of our God. Thy light is now coming, and the glory of the Lord is now rising upon thee. Though darkness hath covered a part of thee hitherto, through the wickedness of those that hated light, yet now the Lord himself (I trust) will rise upon thee, and the glory of the Lord shall be seen upon thee. Now therefore stir up thyself with thankfulness and joy of heart to embrace the things of thy peace, which shall be brought unto thee. See that thou love the Gospel not in word and in show only but in deed and in truth: and not for novelty's sake but for truth's sake, not because it is a new way but because the grace of God which brings salvation is thereby revealed. Though in respect of order and government all things may become new, yet look not after new substantials, new foundations. Thou hast had the foundation truly laid, by many skillful builders, many years ago: only some have built thereupon hay and stubble, instead of gold and precious stones. Let therefore the roof be new, but let the foundation be the same. Take heed of too much of that "new light" which the world is now gazing upon. Some have reported sad things concerning thee in this respect: so much new light breaking forth that the old zeal is almost extinct by it. Herein take heed. "The old way is the good way": this is now ready to be revealed. The time of grace is coming unto thee: this is the accepted season, now is the day of thy salvation. Oh, be wise to consider it, and walk worthy of it, esteeming the Gospel as thy pearl, thy treasure, thy crown, thy felicity! Thou canst not love it too dearly. Make much of it therefore: otherwise, know the neglect of it will bring heaviest wrath, and thy judgment hastenth, and sleepeth not.

And thou, New England, which art exalted in privileges of the Gospel above many other people, know thou the time of thy visitation, and consider the great things the Lord hath done for thee. The Gospel hath free passage in all places where thou dwellest: oh, that it might be glorified also by thee. Thou enjoyest many faithful witnesses, which have testified unto thee the Gospel of the grace of God. Thou has many bright stars shining in thy firmament, to give thee the *knowledge of salvation from on high, to guide thy feet in the way of peace* (Luke 1. 78, 79). Be not high-minded because of thy privileges, but fear because of thy danger. The more thou hast committed unto thee, the more thou must account for. No people's account will be heavier than thine if thou do not walk worthy of the means of thy salvation. The Lord looks for more from thee than from other people: more zeal for God, more love to His truth, more justice and equity in thy ways. Thou shouldst be a special people, an only people—none like thee in all the earth. Oh, be so, in loving the Gospel and ministers of it, having them *in singular love for their work's sake* (I Thess. 5. 13). Glorify thou the word of the Lord, which hath glorified thee. Take heed lest for neglect of either, God remove thy candlestick out of the midst of thee; lest being now as a city upon an hill, which many seek unto, thou be left like a beacon upon the top of a mountain, desolate and forsaken. If we walk unworthy of the Gospel brought unto us, the greater our mercy hath been in the enjoying of it, the greater will our judgment be for the contempt. Be instructed, and take heed.

# JOHN COTTON
## (1584–1652)

## LIMITATION OF GOVERNMENT

THIS MAY serve to teach us the danger of allowing to any mortall man an inordinate measure of power to speak great things, to allow to any man uncontrollableness of speech, you see the desperate danger of it: Let all the world learn to give mortall men no greater power then they are content they shall use, for use it they will: And unlesse they be better taught of God, they will use it ever and anon, it may be make it the passage of their proceeding to speake what they will: and they that have liberty to speak great things, you will finde it to be true, they will speak great blasphemies. No man would think what desperate deceit and wickednesse there is in the hearts of men: and that was the reason why the beast did speak such great things, hee might speak, and no body might controll him: What, saith the Lord in Jer. 3.5. *Thou hast spoken and done evill things as thou couldst.* If a church or head of a church could have done worse, he would have done it: this is one of the straines of nature, it affects boundlesse liberty, and to runne to the utmost extent: What ever power he hath received, he hath a corrupt nature that will improve it in one thing or other; if he have liberty, he will think why may he not use it. Set up the pope as Lord paramount over kings and princes, and they shall know that he hath power over them, he will take liberty to depose one, and set up another. Give him power to make laws, and he will approve, and disprove as he list; what he approves is canonicall, what hee disproves is rejected: give him that power, and he will so order it at length, he will make such a state of religion, that he that so lives and dyes shall never be saved, and all this springs from the vast power that is given to him, and from the deep depravation of nature. Hee will open his mouth, *His tongue is his owne, who is Lord over him,* Psal. 12. 3, 4. It is therefore most wholsome for magistrates and officers in church and common-wealth, never to affect more liberty and authority then will do them good, and the people good; for what ever transcendant power is given, will certainly over-run those that give it, and

3

those that receive it: there is a straine in a mans heart that will sometime or other runne out to excesse, unlesse the Lord restraine it, but it is not good to venture it: it is necessary therefore, that all power that is on earth be limited, church-power or other: if there be power given to speak great things, then look for great blasphemies, look for a licentious abuse of it. It is counted a matter of danger to the state to limit prerogatives; but it is a further danger, not to have them limited: they will be like a tempest, if they be not limited: a prince himselfe cannot tell where hee will confine himselfe, nor can the people tell: but if he have liberty to speak great things, then he will make and unmake, say and unsay, and undertake such things as are neither for his owne honour, nor for the safety of the state. It is therefore fit for every man to be studious of the bounds which the Lord hath set: and for the people, in whom fundamentally all power lyes, to give as much power as God in his word gives to men: and it is meet that magistrates in the commonwealth, and so officers in churches should desire to know the utmost bounds of their own power, and it is safe for both: all intrenchment upon the bounds which God hath not given, they are not enlargements, but burdens and snares; they will certainly lead the spirit of a man out of his way sooner or later. It is wholsome and safe to be dealt withall as God deales with the vast sea; *Hitherto shalt thou come, but there shalt thou stay thy proud waves:* and therefore if they be but banks of simple sand, they will be good enough to check the vast roaring sea. And so for imperiall monarchies, it is safe to know how far their power extends; and then if it be but banks of sand, which is most slippery, it will serve, as well as any brazen wall. If you pinch the sea of its liberty, though it be walls of stone or brasse, it will beate them downe: so it is with magistrates, stint them where God hath not stinted them, and if they were walls of brasse, they would beate them downe, and it is meet they should: but give them the liberty God allows, and if it be but a wall of sand it will keep them: as this liquid ayre in which we breath, God hath set it for the waters of the clouds to the earth; it is a firmament, it is the clouds, yet it stands firme enough, because it keeps the climate where they are, it shall stand like walls of brasse: so let there be due bounds set, and I may apply it to families; it is good for the wife to acknowledg all power and authority to the husband, and for the husband to acknowledg honour to the wife, but still give them that which God hath given them, and no more nor lesse: give them the full latitude that God hath given, else you will finde you dig pits, and lay snares, and cumber their spirits, if you give them lesse: there is never peace where full liberty is not given, nor never stable peace where more then full liberty is granted: let them be duely observed, and give men no more liberty then God doth, nor women, for they will abuse it: the Devill will draw them, and Gods providence leade them thereunto, therefore give them no more then God gives. And so for children; and servants, or any others you are to deale with, give them the liberty and authority you would have them use, and beyond that stretch not the tether, it will not tend to their good nor yours: and also from hence gather, and goe home with this meditation; that certainly here is this distemper in our natures, that we cannot tell how to use liberty, but wee shall very readily corrupt our selves: oh the bottomlesse depth of sandy earth! of a corrupt spirit, that breaks over all bounds, and loves inordinate vastnesse; that is it we ought to be carefull of.

# WADING IN GRACE

## From *The Way of Life* (London, 1641)

FOR FURTHER encouragement hereunto, consider that place, Ezech. 47. 3, 4, 5. It shewes you the marvailous efficacy of the spirit of Grace in the dayes of the Gospel: First a Christian wades in the rivers of God his grace up to the ankles, with some good frame of spirit; yet but weakly, for a man hath strength in his ankle bones, Acts 3. and yet may have but feeble knees, Heb. 12. 12. So farre as you walk in the waters, so far are you healed; why then in the next place, he must wade till he come to the knees, goe a thousand cubits, a mile further, and get more strength to pray, and to walk on in your callings with more power and strength.

Secondly, but yet a man that wades but to the knees, his loynes are not drenched, for nothing is healed but what is in the water. Now the affections of a man are placed in his loynes, God tries the reines; a man may have many unruly affections, though he be padling in the wayes of grace; he may walk on in some eavennesse, and yet have many distempered passions, and may have just cause to complaine of the rottennesse of his heart in the sight of God: why then, thou hast waded but to the knees, and it is a mercy that thou art come so farre; but yet the loynes want healing, why, wade a mile further then; the grace of God yet comes too shallow in us, our passions are yet unmortified, so as we know not how to grieve in measure, our wrath is vehement and immoderate, you must therefore wade untill the *loynes bee girt with a golden girdle;* wade an-end, & think all is not well untill you be so deep, & by this you may take a scantling, what measure of grace is poured out upon you. And if thou hast gone so farre, that God hath in some measure healed thy affections, that thou canst be angry and sin not, &c. it is well, and this we must attain to. But suppose the loyns should be in a good measure healed, yet there is more goes to it then all this; and yet when a man is come thus farre, he may laugh at all temptations, and blesse God in all changes: but yet goe another thousand cubits, and then you shall swimme; there is such a measure of grace in which a man may swimme as fish in the water, with all readinesse and dexterity, gliding an-end, as if he had water enough to swimme in; such a Christian doth not creep or walk, but he runs the wayes of Gods Commandments; what ever he is to doe or to suffer he is ready for all, so every way drenched in grace, as let God turn him any way, he is never drawn dry.

# THE LIFE OF FAITH

From *The Way of Life* (London, 1641)

———

GAL. 2. 20.

*Yet not I, but Christ liveth in me.*

NOW HE corrects, or indeed rather explaines himselfe, how or what kind of life it is that he lives; Not hee, how then? Christ lives in him.

So that in these words, you have a deniall of himselfe, to be the author and roote of his owne life; he denies himselfe to live, even then when he doth live.

Secondly, You have an acknowledgement of the author and roote of his life; Christ lives in his life.

DOCTRINE. *A living Christian lives not himselfe, but Christ in him.*

Or thus:

*The life of a Christian is not his owne life, but the life of Christ Jesus.*

Either of both these expresse these two parts of the verse; A living Christian lives not himself, not his own life, but Christ lives in him.

First, see how a living Christian lives not his owne life, after once he hath had part in the death of Christ, and hath thereby beene initiated into the life and power of Christs death, and so become a mortified and crucified Christian in some measure, such a Christian lives not his own life in this world.

There is a threefold life, *A carnall life, a spirituall life, and a naturall life*; and in some respect, a living Christian lives none of these lives.

A carnall life is expressed in three things, in living to a mans *lusts,* in living to the *world,* and in living to a mans *owne wisedome and reason.*

Now a Christian man lives to none of these; He lives not to his owne lusts: *How shall we that are dead to sin live any longer therein?* Rom. 6. 2. He looks at it as an absurdity, and indeed in some measure monstrous, *ver.* 6. *The body of sin is dead in us, that we should no more serve sin;* and ver. 7. he that is dead with Christ, is *free from sinne:* arme your selves with the same minde; now you live *no longer to the lusts of men,* but to the will of God; this life *Paul* doth not live, he is not lively at his lusts, they are death to him; for though a Christian man may be defiled, and sometimes overtaken, yet so farre as he is a living Christian, so farre he is a dead man to those lusts, they are the deadnesse of his heart, the discouragement of his spirit, the hell of his soule, that he is compassed about with such evils as these be; *Oh wretched man that I am, &c.* Rom. 7. 23, 24. as if it were the death of his life, that he carried about such *a body of death* with him. Now then, saith the Apostle, if I doe that which I hate, *It is no more I that doe it, but sin that dwelleth in me,* Rom. 7. 20. It is the misery of my spirituall life, that I am at any time deadhearted to spirituall duties, and somewhat apt to close with temptations to sinne, whether darted by Satan, or stirred up by my owne corrupt heart; and therefore if there be any life of sin in me, in the least measure, it is the death of my heart.

And secondly, so neither lives he in regard of the *world,* for though you may have a godly man busie in his calling from Sunne rising to Sunne setting, and may by Gods providence fill both his hand and head with businesse, yet a living Christian when he lives a most busie life in this world, yet he lives not a worldly life.

There are foure or five several differences between a Christian his living to the world, and another mans that is not yet alive to God, and hath no fellowship with Christ in his death.

First, a Christian man principally seeks Christ above and before the world, Mat. 6. 33. He doth first look for spirituall things, he had rather have his part in Christ, then in all the blessings of his life, he would first order his heart to Christ, his principall care is about that, and if he doe not so, he looks at it as his death, which a worldly man doth not.

Secondly, As he first and principally seekes Christ, so all the good things he hath, he lookes for them from Christ, he goes not about his businesse in his owne strength, but what he wants he seeks it from Christ, and what he hath he receives it from Christ, Gen. 33. 5, 11. If God blesse him with children, with health, or with estate, or what ever other comfort of this life, he lookes at it as a free gift of Gods grace; he doth not sacrifice to his owne nets, nor to the dexterity of his owne hands, but these are the blessings God hath graciously given to his servant, though common, and such as every one hath, yet not so to him.

Thirdly, A Christian man, as he receives the world from Christ, so he enjoyes them all in Christ; I meane he enjoyes it not in the sense of his owne desert, but he lookes at himselfe lesse then the least of them all, Gen. 32. 10. *I am lesse then the least of all thy faithfulnesse to thy servant.* This is to enjoy all in Christ, not in his own worth, but in the merit of Christ.

Now this a Christian doth, whatever his businesse be, in his worldly businesse, he doth not lead a worldly life.

Fourthly, Hee useth and imployeth all for Christ, In our gates, saith the church, are all manner of pleasant fruits, my Beloved I have kept them all for thee: when he hath many blessings, he considers what he shall doe with them. This is the frame of a living Christian, one whose heart is given to Christ. I have indeed all manner of these things, faire houses, well furnished roomes, pleasant provision of all sorts, but my Beloved I have kept them all for thee, though I have never so much, yet it is all for Christ, 1 Cor. 10. 31. That God may be glorified in Jesus Christ; this is the summe of his eating and drinking, and buying and selling, &c. this is the upshot of all, this is all for Christ, and this is so to live in the world, as not to live like a man of the world, and so he makes good work of his worldly businesse, though in themselves never so intricate.

Fifthly, A living Christian lives unto God, even then when he lives in the world, in that he is willing to leave worldly businesse, and worldly things for Christ, leave them all, rather then part with Christ; this is the resolution of his spirit, and his practise when he is put to it, Psal. 45. 10. Hearken O daughter and consider, *forget thy kindred and thy Fathers house;* let them all goe, forget thy pleasures and treasures in *Pharaohs* court, so shall the King have pleasure in thy beauty, that if any thing stand betweene obtaining of Christ, and the enjoying of the world, let all goe; were the comfort of this life never so precious and glorious, yet forget them all, let them all be as *dead commodity for a living Christ,* Matth. 16. 27. *We have forsaken all and followed thee;* and if afterward the world and Christ should fall out, as sometimes they will, and ere long it will be that a man cannot keep his heart in a comfortable plight with Christ, but it will cost him losse of friends, and sometimes losse of estate, and sometimes losse of life, why yet a Christian will forsake all for Christ, if once the world and Christ come to fall out; and in this case a Christian thinks it no hard choyce, though *Demas* did, 2 Tim. 4. 10. *I passe not at all,* saith a Christian, *so that I may but finish my course with joy,* Acts 20, 23, 24. This is the true life of a Christian in respect of his Christian life, and wherein he differs from a worldly man; for there is no worldly man that lives a worldly life, but his first care is for his estate to settle that well, and when he hath thus provided for him and his, in the remanent of his time he will seek Christ.

And when he gets any thing, he depends much upon his trade, he lives unto himself, and what he hath he thinks he hath deserved it, and he will be much offended with Gods providence if he be crossed in his designs and labours. And that which he hath, for whom doth he keep it? He will say for wife, and children, and kindred; but how they will use it, that is no matter. And if it come to a parting blow, that either the world or Christ we must lose, they think men very unwise that will part with a bird in the hand for two in the bush. They may goe away sorrowfull, but away they will goe, if there bee no remedy, rather let Christ provide for himselfe; for their part, they will beare no such burthens for him; but now a Christian lives not to the world, and if hee should so live, it were rather a swoune of Christianity, then any life and power of Christ.

For *a carnall life,* which is a life of living to a mans owne wisdome and reason, he lives not that life neither, *If any man would be wise in this world, let him become a foole that hee may bee wise,* 1 Corinth. 3. 18, 19, 20. No living Christian but he must deny his owne wisedome, judgement, and understanding, that he may be wise in Christ; You say, what, would you have men senselesse, and mopish, and not understand themselves? No, no, here is the point, True grace doth not destroy a mans wisdome, but rather enlargeth and enlightneth it wonderfully; so as that men by nature are blinde, but spirituall wisedome enlightens the eyes of the blinde. It is an excellent speech, that in the Heb, 11. 1. *Faith is the substance;* in the Originall it is, faith is the *subsistance of things not seene;* the meaning is, that if wee should tell many a man, that the favour of God is more worth then any blessing of this world, the blood of Christ more precious then gold, the spirit of grace the best companion for the soule, &c. these seeme to many a man but fained things, no subsistence in these things: this is but some strong imagination of some melancholy braines, he sees no such matter in them, and he is perswaded there is no such thing, it is onely faith that sees subsistence in these things; to a faithfull Christian there is subsistence in al the promises, there is waight in the examples, threatenings, and Commandments of the word, subsistence in the favour of God, and in the blood of Christ, and in fellowship with the spirit, and in other things there is none at all. Now in this case a man must see all his wisedome to be but folly, all the high thoughts hee had of the world and himselfe, hee must looke at them all as vain; and all the low thoughts he had of religion and the wayes of grace, hee must looke at them all as folly and madnesse; so that here a Christian is dead to his owne wisedome; that which sometimes hee thought to have beene his chiefest good, is now nothing but vanity and vexation of spirit, but when hee comes to see spirituall things have onely true subsistence in them, then he leads a wiser life then ever hee did before.

Now for his *spirituall life:* a living Christian, his whole spirituall life is Christ, and not himselfe, his spirituall life is not this owne life.

There be three parts of spirituall life, which a Christian lives in this world, the fourth (which is the life of glory) he lives in that which is to come.

A life of Justification, a life of Sanctification, a life of spirituall Consolation.

1. A life of Justification, Rom. 5. 18. Now a Christian man lookes for Justification, not from all his spiritual performances, prayer, preaching, receiving sacraments, &c. He lookes at all these as losse, that hee might winne Christ, *Not having his owne righteousnesse,* Philip. 3. 6, 7, 8, 9.

2. For his life of Sanctification, he doth not make account that himself is sufficient, as of himselfe, to thinke a good thought, 2 Cor. 3. 5. When God hath given him grace, yet *he can doe nothing* in any lively manner, unlesse Christ assist him, and help him at every turne, 1 Cor. 15. 10.

*By the grace of God I am that I am, and the grace in mee was not in vaine;* but I laboured more abundantly then they all; *yet not I,* it is not I that have took all this paines; though he had a good calling, and an honest heart, *yet not I,* nay, neither was it the grace of Christ that was in him, but the *grace of God that was with him;* it was the spirit of God breathing in his grace, that made *these spices thus flow forth,* Cant. 4. *ult.* Though he had many precious graces bestowed on him yet not he, nor any grace in him, but the grace of God *with him,* that wrought with him, and acted, and did all he did wherever he came; now blessed be God that makes manifest the savor of his grace, 2 Cor. 2, 12. *to* 15.

3. And thirdly, for his life of Consolation, there goe two things for the making up of a mans consolation, partly Gods favour, and that is better then life, Psal. 63. 3 Psal. 30. 5. *In thy favour is life.*

Secondly, The prospering of Gods work in themselves and others, 1 Thess. 3. 8. *Now we live, if ye stand fast in the Lord:* they were his joy, and his crown and glory; but was that his life of justification, think you? No, nor of his sanctification neither; though the church had falne, yet *Paul* his work had been glorious in Gods sight, and he had still been justified and sanctified; but it was the life of his consolation: this is our life, and the crowne of our rejoycing if you stand fast in the Lord.

Now for a mans *naturall life,* how can a man be said not to live his owne naturall life? Yet a Christian may say, that in some measure he lives not his owne naturall life, but Christ lives in him, Acts 17. 28. *In him we live, move, and have our being:* You say, so hath a carnall man his life from Christ; true, but he acknowledgeth it not; In him was life, and that was the life of men, Joh. 1. 3, 4. A Christian man hath his naturall life from Christ, as from an head that gives both spirituall and naturall life; In him thou hast given me life and breath, and thy visitation hath preserved my being, Job. 12. 10. Christ gave us our life, and he preserves it, wee cannot better explaine it then thus; a wind-mill moves not onely by the wind, but in the wind; so a water-mill hath its motion, not onely from the water, but in the water; so a Christian lives, as having his life from Christ, and in Christ, and further then Christ breathes and assists, he stirs not; Psal. 104, 29, 30. *My times are in thy hands,* Psal. 31. 5. Dan. 5. 23. Thou hast not honoured thy God, *in whose hand thy breath is, and all thy wayes,* it was the sinne of the prophane king not to regard it; All his wayes and turnings, his sicknesse and health, and all his changes, they are all in Gods hands; Jer. 10. 23. *I know that the way of man is not in himselfe;* upon thee have I beene cast, from my mothers wombe, thou hast poured me out like milke, and by thee I was curdled in my mothers wombe, so that I live; What you *Paul?* No, not I; as if it were too broad a word for a Christian man to speake, *Though I live, yet not I.*

Now secondly, how may it be said, that Christ lives in a living Christian; How? as a roote of his life, as the author both of his spirituall and naturall life: for his carnall life, that he is wholly dead unto; but for his other, Christ is the Actor and roote of all, for God hath given him above all *to be head of the Church;* as the members live a reasonable life from the head, so doth the Church from Christ; *Without me you can doe nothing,* John 15. 1, 2. he is called the *Prince of life,* Acts 33. 15. 1 Cor. 15. 45. And this comes to passe partly by Gods acceptance of him as our head; God hath appointed him to bee our head; and also by the communication of his Spirit to us, 1 Cor. 6. 17.

And thirdly, by faith, for it is faith that receives Christ to dwell in us, Ephes 3. 17. so that by these we dwell in Christ, and so live in him, and he in us, for by this meanes Christ is made our roote, Rom. 11. 17. so as we that were by nature *branches of the wild olive,* are now made partakers *of the good olive:* and hence it is, that wee bring forth savoury fruit; some fruits there bee, which if you never transplant them, they will grow wild, but transplant them, and they will bring forth fruit; so take any man that is wild by nature, and let him be crucified with Christ, cut him off from fellowship with *Adam,* and his lusts, and implant him into Christ, and then he is made partaker of the true olive, and so will bring forth good fruit.

USE. It may be first an evident signe of tryall to every one of us, of our owne estates, whether we have part in Christs death yea or no, whether wee be living Christians, or no; Christians we are, wee cannot denie, and so have an outward right to partake with the rest of Gods people; but would you know whether you bee living Christians, or no? Consider, a living Christian lives not himselfe, but Christ lives in him; Christian signifies one *Anointed with the grace of Christ,* 1 John 2. 27. Now for this consider what hath beene said; If thou beest a living Christian, thou livest, yet not thou, but Christ in thee; And let me say this to every Christian soule, and take it as an eternall truth, if to this day thou livest to thy lusts, and livest in any knowne sin, and it is the delight of thy soule to live in pride, and covetousnesse, &c. if you live in any sinne, and desire so to doe, thou maiest be called a Christian, but thou art a dead Christian. But you say, you thank God, you have bid adieu to all your lusts: but it was a shrewd saying of old, *Licitis perimus omnes,* we most of us perish by lawfull things; and therefore I say further, dost thou not live to the world? Thou sayest, It is not lawfull for a man to be diligent in his calling, thou canst not leave thy businesse, as such and such as are bankrupts; Well, God forbids thee not to be diligent in thy calling; let me tell thee, if thou canst so live in the world, as that thy first care is to seeke Christ, before the doing of any worke of thine owne, and if to manage thy calling thou looke for helpe from him, and looke at thy selfe, as unworthy of any mercy from God, and aske thy heart, who is all this for? is it for Christ? canst thou say, I have kept them all for thee? and canst thou come to this resolution, that if Christ and thy calling come to be at variance, yet thou canst part with all to keepe fellowship with Christ? then thou livest in the World, but art not a man of the World; Christ sits next to thy heart all this while, and then thou art well; but otherwise let mee tell thee, if thou canst first be busie about thy calling, and thinke you have wit enough for your owne businesse, and you think you deserve all you have, else you would not bee so much disturbed when you are crossed in it; and if you use them not for Christ, but you lose him in the use of them, and you keepe it, that you and yours may bee some great ones in the world; and if a crosse way come, that Christ and your estates must part, you turne your back upon Christ, and upon all that professe his name; then bee not a lyer against the truth, thou art of the world, and livest to the world, and the Lord Jesus hath yet no hold of thee; and therefore bee sure if it bee so with you, you have failed in one of these; you have stirred about worldly businesse, before you looked for Christ, and gone about them in your owne strength, and in sense of your owne worthinesse of them, which makes you discontent when you are crossed in them, and you consider not for what end you laid up all these; and hence it is, that when it comes to a parting blow, many a Christian is foiled about the world: and therefore looke seriously to it, and if you conceive worldly things have some subsistence in them, but not so of the things of GOD, then it is not Christ that lives in you, but you live to your selves.

USE 2. To cast a just reproofe upon living Christians, that Christian men should not live like Christian men; a shame for Christian men still to live in pride, and uncleannesse, committing the works of darknesse; and therefore bee ashamed that ever you should take up the life of a Christian, and still bee more forward for the world, then for Christ; still to bee impatient for worldly crosses, and still to want serious thoughts for whom is all this, and yet not come to consider how you must part from all these. This may cast much confusion upon the face of a Christian man, that to this day they cannot say that they live unto Christ. Some there be, who say, that they live unto Christ, and some that say, they will not have Christ to reigne over them, Luke 19. 14. Some there be that say; Let us breake his bonds asunder, and cast his cords from us, Psal. 2. but it were a shame that any Christian should do so.

USE 3. To teach us all, in the name of the Lord Jesus Christ, to desire to make knowne to our owne consciences, and to the world, that wee are crucified with Christ, and live to God; let us say, it is not enough for a Christian to live besides his lusts, or that the world is lesse to be regarded then Christ, &c. but I pray you practise this resolution daily, unlesse you have some thoughts of this daily, you will lose your spiritual life daily, and you never finde your hearts lost in worldly businesse; but when you want a heart daily to consider what God cals you to, you must therefore have these thoughts daily. And further, take this counsell, if thou beest troubled about thy justification and peace with God, let this comfort thee, that thou knowest thou livest not by thine owne graces, but by Christ.

USE 4. Of comfort and consolation, to every soule as can truly say, this is the frame of their hearts, they doe not live themselves, but Christ in them; bee not you discouraged at your owne weaknesse, but make account your living in Christ will beare you out, and therefore labour to be loose to the world, and live like those that have a living fountaine to run unto, for supply of what ever you stand in need of, that so all the rest of our time may not be a life of our owne lusts, but of Christ in us.

# CHRISTIAN CALLING

## From *The Way of Life* (London, 1641)

WEE ARE now to speake of living by faith in our outward and temporall life: now our outward and temporall life is twofold, which wee live in the flesh. It is either a civill, or a naturall life, for both these lives we live, and they are different the one from the other: civill life is that whereby we live, as members of this or that city, or town, or commonwealth, in this or that particular vocation and calling.

Naturall life I call that, by which we doe live this bodily life, I meane, by which we live a life of sense, by which we eate and drinke, by which we goe through all conditions, from our birth to our grave, by which we live, and move, and have our being. And now both these a justified person lives by faith; to begin with the former.

*A true beleeving Christian, a justified person, hee lives in his vocation by his faith.*

Not onely my spirituall life, but even my civill life in this world, all the life I live, is by the faith of the Son of God: he exempts no life from the agency of his faith, whether he live as a Christian man, or as a member of this or that church, or commonwealth, he doth it all by the faith of the Son of God.

Now for opening this point, let me shew you what are those severall acts of faith which it puts forth about our occasions, and vocations, that so we may live in Gods sight therein.

First, faith drawes the heart of a Christian to live in some warrantable calling; as soone as ever a man begins to looke towards God, and the wayes of his grace, he will not rest, till he find out some warrantable calling and imployment: an instance you have in the Prodigall son, that after he had received & spent his portion in vanity, and when being pinched, he came home to himself, & comming home to his father, the very next thing after confession and repentance of his sin, the very next petition he makes, is, *Make mee one of thy hired servants;* next after desire of pardon of sin, then put me into some calling, though it be but of an hired servant, wherein he may bring in God any service; a Christian would no sooner have his sinne pardoned, then his estate to be settled in some good calling, though not as a mercenary slave, but he would offer it up to God as a free-will Offering, he would have his condition and heart setled in Gods peace, but his life setled in a good calling, though it be but of a day-labourer, yet make me as one that may doe thee some service; *Paul* makes it a matter of great thankfulness to God, that he had given him ability, and put him in place where he might doe him service, 1 Tim. 1. 12. And in the law, they were counted uncleane beasts that did not divide the hoofe into two, Lev. 11. 3. therefore the camell, though he chewed the cud, yet because he did not divide the hoofe, hee was counted uncleane; and God by the beasts, did signifie to us sundry sorts of men, who were cleane, who not, as you may see in *Peters* vision, in Acts 10. It shewes you then, that it is onely a cleane person, that walkes with a divided hoofe, that sets one foote in his generall, and the other in his particular calling; he strikes with both, he serves both God and man, else he is is an uncleane beast, if he have no calling but a generall, or if no calling but a particular, he is an uncleane creature; but now as soone as ever faith purifies the heart, it makes us cleane creatures, Acts 15. 9. and our callings doe not intefeire one upon another, but both goe an end evenly together, he drives both these plowes at once; *As God hath called every man, so let him walke,* 1 Cor. 7. 19, 20. This is the cleane worke of faith, hee would have some imployment to *fill the head and hand with.*

Now more particularly, faith doth warily observe the warrantablenesse of its calling.

Three things doth faith finde in a particular calling.

First, it hath a care that it be a *warrantable* calling, wherein we may not onely aime at our own, but at the publike good, that is a warrantable calling, *Seek not every man his owne things, but every man the good of his brother,* 1 Cor. 10. 24. Phil. 2. 4. Seek one anothers welfare; faith works all by love, Gal. 5. 6. And therefore it will not think it hath a comfortable calling, unlesse it will not onely serve his owne turne, but the turn of other men. Bees will not suffer drones among them, but if they lay up any thing, it shall be for them that cannot work; he would see that his calling should tend to publique good.

Secondly, another thing to make a calling warrantable, is, when God gives a man *gifts* for it, that he is acquainted with the mystery of it, and hath gifts of body and minde sutable to it: Prov. 16. 20. *He that understands a matter shall finde good;* He that understands his businesse wisely. God leads him on to that calling, 1 Cor. 7. 17. To shew you that when God hath called me to a place, he hath given me some gifts fit for that place, especially, if the place be sutable and fitted to me and my best gifts; for God would not have a man to receive five talents, and gaine but two, he would have his best gifts improved to the best advantage.

Thirdly, that which makes a calling warrantable, is, when it is attained unto by warrantable and direct *meanes*, when a man enterprises not a calling, but in the use of such meanes as he may see Gods providence leading him to it: so Amos manifests his calling against the high priest, Amos 7. 14, 15. *The Lord tooke me, and said unto me, Goe, feed my people:* So he had a warrant for it, Gods hand led him to it in Gods ordinance, and therein he comforted himselfe, whereas another man that hath taken up such a calling without warrant from God, he deales ingenuously, Zach. 13. 5. and leaves it; to shew you that a man ought to attend upon his owne warrantable calling. Now faith that hath respect unto the word of God for all its wayes, he would see his calling ayming at the publique good, he would see gifts for it, and an open doore for his entrance into it, hee would not come unto it by deceit and undermining of others, but he would see the *providence and ordinance* of God leading him unto it, the counsell of friends, and encouragement of neighbours; this is the first work of faith.

2. Another work of faith, about a mans vocation and calling, when faith hath made choyce of a warrantable calling, then he *depends* upon God for the quickning, and sharpening of his gifts in that calling, and yet depends not upon his gifts for the going through his calling, but upon God that gave him those gifts, yea hee depends on God for the use of them in his calling; faith saith not, Give me such a calling and turne me loose to it; but faith lookes up to heaven for skill and ability, though strong and able, yet it looks at all its abilities but as a dead work, as like braided wares in a shop, as such as will be lost and rust, unlesse God refresh and renue breath in them. And then if God doe breathe in his gifts, hee depends not upon them for the acting his work, but upon Gods blessing in the use of his gifts; though he have never so much skill and strength, he looks at it as a dead work, unlesse God breathe in him; and he lookes not at his gifts as breathed onely on by God, as able to doe the work, unlesse also he be followed by Gods blessing. *Blessed bee the Lord my strength, that teacheth my hands to warre, and my fingers to fight,* Psal. 44. 1. He had been trained up to skill that way, yet he rests onely in Gods teaching of him, Psal. 18. 32, 33, 34. *It is the Lord that girds me with strength;* he puts strength into his hands, so that a *bow of steele is broken with my armes;* and therefore it was that when he went against *Goliah,* though he hade before found good successe in his combats with the Lyon and the beare, yet he saith not, I have made my part good enough with them, and so shall I doe with this man; no, but this is the voyce of faith; *The Lord*

*my God that delivered me out of their hands, he will deliver me out of the hand of this Philistim;* hee that gave me strength and skill at that time, hee is the same, *his hand is not shortened:* And then what is this Philistim more then one of them? 1 Sam. 17. 37. And so when hee comes in *Goliahs* presence, and looks in his face, he tels him he comes to him *in the name of the Lord of hosts;* and hee comes not onely in the Lords name, but he *looks up to him for skill and strength to help;* and therefore saith ver. 40. *The Lord will close thee in my hands;* so that by his owne strength shall no flesh prevaile; It *is in vaine,* saith faith, *to rise early, and goe to bed late, but it is God that gives his beloved rest,* Psal. 127. 1, 2, 3. Prov. 3. 5, 6. The strongest Christian is never more foyled, then when he goes forth in strength of gifts received, and his owne dexterity.

Thirdly, we live by faith in our vocations, in that faith, *in serving God, serves men, and in serving men, serves God:* the Apostle sweetly describes it in the calling of servants, Eph. 6. 5. to 8. *Not with eye service as men-pleasers, but as the servants of Christ, doing the will of God from the heart with good will, as unto the Lord, and not unto men;* not so much man, or onely man, but chiefly the Lord; so that this is the work of every Christian man in his calling, even then when he serves man, he serves the Lord; he doth the work set before him, and he doth it *sincerely,* and *faithfully,* so as he may give account for it; and he doth it *heavenly* and *spiritually; He uses the world as if he used it not,* 1 Cor. 7. 31. This is not the thing his heart is set upon, hee lookes for greater matters then these things can reach him, he doth not so much look at the world as at heaven. And therefore that which followes upon this, he doth it all *comfortably,* though he meet with little encouragements from man, though the more faithfull service he doth, the lesse he is accepted; whereas an unbeleeving heart would discontented, that he can finde no acceptance, but all he doth is taken in the worst part; but now if faith be working and stirring, he wil say, *I passe very litle to be judged by you, or by mans judgement,* 1 Cor. 4. 3. I passe little what you say, or what you do, God knows what I have done, & so his spirit is satisfied, 1 Thess. 2. 6. *We were tender over you, as a nurse over her childe;* We wrought not for wages, nor for the praise of you, if so, wee had not been the servants of Christ. A man therefore that serves Christ in serving of men, he doth his work sincerely as in Gods presence, and as one that hath an heavenly businesse in hand, and therefore comfortably as knowing God approves of his way and work.

Fourthly, another act of faith about a mans vocation is this; it *encourageth* a man in his calling to the most homeliest, and difficultest, and most dangerous things his calling can lead and expose himselfe to; if faith apprehend this or that to be the way of my calling, it encourages me to it, though it be never so *homely,* and *difficult,* and *dangerous.* Take you a carnall proud heart, and if his calling lead him to some homely businesse, he can by no meanes embrace it, such homely employments a carnall heart knowes not how to submit unto; but now faith having put us into a calling, if it require some homely employment, it encourageth us to it, he considers, It is my calling, and therefore he goes about it freely, and though never so homely, he doth it as a work of his calling, Luke 15. 19. *Make mee one of thy hired servants:* A man of his rank and breeding was not wonted to hired servile work, but the same faith that made him desirous to be in a calling, made him stoop to any work his calling led him to; there is no work too hard or too homely for him, for faith is conscious, that it hath done most base drudgery for Satan. No lust of pride, or what else so insolent, but our base hearts could be content to serve the devil and nature in it, and therefore what drudgery can be too homely for me to doe for God? Phil. 2. 5, 7. *Let the same minde bee in you that was in Christ Iesus, hee made himselfe of no reputation;* he stood not upon it, that he was borne of God, and equall to the most high, but he made himselfe a servant, and of no reputation, and so to serve God, and save men; and when his Father called him to it, he stooped to a very low employment, rose up from supper, and girded himselfe with a Towell, and washed his disciples feet, Iohn 13. They thought it was a service too homely for him to doe, but he tells them, that even they ought thus to serve one another. So faith is ready to embrace any homely service his calling leads him to, which a carnall heart would blush to be seene in; a faithfull heart is never squeamish in this case, for repentance will make a man revenge himselfe upon himselfe, in respect of the many homely services he hath done for Satan, and so faith encourageth us to the most difficult and homely businesses. Ezra 10. 4. *It is a great thing* thou art now about, yet *arise and bee doing, for the matter belongs to thee:* yea, and though sometimes the work be more dangerous, yet if a man be called to it, faith dares not shrink; it was an hard point that *Herod* was put upon, either now hee must bee prophane, or discover his hypocrisie; now therefore *Iohn* dischargeth his conscience, and though it was dangerous for him to bee so plaine, yet faith encourageth him to it; if it appeare to bee his calling, faith doth not picke and choose, as carnall reason will doe.

Firstly, another act of faith, by which a Christian man lives in his vocation, is, that faith *casts all the failings and burthens of his calling upon the Lord;* that is the proper work of faith, it rolls and casts all upon him.

Now there are three sorts of burthens that befall a man in his calling.

1. *Care about the successe of it;* and for this faith casts its care upon God, 1 Pet. 5. 7. Pro. 16. 3. *Commit thy workes unto the Lord, and thy thoughts shall be established,* Psal. 55. 22. 24. *Cast thy burthen upon the Lord, and he will deliver thee;* faith will commend that wholly to God.

2. A second burthen, is *feare of danger* that may befall us therein from the hand of man. Luke 13. 31. 32. Some bids Christ goe out of the

country, for *Herod* will kill him; what saith Christ to that? *Goe tell that foxe I must worke to day and to morrow, &c.* He casts that upon God and his calling, God hath set me a time, and while that time lasts, my calling will beare me out, and when that time is out, then I shall be perfect.

3. Another burthen, is the burthen of *injuries,* which befalls a man in his calling. I have not hastened that evill day, Lord thou knowest; he had not wronged himselfe nor others in his calling, and therefore all the injuries that befall him in his calling, he desires the Lord to take it into his hands.

Sixtly, Faith hath another act about a mans vocation, and that is, it takes *all successes* that befall him in his calling with *moderation,* hee equally beares good and evill successes as God shall dispense them to him. Faith frames the heart to moderation, be they good or evill, it rests satisfied in Gods gracious dispensation; *I have learned in what estate soever I am, therewith to bee content,* Phil. 4. 11, 12. This he had learned to doe, if God prosper him, he had learned not to be puffed up, and if he should be exposed to want, he could do it without murmuring. It is the same act of unbeleefe, that makes a man murmure in crosses, which puffes him up in prosperity; now faith is like a poyse, it keeps the heart in an equall frame, whether matters fall out well or ill, faith takes them much what alike, faith moderates the frame of a mans spirit on both sides.

Seventhly, the last work which faith puts forth about a mans calling, is this, faith with boldnesse *resignes up* his calling into the hands of God or man; when ever God calls a man to lay downe his calling, when his work is finished, herein the sons of God farre exceed the sons of men; another man when his calling comes to bee removed from him, hee is much ashamed, and much afraid, but if a Christian man be to forgoe his calling, he layes it downe with comfort and boldnesse, in the sight of God and man.

First, *In the sight of God,* 2 Tim. 4. 7. *I have fought the fight, I have kept the faith, and finished my course,* and therefore, *henceforth is laid up for me a crowne of righteousnesse, which God according to his righteous* word and promise will give him, as a reward for his sincere and faithfull walking; he lookes up to God, and resignes up his calling into his hand; he tels *Timothy,* the day of his departure is at hand; and now, this is matter of strong consolation to him; faith beleeving, that God put him into his calling, and hath beene helpfull to him hitherto, and now growne nigh to the period of his calling, here was his comfort, that he had not throwne himself out of his work; but God cals him to leave it, and so he leaves it, in the same hand from whom he received it. A man that in his calling hath sought himselfe, and never looked farther then himselfe, he never comes to lay downe his calling, but he thinks it is to his utter undoing: a swine that never did good office to his owner, till hee comes to lye on the hurdle, he then cryes out; but a sheep, who hath many times before yeelded profit, though you take him and cut his throat, yet hee is as a lamb dumb before the shearer; so a carnall man, that never served any man but himselfe, call him to distresse in it, and he murmures and cries out at it; but take you a Christian man, that is wonted to serve God in serving of men, when hee hath beene faithfull and usefull in his calling, he never layes it downe but with some measure of freedome and boldness of spirit; as it was with the three princes in the furnace, they would live and dye in Gods service, and therefore God marvailously assisted them in their worst houres; the soule knows whom it hath lived upon: this is the life of faith in the upshot of a mans calling, he layes it downe in confidence of Gods acceptance: and for *man,* he hath this boldnesse in his dealings with men, he boldly challenges all the sons of men, of any injury done to them, and he freely offers them restitution and recompense, if any such there should be: It was the comfort of *Samuel* when hee was growne old, and the people were earnest for a king, 1 Sam. 12. 3. he saith unto them; Behold, here am I before you this day, beare witnesse against me this day, *Whose oxe or asse have I taken? &c.* hee makes an open challenge to them all, and they answered, *Thou hast done us no wrong.* This is the comfort of a Christian, when he comes to lay downe his calling, he cannot onely with comfort looke God in the face, but all the sons of men. There is never a Christian that lives by faith in his calling, but hee is able to challenge all the world for any wrong done to them, *We have wronged and defrauded no man,* Acts 20. 26. 2 Cor. 12. We have done most there, where we are least accepted; that is the happinesse of a Christian, those who have beene the most weary of him, have had the least cause.

*Vse* 1. From hence you see a just reproofe of the infidelity found in them that live without a calling, they either want faith, or the exercise of faith; if thou beest a man that lives without a calling, though thou hast two thousands to spend, yet if thou hast no calling, tending to publique good, thou art an uncleane beast; if men walke without a cloven hoofe, they are uncleane: and hast thou a calling, and art never so diligent in it, it is but *dead worke,* if thou want faith. It likewise reproves such Christians, as consider not what gifts they have for this and that calling; he pleades for himselfe, his wife and children, further then himselfe he respects no calling; and this is want of faith in a Christians calling: or if men rest in the strength of their owne gifts, for the performing of their callings, and will serve God in some things, and themselves and theirs in other some, or if we can tell how to be eye-servants, it is but a dead worke, for want of faith; or if thou lose thy selfe, and thy heart is carnall, and not heavenly minded, thou mayest have faith, but that is but a dead worke. And if thou cast not all thy care and burthen upon God, thou wilt be very dead when ill successes fall out; but had we faith, it would support us in our worst successes; and if better successes come, if faith be wanting, our vaine heart will be lifted up; and if Christians be confounded before God and men, when they are to resigne up their callings, it is a signe that either they have no faith, or it puts not forth life and courage into them; and if it so fall out, know that the root of it springs from an unbeleeving heart.

*Vse* 2. It is an Use of instruction to every Christian soule that desires to walke by faith in his calling, If thou wouldst live a lively life, and have thy soule and body to prosper in thy calling, labour then to get into a good calling, and therein live to the good of others; take up no calling, but that thou hast understanding in, and never take it unlesse thou mayest have it by lawfull and just meanes, and when thou hast it, serve God in thy calling, and doe it with cheerfulnesse, and faithfulnesse, and an heavenly minde; and in difficulties and dangers, cast thy cares and feares upon God, and see if he will not beare them for thee; and frame thy heart to this heavenly moderation in all successes to sanctifie Gods name; and if the houre and power of darknesse come, that thou beest to resigne up thy calling, let it bee enough that conscience may witnesse to thee, that thou hast not sought thy selfe, nor this world, but hast wrought the Lords workes; thou mayest then have comfort in it, both before God and men.

*Vse* 3. It is a word of consolation to every such soule, as hath beene acquainted with this life of faith in his calling, bee thy calling never so meane and homely, and never so hardly accepted, yet, if thou hast lived by faith in thy calling, it was a lively worke in the sight of God, and so it will be rewarded when thy change shall come; many a Christian is apt to be discouraged and dismaid if crosses befall him in his calling, but be not afraid, let this cheare up thy spirit, that what ever thy calling was, yet thou camest into it honestly, and hast lived in it faithfully, your course was lively and spirituall, and therefore you may with courage looke up for recompence from Christ.

## PURCHASING CHRIST

From *Christ the Fountaine* (London, 1651)

1 John 5. 12

*He that hath the Son, hath life, and he that*
*hath not the Son, hath not life.*

BECAUSE in Scripture phrase, there are more wayes of having Christ requisite for the knowledge of every soul[,] I thought it therefore not amisse to open those other wayes by which in Scripture we are said to have Christ.

Secondly, as therefore we have him first by worshipping of him, so secondly we have him by purchase; this way of having Christ is expressed to us partly in the parable of the merchant man, Matth. 13. 46, *Who when he had found a pearle of precious price, he sold all that [he] had and bought it;* that is one way of having Christ, to purchase him, to buy him: you have the like also held out in Esa. 55. 1, 2. *Every one that is a thirst, come and buy without money or without price,* wherein the Holy Ghost calleth upon us to receive the Lord Jesus Christ as revealed in his ordinances, and he makes a solemne proclamation to all, to come to *these waters and buy without money?* or how without money? It is true, should a man offer his house full of treasure for Christ, it would be despised Cant. 8. 7. and when *Simon Magus* offered to buy the gifts of the Holy Ghost for money, it was rejected with a curse. Act. p. 8, 9, 10, and if the gift of the Holy Ghoast cannot be bought for money, how can the Lord Jesus Christ be bought for money?

And yet thus much I say, that many times without laying out of money, he cannot be had, without parting with money we cannot get him, the case so stands that sometimes, the holding fast a mans money lets go the Lord Jesus Christ, you have a famous example in the Young man, Matth. 19. 21. *to* 24. Where our Saviour shewes how hard a thing it is for a rich man to enter into the kingdome of Heaven, because it is hard for a rich man to part with all that he hath, when God calls for it at his hands, so that without mony sometimes Christ cannot be had; And yet for mony he cannot be had, it was upon the point of mony, that the Lord Jesus parted with the *Pharisees,* Luke 16. 11. 12. *If you be unfaithfull with the mammon of iniquity, who will trust you with true treasure;* if you use not outward things well, who will give you saving grace in Jesus Christ? so that sometimes for want of spending of money in a right way, many a man looses the Lord Jesus; so that though Christ cannot be had for money, yet sometimes without expence of mony he cannot be had.

For opening of this point there are three cases in which money must be layed out, or else Christ cannot be had, and in refusing to lay out money, we refuse life in him.

First, when the Lord by some speciall command requires it, as was the case of the young man in the Gospel, there was a speciall commandement given to him, not given to every man, nor to every rich man, nor scarce any man in ordinary course now adayes, yet then given to him; and now to stick for money, and rather lose eternall life then his goods, in such a case as this, he loseth his life in Christ; and upon the same poynt, or the like, broke *Ananias* and *Saphira,* it was the common resolution of the church of God in that age to sell all that they had, and to give to the

poore, and to live after the same rate that other men did, a like proportion
to every man; and to distribute faithfully to every man as every man had
need, and as the Apostles saw cause; and when they come and keep back
part of the price for which their possessions was sold, you see how bitter
a curse from the presence of the Lord fell upon them, they were cut off
from the congregation of Gods people, and it is much to be feared, cut
off from the Lord Jesus Christ, and from all hope of eternall life, and to
stand as a terrible example to the whole church of God, to shew what a
dangerous thing it is to stand upon termes with Christ, and not to part
with money for him; they could not have fellowship with the people of
God, unlesse they parted with all they had, and live upon the common
distribution; but this case is not alwayes.

But secondly, there is another time, namely, when in case of
persecution the market of Christ goes at so high a rate, that a man cannot
have Christ with any comfort in his soule, or peace to his conscience, or
purity of heart or life, unlesse he hazzard all his estate, or a good part of
it: in buying and selling of a precious commodity, a good chapman will
have it what ever it cost him: so Christ is sometimes at an higher, and
sometimes at a lower rate, but whatever he costs him, he will have him;
it is spoken in commendation of the *Hebrews,* that *they suffered joyfully the
spoyling of their goods,* Heb. 10. 34. to shew you, that sometimes it comes
to that passe, that unlesse a man be content to part with all his goods, he
cannot have the recompence of reweard, the Lord Jesus Christ to his
soule; and therefore the servants of God have been content to loose all
that they had, and willing to resigne up all for the maintaining the
integrity of their spirits, and the purity of their hearts and lives in the
presence of God, and then let all goe, they can *suffer the spoyle of all
joyfully.*

3. It is in case that by Gods providence you be cast to live in such
congregations, where you cannot have the ordinances of God but at a
great charge, as it is the case of many places, that unlesse they be at charge
for the ministery of the Gospel it cannot be had; then we must
communicate freely that way, then *be not deceived, God is not mocked, for
what a man sowes that shall he also reap,* Gal. 6. 6, 7, 8. Where the Apostle
doth encourage men at such a time as this, when the Gospel, cannot be
had but at great charge, then lay out liberally for the Gospel of Christ,
and he calls it, a sowing to the spirit; as a man that layes out his money
for an earthly commodity, for a good bargaine, he reapes corruption; so
he that sowes of the spirit, shall of the spirit reape life everlasting. When
a man layes out his money unto spirituall ends, to obtaine the free passage
of the ordinances of Christ, to enjoy the liberty of the Gospel, he thereby
sowes to the spirit, and shall of the spirit reap life everlasting; for this is
the blessing promised unto it, such as so sow, *shall of the spirit reap life*

*everlasting;* so that when a man out of a good and honest heart, and an hungering desire after Gods ordinances, shall be willing to be at charge for them, he hath this promise made to him, and it shall be fulfilled, *He shall of the spirit reap life everlasting.* But yet, when a man hath layed out his money for this end, if he then thinke his money is worthy of Christ, he gets him not; but this is the first way of having Christ by way of purchase, a seasonable laying out our money for him as God requires it.

Secondly, Christ is to be purchased, not so much by money, as chiefly this purchase must be made by parting with all those many and strong Lusts, and Corruptions, and sinfull rebellions of heart, by which we keep off Christ from coming into our hearts; this is that which the Prophet *Esay* directs us to, Esa. 55. 7. *Let the wicked forsake his way, and the unrighteous man his thoughts,* &c. where he tels us what we must give for Christ, for sinne is neither money nor moneys worth; but he makes a good bargaine that parts with his sins, though he should get no Christ for his parting with them. He speakes of the first and principall part of the life of a Christian man, the life of his justification that springs from pardon of sinne; let a man forsake those sins and lusts that he hath been most carried captive with; let a wicked man forgoe his thoughts and wayes, both his secret and open sins, and let him *then turne to God, and he will abundantly pardon;* then God will receive him graciously, to the justification of life. This is the thing that we must doe, this was the point upon which sundry of them that have been hopefull for religion, have broken off from Christ, and Christ from them; they have forsooke him, and he left them; *Jehu* stuck upon this very point, he would goe a great way, but when it comes (as he thinkes) to hazzard his title to the crowne, then he will set up the *golden Calves;* when he saw that all must be parted with, rather then he would forgoe that, without which he could not maintaine his kingdome, he would rather loose Christ, then venture the losse of that, 2 King. 10. 29. 31. *He regarded not to walke in all the Commandments of the Lord,* and then as he cut short with God in reformation, and did not fulfill to walke after the Lord, therefore God cut *Jehu* short of all the hopes of grace that ever he might have attained, to vers. 32. so that if we cut at a scanting with God, and will part with some lusts and corruptions, but not with others, then will God cut you short of all your hopes of eternall life: and it was upon the same termes that *Herod* fell short of Christ, Mar. 6. 10. Luk. 3. 18. he had done many things according to *Johns* Ministry, but when God would cut him short of *Herodias* his darling Lust, that nothing might lye between God and him, but might now become fit for Christ, because he would not cut himselfe short of *Herodias,* and cut short his reformation there, then this was added to all his other sins, he *shut up* John *in prison,* and afterward cut off his head also; so that when there is any sinne, whether honour or pleasure, or any comfort in this life, that men will not be content to cut themselves short of, it is the way to utter ruine; God will not be abundantly ready to pardon such. And so was it with *Dæmas,* when the love of money did so prevaile with his heart, after he had been much esteemed of the Apostles, and mentioned honourably in their writings, yet in the end it is said of him, *He hath forsaken me, and loved this present world,* 2 Tim. 4. 10. Love of the world had so prevailed with him, that he fell off from *Paul,* and from the Lord, whose servant *Paul* was, and from fellowship in the Gospel, and so did not finde Christ; this rule is universally to be followed, and the care of it not to be neglected in any case, that our sins are to be put out of our hearts and hands, as ever we looke to finde Christ, and life in him; notable is that expression recorded in Judg. 10. 10. to 16. The people come and *cry to the Lord,* to deliver them out of the hands of their enemies; but they had got to themselves other gods, and now he would deliver them no more; When the people heard that, that God would not deliver them, and could finde no acceptance from him, so long as they continued in such a sinne; they thereupon goe and put away all their Idols, and leaves not one to be seen among them; and when God sees that they had put them away, the text saith, *that his soule was grieved for their misery,* and his bowels rowled within him for them, and he delivered them: so that when men are willing to fore-go their honourable sinnes, their sweet and delightfull sinnes, their profitable sinnes, and those wherewith they have been most captivated; and he knowes one may as well pull their hearts out of their bellies, as some sinnes out of them; but when he sees men are willing to fore-go their most darling delightfull sins, willing to breake off all impediements that stand between God and them, the soule of God is grieved in such a case, and it pitties him now that such a soule should be without him; and then it will not be long ere God stirres them up meanes of deliverance, and he himselfe will reveale himselfe unto them. Notable is that speech, Hos. 14. 3. 8. when they *take words to themselves,* and promise to leave all their evil wayes, whereby they sinne against God, they make this request to God, that *he would take away their iniquities from them;* and least God should answer them, but be you doing something in the meane time; they professe, that for their owne parts they will set about the doing of their iniquities away, and they say; Ashur *shall not save us, and we will have no more to doe with them;* wherein he shewes you, that God lookes not that only his people shall pray him to take away their iniquities, for we may pray so long enough, and not finde it done; but when we desire God to doe it, and set our hearts and hands to it, and now with heart and hand say, *Ashur shall not save us, nor will we say any more to the workes of our hands, ye are our gods;* then saith God in vers. 4. *I will heale their back-slidings, and will love them freely,* &c. God is then abundantly ready to pardon, when men forsake their owne wayes and thoughts, and throw away the sins that hang about them, God will say of such a people, *I will heale them, and love them freely, mine anger is turned away from them.* And you may presume, when Gods anger is turned away, it is by and through Christ, or else there is no healing; and therefore in vers. 8. *Ephraim* saith, *What have I to doe any more with Idols;* the heart of a Christian, or of a nation, shall openly acknowledge, that they will have no more fellowship with these abominations; and then saith God, *I have heard him, and observed him.* God heares us, and understands what we say, and observes us well, and offers to be a covert to us from the storme, when we begin solemnly to abandon such evils, then he heares us, and answers us according to the desire of our hearts; you have many a soule that cryes to God, take away our iniquity, and many petitions we put up to God to that purpose; and that sometimes with many bitter moanes, but God heares it not; we pour out our plaints in vaine, and he regards it not; but when we come to God, and desire him not only to take them from us, but begin to consider our owne wayes and iniquities, and to put them from us, out of our hearts and hands, and we wil no more take such bad wayes, as heretofore we have done; we *will no more ride upon horses,* nor run to forreigne princes for succour; then God heares, and grants graciously whatever his poore people begge at his hands, and answers it according to all the desire of their hearts, then the Lord presently gives us the Lord Jesus Christ, and life and healing in him; and this is the second way of having Christ by purchase. . . .

Fourthly, there is yet something more then all this, a further price to pay, if we mean to purchase Christ; and that is, that we part with all our good parts, and all the good common gifts of grace, which are found sometimes in good nature, and sometimes in the children of the church, we must part with them all that we may win Christ 1 Cor. 3. 18. *If any man among you seem to be wise in this world, let him become a foole that he may be wise:* who ever would be a wise man, (as a wise man he cannot be, if hee have not his part in Christ) he must lay aside his serious and sad deliberation, and communication with flesh and blood, and all things in the way of God, that he thinkes will be prejudiciall, if any man be so wise, as to see this and that danger in a Christian course, let him become a foole; else he shall never become a Christian: if a man will be content to forsake all for Christ, he must first be a foole, and be content to bee counted a foole, and heare every carnall man to count him a foole. And I speak not onely of carnal and civill wisdom, that, that only is to be denyed in the case, but common graces, which many times choakes all the hypocrites in the bosome of the church; they are commonly choaked upon this point, upon these things they trust, and doe therefore verily beleeve, that this and that interest, God hath in them, and they in God;

because they have received such and such gifts from him, and this is the case formerly mentioned, Matth. 7. 22, 23. they pleaded their spirituall gifts, though common gifts, and such as may be found in *workers of iniquity,* they *prayed to God,* a common gift; and they *prophesied in his name,* they had prophetical gifts; some measure of the spirit of ministery, and they were able *to cast out devills in Christs name;* now when as men do trust upon these, and settle themselves upon such a change, truly, hereby they loose that power in Christ which else they might have had. It a wonder to see what a change propheticall gifts will work in a man, 1 Sam. 10. 10, 12. He, there *Saul* had a spirit of prophesie came upon him, and the people wondred at it, it works a strange change in a man, and so in the next chap. the 19 and 23 ver. He prophesied til he came at such a place, so that you shall see a man that is trained up in any good order, though sometimes given to loose company; when once God begins to poure into him any spirituall gift, to inlighten his mind, and to inlarge his affection, that hee begins to have some love to, and some joy in the Word, and some sorrow in hearing of the Word, and some comfort in meditation: its wonder to see what a change this will work in the spirit; he forthwith begins to abandon his loose courses, and sets himselfe to a more strict course, then hee begins to see his acquisite learning is but a small matter to edification; hee prizes his spirituall gifts, and hee is able now to doe much; and when a mans heart is thus changed by propheticall gifts, it workes in a man such confidence in his soule, that he thinkes all the congregation shall perish before he can perish, and if ministers, may be thus deceived by common gifts and graces, how much more may their poor hearers bee deceived, when they by hearing the Word find such comfort, and illumnination, and inlargements, that they thereby finde a great change wrought in them; and yet if ministers may bee so much deceived, in presuming vainly of their good estate, which was not so, then much more common Christians: should any man presume at *Fælix his trembling,* Act. 24. 25. *At Jehues zeale,* 2 King. 10. 16. *At Ahabs humiliation,* 1 King. 21, 28, 29. *At Herods joy* in hearing, you know what became of all these, these be graces of God, though but common graces, and if the Prophets were deceived, may not these be deceived also, that have neither Christ nor any part in him; and therefore a man that would bee sure not to goe without Christ, nor without life in him; he must not trust in any spirituall gift he hath received, though his mind be inlightened, sometimes to feare, sometimes to joy, to humiliation, to inlargement, to zealous reformation, yet rest in none of these, for these may have and yet want Christ, and life in him; common graces may and will deceive you, a man may have all these, and yet not prize Christ, as his cheifest good; he may have all these, and yet not worship him: notwithstanding all these, there may bee some iniquity in their hands for which cause God will not shew mercy to them: See and observe, if in the midst of all these you do not *worke some iniquity;* they were *workers of iniquity* always at the best, Matth. 7. 23. You may be workers of iniquity, notwithstanding all these; and therefore consider if there be not some veine of pride, and hypocrisie, and covetousnesse, that cleaves fast to your hearts, which you allow your selves in, which if you doe, these very gifts will bee your ship-wracke, your anchor will breake, and your ship will bee carryed away, and you fall downe in destruction; but see that your hearts bee cleane, and see that there bee not an ill thought or way that you allow your selves in, and if so, then your heart will lay hold upon God, and you will prize Christ, and then it is a signe those gifts you have are not in hypocrisie; for in an hypocrite, they are alwayes found with some sinne, which if a man doe not willfully shut his eyes against hee may see, for our Saviour speakes of such a sinne in them, as the rest of the people of God may know them to be counterfeits, from verse 15 to 23. *You shall know them by this, doe men gather grapes of thornes, or figges of thistles?* have not they their ill haunts, but put away these from you, if you mean to have Christ.

# SWINE AND GOATS

From *The New Covenant, or A Treatise, Unfolding the Order and Manner of the Giving and Receiving of the Covenant of Grace to the Elect* (London, 1654)

ALL THE men in the world are divided into two ranks, godly or ungodly, righteous or wicked; of wicked men two sorts, some are notoriously wicked, others are hypocrites: Of hypocrites two sorts (and you shall find them in the church of God) some are washed Swine, others are Goats.

1. The Swine are those of whom our Saviour Christ saith, *That they returne unto their wallowing in the mire;* like unto these are such men who at the hearing of some sermon have been stomach sick of their sins, and have rejected their wicked courses, but yet the swines hearts remaineth in them, as a swine when he cometh where the puddle is, will readily lye down in it: so will these men wallow in the puddle of uncleannesse when their conscience is not pricked for the present: but these are a grosser kind of hypocrites.

2. There is another sort that goe far beyond these, and they are Goats, so called, Matth. 25. 32, 33. and these are clean beasts such as chew the cudd, meditate upon ordinances, and they divide the hoofe, they live both in a generall and particular calling, and will not be idle; they are also fit for sacrifice; what then is wanting? Truly they are not *sheep* all this

while, they are but *goats,* yet a goat doth loath that which a swine will readily break into; but where then doe they fall short of the nature of sheep? A difference there is, which standeth principally in these particulars.

1. The goat is of a capricious nature, and affecteth eminency, his gate also is stately, Prov. 30. 30 *Agur* reckoneth the he-goat among the 4 things that are comely in going: and they are full of ambition, they cannot abide swamps and holes, but will be climbing upon the tops of mountains; there is not that plain lowly sheepish frame that attendeth unto the voyce of the shepheard, to be led up and downe in fresh pastures: they attend upon their ends, and will outshoot God in his own bowe, and therefore when they have done many things for Christ, he will say unto them, *Depart from me, ye workers of iniquity.* More eminency they did affect, then they were guided unto. Thus it was with *Jehu,* who in his zeal for God thought to promote himselfe, and herein he will not be perswaded of his sin, and therefore going into crooked wayes, he cometh at length to cleave unto the sins of *Jeroboam* the son of *Nebat,* who made *Israel* to sin; yet notwithstanding, you may rec[e]ive a goat into church-fellowship for all his capricious nature, and he will be a clean creature, and of much good use. The five foolish Mat. 25. 2. were all of them *Virgins,* all of them abhorring idolatry, and all go forth to meet the bridegroome, and yet they are foolish and never shall you make them wise, to be all for Christ, onely hearing and obeying his voyce.

2. They are of a rankish nature all of them, specially the old goats will have an unsavory relish, far from that pleasant sweetnesse that is in a sheep; and herein hypocrites are greatly different from the sheep of Christ, as the Prophet speaketh, Ezek. 34. 21. and they marre the pastures with their feet, and will be at length mudling the faire waters of the sanctuary also; and in your best sanctification they fall far short of a sheep-like frame of spirit, diligently to heare the voyce of the shepheard, this will not be found in the sanctification of the best hypocrite under Heaven, they may goe far and yet fall away, and this is no arminianism, but if you search the Scriptures diligently, you will find these things to be true.

## HYPOCRITES AND SAINTS

TRULY IT is hard to perceive when men differ, and therefore it is not an easie matter to make such use of sanctification, as by it to beare witnesse unto justification: and it will be a very hard case and much more difficult, when men cannot feele the presence of spirituall gifts, but want spirituall light: and when they doe fine faith in themselves, they doe finde it in hypocrites also, even in hypocrites also, even faith to seeke the Lord, & faith to waite upon him, and faith to apply him, saying, *My God,* and faith to stay upon the *God of Israel;* and yet these men doe vanish away in hypocrisie; this hypocrites may doe; seeing therefore what easines of errour may befall Christians, whether this or that grace be of the right stampe or no, it will behove Christians to be wary, for even eagle-eyed Christians will have much adoe so to discerne of sanctification in themselves, before they see their justification, as to cut off all hypocrites from having the like in them, for the sanctified frame of Gods children, and that which seemeth to be like it in hypocrites, both of them spring from the Holy Ghost, and both from faith: but now the Spirit of God hath further worke in his own people, beyond what he worketh upon others, though he melteth both, yet hypocrites are melted as iron, which will returne againe to his former hardnes, but his owne people are melted into flesh, which will never return to his hardnes more, neither can they rest in any measure of softnes unto which they have attained, but still are carryed toward Jesus Christ; so that the one is a temporary faith, and the other persevereth; though both worke in the name of Christ, yet this difference will be found between them, not only when hypocrites come to be blasted, but even in the middest of their profession: as for the faith of the Gospell of Jesus Christ, it is never president of its own power, but his strength lyeth out of himselfe in Christ; whereas hypocrites and legall Christians are confident of their faith, that they can make use of it unto such and such ends, they think they need no more but look up to Christ, and their worke is at an end; and such strength they finde in themselves, as that they doe not feare, but that they shall carry an end all their worke to Gods glory and their own: whereas the strongest faith even of the *Thessalonians* (whose faith was such, as none of all the churches went before them) if it be not supplyed and strengthened, they know, & the Apostle *Paul* knoweth that it will warpe & shrinke. This may we see by comparing, 1 Thes. 1. 3. with Chap. 3. 2, 10. And the faithfull people of God, Isa. 26. 12. acknowledge him to *worke all their works for them.* And therefore as there is a reall difference in the presence of the spirit; so also in the worke of faith in hypocrites, and the children of God, for the one putteth confidence in himselfe in the gift received, and the other in *Jehovah.* This is the first difference of sanctification.

2. There is difference also in the rule whereby they are guided, though both seeke to the word of God & take delight in that, insomuch as you shall not be able to difference them there, yet a great difference there is in the apprehension of the word: the one is so confident of the comfort that he hath in the word, and he will be ready to take it ill at Gods hand, if he finde not acceptance before him: Now the other see the need they have of the Lord to maintaine their comfort for them. This manner of

affection we finde in *David,* when the Lord had brought him and his people into a sweet frame and temper of spirit to offer willingly towards the building of the temple; what saith *David* now? Doth he thinke this to be enough? No, no, but he prayeth to the Lord, 1 Chron. 29. 18. *O Lord God of Abraham, Isaack, and Israel our fathers keepe this for ever in the imagination of the thoughts of the heart of thy people, and prepare their heart unto thee.* Thus is he sensible that these comforts would soone faile them, & they should againe waxe barren and uncomfortable. And here is the nature of true consolation in Christ, to looke up unto the Lord to preserve and maintaine it, and so he is still drawne neerer & neerer to Christ. But now though both attend unto the word, as their rule of sanctification, if you take it in the way, in which the one and the other hold it forth, yet there is a great difference. Psal. 119. 6. *Then shall I not be ashamed,* &c. Here is a rule; what, may not hypocrites walke according to this rule? Truly they professe no lesse, and they think it enough, if they have but a rule in their eye, and therefore under a spirit of bondage they are confident and say, *What soever the Lord commandeth us, we will heare it and doe it,* Deut. 5. 27. And what saith *Balaam; though* Balaack *would give me an house full of silver and gold, I cannot goe beyond the Commandment of the Lord,* Numb. 22. 18. And yet he loved the wages of iniquity; and indeed those that undertake so much in their owne strength, they come afterward to be weary of the Lord, and weary of his Commandments; as Amos 8. 5. and they say at last, *It is in vaine to serve God, and what profit is it that we have kept his ordinances?* Mal. 3. 14. These are but like washed swine, that will crop grasse for a while in a faire pasture, but if you keepe them long there, they will not delight in such manner of feeding, but will rather choose to go into the mire; but as for goats they will delight in the Commandments of the Lord, Isa. 58. 2. It is not a very hard thing unto them, nor grievous for them to keep solemne fasting dayes together, they come willingly, they delight to come, therefore the difference will be hardly discovered, and unles you be a Christian of a very cleere discerning, you will not finde the difference.

# THOMAS HOOKER
## (1586–1647)

## HARTFORD ELECTION SERMON
### (Hartford, 1638)

TEXT (Deut. 1. 13): *Take you wise men, and understanding, and known among your tribes, and I will make them rulers over you.* Captains over thousands, and captains over hundreds—over fifties, over tens, etc.

Doctrine. I. That the choice of public magistrates belongs unto the people by God's own allowance.

II. The privilege of election, which belongs to the people, therefore must not be exercised according to their humors, but according to the blessed will and law of God.

III. They who have the power to appoint officers and magistrates, it is in their power also to set the bounds and limitations of power and place unto which they call them.

Reasons. 1. Because the foundation of authority is laid, firstly, in the free consent of the people.

2. Because by a free choice the hearts of the people will be more inclined to the love of the persons [chosen] and more ready to yield [obedience].

3. Because of that duty and engagement of the people.

Uses. The lesson taught is threefold:

First. There is matter of thankful acknowledgment in the [appreciation] of God's faithfulness towards us, and the permission of these measures that God doth command and vouchsafe.

Secondly. Of reproof: to dash the conceits of all those that shall oppose it.

Thirdly. Of exhortation: to persuade us, as God hath given us liberty, to take it.

And lastly: as God hath spared our lives and given them in liberty, so to seek the guidance of God, and to choose in God and for God.

# A TRUE SIGHT OF SIN, MEDITATION, WANDERING THOUGHTS, REPENTANT SINNERS AND THEIR MINISTERS

From *The Application of Redemption By the Effectual Work of the Word, and Spirit of Christ, for the Bringing Home of Lost Sinners to God. The Ninth and Tenth Books.* (London, 1659)

### *Wherein this true sight, and apprehension of sin properly discovers it self.*

I ANSWER, a true sight of sin hath two conditions attending upon it; or it appears in two things: We must see sin, 1. Cleerly. 2. Convinctingly, what it is in it self, and what it is to us, not in the appearance and paint of it, but in the power of it; not to fadam it in the notion and conceit only, but to see it with application.

We must see it cleerly in its own nature, its native color and proper hue: it's not every slight conceit, not every general and cursorie, confused thought or careless consideration that will serve the turn, or do the work here, we are all sinners; it is my infirmity, I cannot help it; my weakness, I cannot be rid of it; no man lives without faults and follies, the best have their failings, *In many things we offend all.* But alas all this wind shakes no corn, it costs more to see sin aright than a few words of course; it's one thing to say sin is thus and thus, another thing to see it to be such; we must look wis[e]ly and steddily upon our distempers, look sin in the face, and discern it to the full; the want whereof is the cause of our mistaking our estates, and not redressing of our hearts and waies, Gal. 6. 4. *Let a man prove his own work.* Before the goldsmith can sever and see the dross asunder from the gold, he must search the very bowels of the mettal, and try it by touch, by tast, by hammer, and by fire; and then he will be able to speak by proof what it is; so here. We perceive sin in the crowd and by hearsay, when we attend some common and customary expressions taken up by persons in their common converse, and so report what others speak, and yet never knew the truth, what either others or we say, but we do not single out our corruptions and survey the loathsomness of them, as they come naked in their own natures; this we ought to do: there is great ods betwixt the knowledg of a traveller, that in his own person hath taken a view of many coasts, past through many countries, and hath there taken up his abode some time, and by experience hath been an eye-witness of the extream cold, and scorching heats, hath surveyed the glory and beauty of the one, the barrenness and meanness of the other; he hath been in the wars, and seen the ruin and desolation wrought there; and another that sits by his fire side, and happily reads the story of these in a

Book, or views the proportion of these in a map, the ods is great, and the difference of their knowledg more than a little: the one saw the country really, the other only in the story; the one hath seen the very place, the other only in the paint of the map drawn. The like difference is there in the right discerning of sin; the one hath surveyed the compass of his whol course, searched the frame of his own heart, and examined the windings and turnings of his own waies, he hath seen what sin is, and what it hath done, how it hath made havock of his peace and comfort, ruinated and laid wast the very principles of reason and nature, and morality, and made him a terror to himself, when he hath looked over the loathsom abominations that lie in his bosom, that he is afraid to approach the presence of the Lord to bewail his sins, and to crave pardon, lest he should be confounded for them, while he is but confessing of them; afraid and ashamed lest any man living should know but the least part of that which he knows by himself, and could count it happy that himself was not, that the remembrance of those hideous evils of his might be no more; another happily hears the like preached or repeated, reads them writ or recorded in some authors, and is able to remember and relate them. The ods is marvelous great. The one sees the history of sin, the other the nature of it; the one knows the relation of sin as it is mapped out, and recorded; the other the poyson, as by experience he hath found and proved it. It's one thing to see a disease in the book, or in a mans body, another thing to find and feel it in a mans self. There is the report of it, here the malignity and venom of it.

But how shall we see cleerly the nature of sin in his naked hue?

This will be discovered, and may be conceived in the particulars following. Look we at it: first, as it respects God. Secondly, as it concerns our selves. As it hath reference to God, the vileness of the nature of sin may thus appear.

It would dispossess God of that absolute supremacy which is indeed his prerogative royal, and doth in a peculiar manner appertayn to him, as the diamond of his crown, and diadem of his deity, so the Apostle, *He is God over all blessed for ever,* Rom. 9. 5. All from him and all for him, he is the absolute first being, the absolute last end, and herein is the crown of his glory. All those attributes of wisdom, goodness, holiness, power, justice, mercy, the shine and concurrency of all these meeting together is to set out the unconceivable excellency of his glorious name, which exceeds all praise, *Thyne is the kingdom, the power and the glory,* the right of all and so the rule of all and the glory of all belongs to him.

Now herein lyes the unconceavable hainousness of the hellish nature of sin, it would justle the almighty out of the throne of his glorious soveraignty, and indeed be above him. For the will of man being the chiefest of all his workmanship, all for his body, the body of the soul, the mind to attend upon the will, the will to attend upon God, and to make choyce of him, and his wil, that is next to him, and he onely above that: and that should have been his throne and temple or chair of state, in which he would have set his soveraignty for ever. He did in an especial manner intend to meet with man, and to communicate himself to man in his righteous law, as the rule of his Holy and righteous will, by which the will of *Adam* should have been ruled and guided to him, and made happie in him; and all creatures should have served God in man, and been happy by or through him, serving of God being happy in him; but when the will went from under the government of his rule, by sin, *it would be above God, and be happy without him,* for the rule of the law in each command of it, holds forth a three-fold expression of soveraignty from the Lord, and therein the soveraignty of all the rest of his attributes.

1. The powerful supremacy of his just will, as that he hath right to dispose of all and authority to command all at his pleasure; *What if God will?* Rom. 9. 22 *My Counsel shall stand and I wil do all my pleasure,* Isa. 46. 10. And as its true of what shal be done upon us, so his wil hath soveraignty of command in what should be done by us we are to say *the will of the Lord be done; Davids* warrant was *to do all Gods wils* Acts. 13. 22. and our Saviour himself professeth, John. 6. 38. *that he came not to do his own will but the will of him that sent him,* and therefore his wrath and jealosie and judgment will break out in case that be disobeyed.

2. There is also a fulness of wisdom in the law of God revealed to guide & direct us in the way we should walk, Psal. 19. 7. *The law of God makes wise the simple,* 2. Tim. 3. 15. *It's able to make us wise unto salvation.*

3. There's a sufficiency of God to content and satisfy us. *Blessed are they who walk in his wayes, and blessed are they that keep his testimonies.* Psal. 119. 1. 2. *Great prosperity have they that love the law, and nothing shal offend them,* ver. 16. and in truth there can be no greater reward for doing wel, than to be enabled to do well, he that hath attayned his last end he cannot go further, he cannot be better;

Now by sin we justle the law out of its place, and the Lord out of his glorious soveraignty, pluck the crown from his head, and the seepter out of his hand, and we say and profess by our practice, there is not authority and power there to govern, nor wisdom to guide, nor good to content me, but I will be swayed by mine own wil and led by mine own deluded reason and satisfied with my own lusts. This is the guise of every graceless heart in the commission of sin; so *Pharaoh who is the Lord? I know not the Lord, nor will I let Israel go.* Exod. 5. 2. in the time of their prosperity see how the Jews turn their backs and shake off the authority of the Lord, *we are Lords* (say they) *we will come no more at thee.* Jer. 2. 31. *and our tongues are our own who shal be Lords over us?* Psal. 12. 4. So for the wisdom of the world, see how they set light by it as not worth the looking after it Jer. 18.

12. *we wil walk after our own devices & we wil every one do the imagination of his own evil heart, yea they sett up their own traditions,* their own Idols and delusions, and Lord it over the law, *making the command of God of none effect* Math. 15. 8. 9. So for the goodness of the word; Job. 22. 17. Mat. 3. 14. *It is in vayn to serve God and what profit is there that we have kept his ordinances, yea his Commandments are ever grievous,* Its a grievous thing to the loose person he cannot have his pleasures but he must have his guilt and gall with them; its grievous to the worldling that he cannot lay hold on the world by unjust means, but conscience layes hold upon him as breaking the law. Thou that knowest and keepest thy pride and stubbornness and thy distempers, know assuredly thou dost justle God out of the throne of his glorious soveraignty and thou dost profess, Not Gods wil but thine own (which is above his) shall rule thee, thy carnal reason and the folly of thy mind, is above the wisdome of the Lord and that shal guide thee; to please thine own stubborn crooked pervers spirit, is a greater good than to please God and enjoy happines, for this more contents, thee; that when thou considerest but thy course, dost thou not wonder that the great and terrible God doth not pash such a poor insolent worm to pouder, and send thee packing to the pitt every moment.

2. It smites at the essence of the Almighty and the desire of the sinner, is not only that God should not be supream but that indeed he should *not be at all,* and therefore it would destroy the being of Jehovah. Psal. 81. 15. Sinners are called *the haters of the Lord.* John. 15. 24. *They hated both me and my Father.* Now he that hates endeavours if it be possible the annihilation of the thing hated, and its most certain were it in their power, they would pluck God out of Heaven the light of his truth out of their consciences, and the law out of the societies and assemblies where they live, that they might have elbow room to live as they list. Nay what ever they hate most and intend, and plott more evil against in al the world, they hate God most of all, and intend more evil against him than against all their enemies besides, because they hate all for his sake, therefore wicked men *are said to destroy the law* Psal. 126. 119 the adulterer loaths that law that condemns, uncleaness; the earthworm would destrow that law that forbids covetousness, they are sayd to *hate the light* John 3. 21. To hate the saints and servants of the Lord John 15. 18. *The world hates you,* he that hates the Lanthorn for the lights sake, he hates the light much more, he that hates faithful because of the image of God, and the grace that appears there, he hates the God of all, grace and holiness, most of all, so God to *Zenacharib,* Isa. 37. 28. *I know thy going out and thy comming in, and thy rage against me,* oh it would be their content, if there was no God in the world to govern them, no law to curbe them, no justice to punish, no truth to trouble them, learn therfore to see how far your rebellions

reach, it is not arguments you gainsay, not the counsel of a minister you reject, the command of a magistrate ye oppose, evidence of rule or reason ye resist; but be it known to you, you fly in the very face of the Almighty, and it is not the Gospel of grace ye would have destroyed, but the spirit of grace, the author of grace the Lord Jesus, the God of all grace that ye hate.

It crosseth the whol course of Providence, perverts the work of the creature and defaceth the beautiful frame, and that sweet correspondence and orderly usefulness the Lord first implanted in the order of things; the heavens deny their influence, the earth her strength, the corn her nourishment, thank sin for that. Weeds come instead of herbs, cockle and darnel instead of wheat, thank sin for that, Rom. 8. 22. *The whol creature* (or creation) *grones under vanity,* either cannot do what it would or else misseth of that good and end it intended, breeds nothing but vanity, brings forth nothing but vexation, It crooks all things so as that none can straiten them, makes so many wants that none can supply them, Eccles. 1. 15. This makes crooked servants in a family no man can rule them, crooked inhabitants in towns, crooked members in congregations, ther's no ordering nor joynting of them in that comly accord, and mutual subjection; know they said, *the adversary sin hath done all this.* Man was the mean betwixt God and the creature to convey all good with all the constancy of it, and therefore when man breaks, Heaven and earth breaks all asunder, the conduit being cracked and displaced there can be no conveyance from the fountain.

In regard of our selves, see we and consider nakedly the nature of sin, in four particulars.

Its that which makes a separation between God and the soul, breaks that union and communion with God for which we were made, and in the enjoyment of which we should be blessed and happie, Isai. 59. 1. 2. *Gods ear is not heavy that it cannot hear nor his hand that it cannot help, but your iniquities have separated betwixt God and you & your sins have hid his face that he wil not hear for he professeth,* Psal. 5. 4. *that he is a God that wills not wickedness neither shal iniquity dwell with him. Into the new Jerusalem shal no unclean thing enter, but without shal be doggs* Rev. 21. 27. The Dogs to their kennel, and hogs to their sty and mire: but if an impenitent wretch should come into Heaven, the Lord would go out of Heaven; *Iniquity shall not dwell with sin.* That then that deprives me of my greatest good for which I came into the world, and for which I live and labor in the world, and without which I had better never to have been born; nay, that which deprives me of an universal good, a good that hath all good in it, that must needs be an evil, but have all evil in it: but so doth sin deprive me of God as the object of my will, and that wills all good, and therefore it must bring in truth all evil with it. Shame takes away my honor, poverty my wealth, persecution my peace, prison my liberty, death my life, yet a man may still be a happy man, lose his life, and live eternally: but sin takes away my God, and with him all good goes; prosperity without God will be my poyson, honor without him my bane; nay, the word without God hardens me, my endeavor without him profits nothing at all for my good. A natural man hath no God in any thing, and therefore hath no good.

It brings an incapability in regard of my self to receive good, and an impossibility in regard of God himself to work my spiritual good, while my sin continues, and I continue impenitent in it. An incapability of a spiritual blessing, *Why transgress ye the Commandment of the Lord that ye cannot prosper do what* ye can, 2 Chron. 24. 20. And *he that being often reproved hardens his heart, shal be consumed suddenly and there is no remedy,* He that spils the physick that should cure him, the meat that should nourish him, there is no remedy but he must needs dye, so that the commission of sin makes not only a separation from God, but obstinate resistance and continuance in it, maintains an infinit and everlasting distance between God and the soul: so that so long as the sinful resistance of thy soul continues; God cannot vouchsafe the comforting and guiding presence of his grace; because it's cross to the covenant of grace he hath made, which he will not deny, and his oath which he will not alter. So that should the Lord save thee and thy corruption, carry thee and thy proud unbeleeving heart to heaven he must nullify the Gospel, (Heb. 5. 9. *He's the author of salvation to them that obey him*) and forswear himself, (Heb. 3. 18. *He hath sworn unbeleevers shall not enter into his rest*) he must cease to be just and holy, and so to be God. As *Saul* said to *Jonathan* concerning *David,* 1 Sam. 20. 30, 31. *So long as the son of* Jesse *lives, thou shalt not be established, nor thy kingdom:* So do thou plead against thy self, and with thy own soul; so long as these rebellious distempers continue, grace and peace, and the kingdom of Christ can never be established in thy heart. For this obstinate resistance differs nothing from the plagues of the state of the damned, when they come to the highest measure, but that it is not yet total and final, there being some kind of abatement of the measure of it, and stoppage of the power of it. Imagine thou sawest the Lord Jesus coming in the clouds, and heardest the last trump blow, *Arise ye dead, and come to judgment:* imagine thou sawest the judg of all the world sitting upon the throne, thousands of angels before him, and ten thousands ministring unto him, the sheep standing on his right hand, and the goats at the left: suppose thou heardest that dreadful sentence, and final doom pass from the Lord of life (whose word made Heaven and earth, and will shake both) *Depart from me ye cursed;* how would thy heart shake and sink, and die within thee in the thought thereof, wert thou really perswaded it was thy portion? Know, that by thy dayly continuance in sin, thou dost to the utmost of thy power execute that Sentence upon thy soul: it's thy life, thy labor, the desire of thy heart, and thy dayly practice to depart away from the God of all grace and peace, and turn the tomb-stone of everlasting destruction upon thine own soul.

It's the cause which brings all other evils of punishment into the world, and without this they are not evil, but so far as sin is in them. The sting of a trouble, the poyson and malignity of a punishment and affliction, the evil of the evil of any judgment, it is the sin that brings it, or attends it, Jer. 2. 19. *Thine own wickedness shall correct thee, and thy back slidings shall reprove thee, know therefore that it is an evil, and bitter thing that thou hast forsaken the Lord.* Jer. 4. 18. *Thy waies and doings have procured these things unto thee, therefore it is bitter, and reacheth unto the heart.* Take miseries and crosses without sin, they are like to be without a sting, the serpent without poyson, ye may take them, and make medicines of them. So *Paul* 1 Cor. 15. 55. he plaies with death it self, sports with the grave. *Oh death, where is thy sting? Oh grave where is thy victory? the sting of death is sin.* All the harmful annoyance in sorrows and punishments, further than either they come from sin, or else tend to it, they are rather improvements of what we have than parting with any thing we do enjoy, we rather lay out our conveniences than seem to lose them, yea, they encrease our crown, and do not diminish our comfort. *Blessed are ye when men revile you, and persecute you, and speak all manner of evil of you for my sake, for great is your reward in Heaven:* Matth. 5. 11. There is a blessing in persecutions and reproaches when they be not mingled with the deserts of our sins; yea, our momentary short affliction for a good cause, and a good conscience, works an excessive exceeding weight of glory. If then sin brings all evils, and makes all evils indeed to us, then is it worse than all those evils.

It brings a curse upon all our Comforts, blasts all our blessings, the best of all our endeavors, the use of all the choycest of all Gods ordinances: it's so evil and vile, that it makes the use of all good things, and all the most glorious, both ordinances and improvements evil to us. Hag. 2. 13. 14. When the question was made to the priest; *If one that is unclean by a dead body touch any of the holy things, shall it be unclean? And he answered, yea. So is this people, and so is this nation before me, saith the Lord; and so is every work of their hands, and that which they offer is unclean:* if any good thing a wicked man had, or any action he did, might be good, or bring good to him, in reason it was the services and sacrifices wherein he did approach unto God, and perform service to him, and yet *the sacrifice of the wicked is an abomination to the Lord,* Prov. 28. 9. and Tit. 1. 15. *To the pure all things are pure; but to the unbeleeving there is nothing pure, but their very consciences are defiled.* It is a desperate malignity in the temper of the stomach, that should turn our meat and diet into diseases, the best cordials and preservatives into poysons, so that what in reason is appointed to nourish a man should kill him. Such is the venom and malignity of sin, makes the use of the best things become evil, nay, the greatest evil to us many times; Psal. 109. 7. *Let his prayer be turned into sin.* That which is appointed by God to be the choycest means to prevent sin, is turned into sin out of the corrupt distemper of these carnal hearts of ours.

Hence then it follows; *that sin is the greatest evil in the world, or indeed that can be.* For, That which separates the soul from God, that which brings all evils of punishment, and makes all evils truly evil, and spoils all good things to us, that must needs be the greatest evil, but this is the nature of sin, as hath already appeared.

But that which I will mainly press, is, sin is only opposite to God, and cross as much as can be to that infinite goodness and holiness which is in his blessed majesty; it's not the miseries or distresses that men undergo, that the Lord distasts them for, or estrangeth himself from them, he is with *Joseph* in the prison, with the three children in the furnace, with *Lazarus* when he lies among the dogs, and gathers the crums from the rich mans table, yea with *Job* upon the dung-hil, but he is not able to bear the presence of sin: yea, of this temper are his dearest servants, the more of God is in them, the more opposite they are to sin where ever they find it. It was that he commended in the Church of *Ephesus, That she could not bear those that were wicked,* Rev. 2. 3. As when the stomach is of a pure temper and good strength, the least surfet or distemper that befals, it presently distasts and disburdens it self with speed. So *David* noted to be *a man after Gods own heart.* He professeth, 101. Psal. 3. 7. *I hate the work of them that turn aside, he that worketh deceit shall not dwell in my house, he that telleth lyes, shall not tarry in my sight.* But when the heart becomes like the stomach, so weak it cannot help it self, nor be helped by physick, desperate diseases and dissolution of the whol follows, and in reason must be expected. Hence see how God looks at the least connivance, or a faint and feeble kind of opposition against sin, as that in which he is most highly dishonored, and he follows it with most hideous plagues, as that indulgent carriage of *Ely* towards the vile behavior of his sons for their grosser evils, 1 Sam. 2. 23. *Why do you such things, It's not well my sons that I hear such things: it is not well,* and is that all? why, had they either out of ignorance not known their duty or out of some sudden surprisal of a temptation neglected it, it had not been well, but for them so purposedly to proceed on in the practice of such gross evils, and for him so faintly to reprove: the Lord looks at it as a great sin thus feebly to oppose sin, and therefore verse 29. He tells him, *That he honored his sons above God,* and therefore he professeth, *Far be it from me to maintain thy house and comfort, for he that honors me I wil honor, and he that despiseth me shall be lightly esteemed,* verse 30. Hence it is the Lord himself is called *the holy one of Israel,* 1. Hab. 12. *Who is of purer eyes than to behold evil, and cannot look upon iniquity,* no not in such as profess themselves saints, though most deer unto him, no, nor in his Son the Lord Jesus, not in his saints, Amos. 8. 7. *The Lord hath sworn by himself, I abhor the excellency of* Jacob; what ever their excellencies, their priviledges are, if they do not abhor sin, God will abhor them, Jer. 22. 24. *Though* Coniah *was as the signet of my right hand, thence would I pluck him.* Nay, he could not endure the appearance of it in the Lord Christ, for when but the reflection of sin (as I may so say) fell upon our Savior, even the imputation of our transgressions to him, though none iniquity was ever committed by him, the father withdrew his comforting presence from him, and let loose his infinite displeasure against him, forcing him to cry out, *My God, my God, why hast thou forsaken me?*

Yea, sin is so evil, (that though it be in nature, which is the good creature of God) that there is no good in it, nothing that God will own; but in the evil of punishment it is otherwise, for the torments of the devils, and punishments of the damned in Hell, and all the plagues inflicted upon the wicked upon earth, issue from the righteous and revenging justice of the Lord, and he doth own such execution as his proper work, Isa. 45. 7. *Is there any evil in the city,* viz. of punishment, *and the Lord hath not done it? I make peace, I create evil, I the Lord do all these things:* it issues from the justice of God that he cannot but reward every one according to his own waies and works; those are a mans own, the holy one of Israel hath no hand in them; but he is the just executioner of the plagues that are inflicted and suffered for these; and hence our blessed Savior becoming our surety, and standing in our room, he endured the pains of the second death, even the fierceness of the fury of an offended God; and yet it was impossible he could commit the least sin, or be tainted with the least corrupt distemper. And it's certain it's better to suffer all plagues without any one sin, than to commit the least sin, and to be freed from all plagues. Suppose that all miseries and sorrows that ever befel all the wicked in earth and Hell, should meet together in one soule, as all waters gathered together in one sea: suppose thou heardest the devils roaring, and sawest Hell gaping, and flames of everlasting burnings flashing before thine eyes; it's certain it were better for thee to be cast into those inconceivable torments than to commit the least sin against the Lord: thou dost not think so now, but thou wilt find it so one day.

# MEDITATION

*Meditation is a serious intention of the mind whereby wee come to search out the truth, and settle it effectually upon the heart.*

*An intention of the mind;* when one puts forth the strength of their understanding about the work in hand, takes it as an especial task whereabout the heart should be taken up and that which wil require the whol man, and that to the bent of the best ability he hath, so the word is used Jos. 1. 8. *Thou shalt not suffer the word to depart out of thy mind, but thou shalt meditate therein day and night,* when either the word would depart away or our corruptions would drive it away, meditation layes hold upon it and wil not let it go, but exerciseth the strength of the attention of his thoughts about it, makes a business of it as that about which he might do his best, and yet fals short of what he should do in it. So *David* when he would discover where the stream and overflowing strength of his affections vented themselves, he points at this practice as that which employes the mind to the ful. Psal. 119. 197. *Oh how I love thy law, it is my meditation all the day,* love is the great wheel of the soul that sets al on going, and how doth that appear? it is my meditation day and night; the word in the original signifyeth to swim, a man spreads the breadth of his understanding about that work, and layes out himself about the service wherein there is both difficulty and worth.

*Serious.*] Meditation is not a flourishing of a mans wit, but hath a set bout at the search of the truth, beats his brain as wee use to say, hammers out a buisiness, as the gouldsmith with his mettal, he heats it and beats it turnes it on this side and then on that, fashions it on both that he might frame it to his mind; meditation is hammering of a truth or poynt propounded, that he may carry and conceive the frame and compass in his mind, not salute a truth as we pass by occasionally but solemnly entertain it into our thoughts; not look upon a thing presented as a spectator or passenger that goes by: but lay other things aside, and look at this as the work and employment for the present to take up our minds. It's one thing in our diet to take a snatch and away, another thing to make a meal, and sit at it on purpose until wee have seen al set before us and we have taken our fil of al, so we must not cast an eye or glimpse at the truth by some sudden or fleighty apprehension, a snatch and away, but we must make a meal of musing. Therefore the psalmist makes it the main trade that a godly man drives, professedly opposite to the carriage of the wicked, whether in his outward or inward work, in his disposition or expression of himself in his common practice; whereas they walk in the corrupt counsels of their own hearts, stand in the way of sinners, not only devise what is naught, but practice and persevere in what they have devised, and sit in the seat of the scorners; a blessed man his rode in which he travels, his set trade *he meditates in the Law of God day and night:* that is the counsel in which he walks, the way in which he stands, the seat in which he sits. Look at this work as a branch of our Christian calling, not that which is left to our liberty, but which is of necessity to be attended and that in good earnest as a Christian duty, which God requires, not a little available to our spiritual welfare.

The end is doubly expressed in the other part of the description.

1. *The searching of the truth.*

2. *The effectual setling of it upon the heart.*

*The search of the truth:* Meditation is a coming in with the truth or any cause that comes to hand, that we may enquire the ful state of it before our thoughts part with it, so that we see more of it or more clearly and fully than formerly we did, this is one thing in that of the Prophet Hos. 6. 3. *Then shall yee know if you follow on to know,* when we track the footsteps of the truth, in al the passages, until we have viewed the whol progresse of it, from truth to truth from point to point. *This it is to dig for wisdom,* Prov. 2. 2. When men have found a mine or a veyn of silver, they do not content themselves, to take that which is uppermost and next at hand within sight which offers it self upon the surface of the earth, but they dig further as hoping to find more, because they see somewhat. So meditation rests not in what presents it self to our consideration, but digs deeper gathers in upon the truth, and gaynes more of it then did easily appear at the first, and this it doth.

1. *When it recals things formerly past, sets them in present view before our consideration and judgment* Meditation sends a mans thoughts afar off, cals over and revives the fresh apprehension of things done long before, marshals them al in rank together, brings to mind such things which were happily quite out of memory, & gone from a man, which might be of great use and special help to discover our condition according to the quality of it; may be conscience starts the consideration but of one sin, but meditation looks abroad, and brings to hand many of the same, and of the like kind and that many dayes past and long ago committed, this distemper now sticks upon a man and brings him under the arrest of conscience and the condemnation thereof. But saies meditation let me mind you of such and such sins at such and such times, in such and such companies, committed and multiplyed both more and worse than those that now appear so loathsom and so troublesom to you; meditation is as it were the register and remembrancer, that looks over the records of our daily corruptions, and keeps them upon file, and brings them into court and fresh consideration Job. 13. 26. *Thou makest me to possess the sins of my youth:* this makes a man to renew the sins of his youth, makes them fresh in our thoughts, as though new done before our eyes. This interpreters make the meaning of that place Job. 14. 17. *My trangression is sealed up in a bag, and thou sewest up mine iniquity,* though God do thus, yet he doth it by this means in the way of his Providence, *i.e.* by recounting and recalling our corruptions to mind, by serious meditation we sew them all up together, we look back to the linage and pedegree of our lusts, and track the abominations of our lives, step by step, until we come to the very nest where they are hatched and bred, even of our original

corruption, and body of death, where they had their first breath and being, links al our distempers together from our infancy to our youth, from youth to riper age, from thence to our declining daies. So *David*, from the vileness of his present lusts is led to the wickedness *in which he was warmed*, Psal. 51. 5. This was typed out in the old law by *the chewing of the cud;* Meditation cals over again those things that were past long before, and not within a mans view and consideration.

Meditation *takes a special Survey of the compass of our present condition, and the nature of those corruptions that come to be considered:* it's the traversing of a mans thoughts, the coasting of the mind and imagination into every crevis and corner, pryes into every particular, takes a special view of the borders and confines of any corruption or condition that comes to be scanned, Psal. 119. 59. *I considered my waies, and turned my feet unto thy testimonies;* he turned them upside down, looked through them as it were; a present apprehension peeps in as it were through the crevis or key-hole, looks in at the window as a man passeth by; but Meditation lifts up the latch and goes into each room, pries into every corner of the house, and surveys the composition and making of it, with all the blemishes in it. Look as the searcher at the sea-port, or custom-house, or ships, satisfies himself not to over-look carelessly in a sudden view, but unlocks every chest, romages every corner, takes a light to discover the darkest passages. So is it with meditation, it observes the woof and web of wickedness, the ful frame of it, the very utmost Selvage and out-side of it, takes into consideration all the secret conveyances, cunning contrivements, all bordering circumstances that attend the thing, the consequences of it, the nature of the causes that work it, the several occasions and provocations that lead to it, together with the end and issue that in reason is like to come of it, Dan. 12. 4. *Many shall run to and fro, and knowledg shall encrease:* Meditation goes upon discovery, toucheth at every coast, observes every creek, maps out the dayly course of a mans conversation and disposition.

The second end of meditation is, *It settles it effectually upon the heart.* It's not the pashing of the water at a sudden push, but the standing and soaking to the root, that loosens the weeds and thorns, that they may be plucked up easily. It's not the laying of oyl upon the benummed part, but the chafing of it in, that suppleth the joynts, and easeth the pain. It is so in the soul; application laies the oyl of the word that is searching and savory, meditation chafeth it in, that it may soften and humble the hard and stony heart: application is like the conduit or channel that brings the stream of the truth upon the soul; but meditation stops it as it were, and makes it soak into the heart, that so our corruptions may be plucked up kindly by the roots.

This settling upon the heart appears in a three-fold work.

*It affects the heart with the truth attended,* and leaves an impression upon the spirit answerable to the nature of the thing which is taken into meditation: 2 Pet. 2. 8. It's said of *Lot, in seeing and hearing, he vexed his righteous soul.* Many saw and heard the hideous abominations, and were not touched nor affected therewith. No more had he been, but that he vexed and troubled his own righteous soul, because he was driven to a dayly consideration of them which cut him to the quick. The word is observable, it signifies to try by a touch-stone, and to examine, and then upon search to bring the soul upon the rack: therefore the same word is used, Matth. 14. 24. *The ship was tossed by the waves;* the consideration of the abominations of the place raised a tempest of trouble in *Lots* righteous soul. This the wise man calls *laying to the heart,* Eccles. 7. 1, 2. *It's better to go to the house of mourning than to the house of laughter; for this is the end of all men, and the living will lay it to his heart.* When the spectacle of misery and mortality is laid in the grave, yet savory meditation laies it to a mans heart, and makes it real there in the work of it. The goldsmith observes that it is not the laying of the fire, but the blowing of it that melts the mettal: so with meditation, it breaths upon any truth that is applied, and that makes it really sink and soak into the soul; and this is the reason why in an ordinary and common course of Providence, and Gods dealing with sinners, (leaving his own exceptions to his own good pleasure) that the most men in the time and work of conversion have that scorn cast upon them, *that they grow melancholly.* And it's true thus far in the course of ordinary appearance; the Lord usually never works upon the soul by the ministry of the word to make it effectual, but he drives the sinner to sad thoughts of heart, and makes him keep an audit in his own soul by serious meditation, and pondering of his waies; otherwise the word neither affects throughly, nor works kindly upon him.

*It keeps the heart under the heat and authority of the truth that it's taken up withal, by constant attendance of his thoughts.* Meditation keeps the conscience under an arrest, so that it cannot make an escape from the evidence and authority of the truth, so that there is no way, but either to obey the rule of it, or else be condemned by it. But escape it cannot, Meditation meets and stops al the evasions and sly pretences the fals-hearted person shal counterfeit. If a man should deny his fault, and himself guilty, Meditation will evidence it beyond all gainsaying, by many testimonies which Meditation wil easily cal to mind; remember ye not in such and such a place: upon such an occasion, you gave way to your wicked heart to do thus and thus; you know it, and God knows it, and I have recorded it: if the sinner would lessen his fault, Meditation aggravates it; or if he seem to slight it, and look at it as a matter of no moment, yet Meditation will make it appear, there is greater evil in it, and greater necessity to bestow his thoughts upon it than he is aware of.

Hence it is Meditation laies siege unto his soul, and cuts off al carnal pretences that a wretched self-deceiving hypocrite would relieve himself by; and stil lies at the soul, this you did, at that time, in that place, after that manner; so that the soul is held fast prisoner, and cannot make an escape; but as *David* said, Psal. 51. 3. *My sins are ever before me:* consideration keeps them within view, and will not suffer them to go out of sight and thoughts; and therefore it is *Paul* joyns those two together, 1 Tim. 3. 15. *Meditate in these things, and be in them.*

It provokes a man (by a kind of over-bearing power) to the practice of that with which he is so affected: a settled and serious Meditation of any thing, is as the setting open of the flood-gates, which carries the soul with a kind of force and violence, to the performance of what he so bestows his mind upon; as a mighty stream let out turns the mill. Phil. 4. 9. *Think of these things, and do them:* thinking men are doing men. Psal. 39. 3. *While I was thus musing, the fire brake out, and I spake:* the busie stirring of Meditation is like the raising of a tempest in the heart, that carries out all the actions of the man by an uncontroulable command. *I considered my waies, and turned my feet unto thy Statutes:* right consideration, brings in a right reformation with it.

## WANDERING THOUGHTS

The marriner, because the channel is narrow, and the wind somwhat scant, he toucheth in many places, tacks about, and fetcheth many points, but stil because it's to attain the haven; therfore each man in reason concludes, that was the cause that invited him to al that variety in his course. It's so in the carriage of the soul; the cause why a man fetcheth such a compass, and tacks about in his own contrivements; now this, now that; one while one way, another while this or that presented and pursued busily; yet in the issue we land al our thoughts, and look at the last how to bring in content to such a lust: it's certain the vanity of that lust occasioned and drew the vanity of thy thoughts after it.

The cause being thus conceived, the cure is fair and easie to comprehend; namely, *cure these inordinate and raging lusts,* and thence wil follow a stil and quiet composure of mind; purge the stomach if it be foul, and that wil ease the pain of wind in the head, because that is caused by the fumes that arise from thence. Take off the plummet, or lessen but the weight of it, the minutes though they hurried never so fast before, yet wil not move at all, or at least very slowly and quietly. So here, take off the poyse of the affections, purge away these noysom lusts which carry and command the head, and send up dunghil steams which distemper the mind, and disturb it, and those windy imaginations wil cease, and those thoughts of the mind like the minutes, either wil not move, or move in order and manner as may help and not hinder. Here the great skil and care ought to be to labor the clensing and sanctification of such affections which are most tainted, and where the vein and sourse of original corruption, either through custom, or constitution, or company, hath vented it self most usually, and so hath taken up the soul, and gained, and so exercised greater power over it. For as in bruised or weak parts, all the humors run thither, so commonly this corruption is the sink and drain of the soul, all distempered thoughts, and other inferior lusts, empty themselves, and become servants unto this. If once the affections had gained such a tast and rellish of the sweetness that is in Christ, and his truth, that al these baggage and inferior things here below seemed sapless, and that the heart were endeared to him & his truth, and carried strongly after both: this would carry the thoughts vehemently, & keep them so strongly to both, that they would be so far from wandring away from Christ, that they would not be taken from bestowing the strength of their intentions about him, Psal. 119. 97. *Oh how I love thy law, it is my meditation all the day;* verse 93. *I will never forget thy precepts, for thereby thou hast quickened me;* ver. 23. *Princes sate and spake against me, but thy servant did meditate in thy statutes.* In reason he would have conceived it was high time for him to bethink himself how to prevent their fury, & it would cost him sad thoughts of heart how to provide for his succor and safty; no truly, *Thy servant did meditate in thy law.*

*Possess thy heart with an actual consideration, and a holy dread of the glorious presence of the Almighty,* who sees and pondereth all thy paths, and therefore wil take an account, and that strictly, of all the outstrainings of thy thoughts when thou comest to give attendance upon him, and to draw neer into his presence, in some peculiar and spiritual service: there is a kind of heedless wantonness which like a canker breeds in our atheistical dispositions, whereby we see not the rule that should guide us, we lay aside also the consideration of that power that doth rule us, and wil bring us to judgment, and so missing the guide that should shew us the path, and the power that should awe us, and constrain us to keep the rode, a mans mind powrs out it self to every vanity that next offers it self unto its view. Whereas were we aware of his presence, and awed with it, it would cause us to eye him, and attend him in his way and work, wherein he commands us to walk with him. As it is with trewantly schollers who are sporting and gaming out of their place, and from any serious attendance upon their books, when nothing wil stil them, and force them to their studies, as soon as ever there is but the least inkling of the Master, or any eye they can cast upon his approach, they are all as stil as may be, repair presently to their place, fal close, and let their minds to their work; O Master, Master, our Master is yonder; there follows stilness and attendance presently. Our trewantly and wanton minds are of this temper, we are apt to straggle out of our places, or from giving attendance to those special services which the Lord cals for at our hands, and to lay out themselves upon things that are not pertinent, and further than we are awed with the apprehension of Gods sight and presence, who cals for the dayly attendance of our thoughts when we draw neer unto him, doth see and observe our carelessness, and wil proceed in Judgment, and execute punishment upon us for it, it's scant possible to hold the bent of our thoughts awfull, to the business we have in hand. It was the curse which attended *Jonah* when he departed away from the presence of the Lord, and from following his command, he followed *lying vanities,* Jonah, 2. 8. And it's the peculiar plague which is appointed in the way of Providence, and the Lords righteous proceedings to befal al who bestow not their hearts upon him, Eph. 4. 21. *They walk in the vanity of their minds*; and the reason is rendred, *they are strangers from the life of God.* When our thoughts start aside from under the government of Gods wisdom, the rule of truth and stability, they wander up and down in the waies of error and vanity, and find no end or measure, follow vanity, and become vain, nor can they attain any stability before they return thither. As your vagabond beggars, and vagrant persons in the country from whence we came, there is no possibility to fasten them to any imployment, or settle them in any place before they come under the eye of authority, and power of the magistrate. So fares it with our vagabond and vagrant thoughts; further than they are under the eye of God, and awed with his presence, it's not possible to stop them from the pursuit of vanity, or confine them to settled consideration of that which concerns our duty and comfort. The rule is one, like it self accompanied with stability and rest; if once we go astray from that, there is neither end nor quiet in error, but restlessness and emptiness. The sea, while it keeps the channel, the course is known, and the marriners can tel how to advantage their passage; but if once it exceeds the banks, no man can tel whither it wil go, or where it will stay. Our imaginations are like the vast sea, while we eye the rule, and are ordered by the authority of it, we know our compass; but once go off, and we know not whither we shal go, or where we shal stay.

Be *watchfully careful to observe the first wandrings and out-strayings of thy thoughts,* how they first go off from the attendance to the work in hand, and look off from the matter, thou settest thy self to meditate in; immediately recal them back, bring them to their task again, and set them about their intended work. If often they fly out and follow fresh occasions that Satan or a mans corruptions shal suggest take them at the first turn and often again settle them upon the service, until at last by constant custom our mind and thoughts wil buckle handsomly to their business, after they be kept in by a daily care; I have heard hunts-men say when they have young dogs, raw and that hath not been entered nor accquainted with their sport, if a fresh game come in view, or some other unexpected prey cross them in their way, they forsake the old sent and follow that which is in their eye, but their manner is to beat them off, and cal them away from that, and then to bring them to the place where they left their former pursuit, and there set them to find the sent afresh, until at last being often checked and constantly trayned up they wil take and attend the first game, so here, with our wandring minds which are not trayned up to this work of meditation, if they begin to fly off and follow a new occasion, suffer not thy thoughts to range, but bring your mind back again, and set it upon the former service, and then by thy constant care and Gods blessing thy mind wil fal in sweetly and go away with the work, or as men use to do with some kind of wand that is warped & bent somwhat much one way, they bend it a little, at the first & there hold it. Bend it & hold it, at last it comes fully to the fashion they desire it. So here often bend and hold thy mind bent to the work in hand, Heb. 2. 1. *let us give earnest heed to the things wee have heard;* our roving thoughts are like riven vessels, if the parts be not glewed and the breaches brought together again by strong hand, they wil leak out, so here &c.

## REPENTANT SINNERS AND THEIR MINISTERS

Doct. They whose hearts are pierced by the ministry of the word, they are carryed with love and respect to the ministers of it.

*Men and brethren,* they be words of honor & love, & they spoke them seriously and affectionaley, they mocked them before, and they now embrace them, they cared not what tearms of reproach they cast upon their persons, they know not now what titles of love and tenderness to put upon them, they now fal at their feet as clients, who flouted them before as enemies, so it was with the jalour Acts 16. 30, 31, 34. how kindly doth he *Paul* and *Silas* whome erewhile he handled so currishly, beyond the bounds of reason and humanity, he entertains them in the best room of his house who before thought the worst place in the prison too good for them. He baths their wounded parts which he had whipped and stocked before, fears and trembles before them as his counsellors, whom he handled most harshly before as prisoners; he feasts them as his guests whom he had struck as malefactors; the wind was in another dore, the man is of another mind yea is another man than he was. God had no sooner opened the heart of *Lydia* to attend the word but her affections were exceedingly enlarged, towards the dispensers thereof. Acts 16. 15. So that the cords of her loving invitation led *Paul* and held him captive, he professed *she compelled them i.e.*

by her loving and affectionate expressions, prevailed with them for a stay. And while *Paul* had the *Galathians* under the pangs of the new birth and Christ was now *forming in them,* they professed they *would have plucked out their eyes* and have given them to the Apostle, Gal. 4. 15.

*Naaman* hath no sooner his leprosy healed, and his heart humbled and cut off from his corruption, but he professed himself and what he had is at the devotion of the Prophet, and that not out of complement but in truth, 2 Kings 5. 15. *Take a blessing from thy servant.*

Reasons are two.

*They see and know more than formerly they did,* when happily the crooked counsels of others deceived them, and their own carnal reason couzened and deluded their own souls that they mis-judged the men and their doctrine also. As that they did not speak the truth, or else had some crooked and self-seeking ends in what they spak; as either to gratify other mens humors whom they would please or else to set up their own persons and praise and esteem in the apprehensions of others as singular men and more than of an ordinary frame; and therefore would wind men up to such a high pitch of holiness, and force them to such a singular care to fly the very appearance of al evil, when its more than needs and more than God requires, and more than any man can do but now they find by proof and are forced out of their own sence and feeling to acknowledg the truth of what they have spoken, and what they have heard, & themselves also, to be the faithful embassadors of the Lord Jesus, and therefore worthy to be believed and attended in their dispensations and honored of al. *So Paul* 2 Cor. 4. 3. *We hope we are made manifest unto your consciences* thus the Woman of *Samaria* when our Savior came home to the quick and met with the secrets of her heart, she then fel from her taunting and slighting of our Savior to admiring of him, *Come faith she behould the man that told me al that ever I did, is not he the Christ.* John, 4. 29. Look as *Nabuchadnezzar* said, Dan. 4. last, now I know the God of *Daniel* is the true God, *and now I praise the living God,* so when they have been in the fire, and God hath had them upon the anvil, now I know what sin is, now I know what the danger is, now I know what necessity there is to part with sin; when the patient hath found the relation and direction of the physitian hath proved real it makes him prize and honor his skil and counsel, for ever; and for ever to have his custom, As the Pythonist was compelled from the power of *Pauls* administration to confess, *these are the servants of the living God which shew unto us the way of salvation,* so here.

As they see more and can therefore judge better of the worth of persons and things; *so their conscience now hath more scope, and the light of reason hath more liberty, and allowance to express that they know, and nothing now can withstand and hinder;* for while men are held captive under the power of their lusts and corruptions of their hearts, in which they live, and which for the while they are resolved to follow; though their reason happily do yield it, and their own hearts and consciences cannot but inwardly confess it, the persons are holy, the sins are vile which they condemn, and dangers dreadful which they forewarn; yet to profess so much openly to others, and to the world were to judg themselves while they would acquit others, and condemn their own courses, while they should praise and honor the carriages and persons of others, and therefore darken the evidence of the word by carnal cavils and reproaches, stifle the wittness of conscience, and stop its mouth that it cannot speak out. Thus Rom. 1. 18. *they hold down the truth in unrighteousness.* When the truth that is by their judgments assented unto, and by their hearts yeilded, and therefore should break out and give in testimony to the good wayes of God: their corrupt and unrighteous and rebellious hearts hold it prisoner, wil not suffer it either to appear unto others or prevail with themselves; As it fared with the Scribes & Pharisees when the wonder was wrought by *Peter,* say they Acts, 4. 16. *that indeed a notable miracle hath been done by them is manifest to all that dwel in Jerusalem, and we cannot deny it* (q. d. they would have done it if they could) *but that it spread no further, let us charge them straitly that they speak no more in this name.* But here when the conscience of a poor sinner is convinced, and the heart wounded, and that resistance and gainsaying distemper is taken off and crushed, now conscience is in commission and hath his scope & the coast is now clear that reason may be heard, now the broken hearted sinner wil speak plainly, these are the guides that God hath set up, their direction I wil attend, these are the dear and faithful servants of the Lord whom I must honor, and with them I would betrust my soul, not with the blind guides, and false teachers, who daub with untempered morter and are not trustie to God, nor their own souls, and therefore cannot be to me. Oh send for such though in their life time they could not endure the sight, abide the presence, nor allow them a good word, reviled their persons and proceedings and professions, (yea that they wil confess) but it was directly against their own judgment and knowledg and conscience, myne own heart often gave my tongue the lye, when I did so speak and so disparage their conversation, otherwise I must have condemned mine own course and conscience also, but the Lord is with them, and the truth is with them, and a Blessing wil undoubtedly follow them. Ask why these poor pierced sinners did not go to the Scribes, they would tel the truth. Oh it was they that deceived us, led and drew us to the commission of this hellish wickedness; we cannot cal them teachers but murtherers, they could never help themselves, therefore not help us.

INSTRUCTION, *Sound contrition and brokenness of heart brings a strange &*

*a sudden alteration into the world, varies the price and valew of things and persons beyond imagination, turnes the market upside down;* makes the things appear as they be, & the persons to be honored and respected as they are in truth, that look what the truth determines, reason approves, and conscience witnesseth, that account is current in the hearts and apprehensions of those, whose hearts have been pierced with godly sorrow for their sins. Because such judg not by outward appearance as it is the guise of men of corrupt minds, but upon experience, that which they have found and felt in their own hearts, what they have seen and judged in their own spirits, they cannot but see so and judg so of others. Those who were mocked as *men ful of new wine,* are now the precious servants of the Lord, flouted to their faces not long since, now they attend them, honor and reverence them, yea fal at their very feet. It was before men and drunkards, now men and bretheren, the world you see is wel amended but strangely altered. It was said of John Baptist the fore-runner of our Savior, and the scope of whose doctrine was mainly to prepare the way for the Lord, it's said of him that *Elias* is come and hath reformed al, set a new face and frame in the profession of the Gospel, Math. 17. 11. *Turned the disobedient to the wisdom of the just men, the hearts of children to the fathers,* that though they were so degenerate that *Abraham* would not own them had he been alive, yet when the ministery of John had hammered and melted them for the work of our Savior, they became to be wholly altered, their judgments altered and their carriage also. For in truth the reason why men see not the loathsomness of other mens sins, or else have not courage to pass a righteous sentence upon them, It is because they were never convinced to see the plague sore of their own corruptions, never had their hearts affected with the evil of them in their own experience but their own conscience was misled out of authority, and stifled that it durst not outwardly condemn that which inwardly they could not but approve. They therefore who either do not see their own evil, or dare not proceed in open judgment to condemn, they wil either not see or not pass a righteous judgment upon others, so *Paul* intimates to *Agrippa,* Acts, 26. 8. 9. *let it not seem strange Oh king for I my self did think I should do many things against the name of Jesus, which I also did. q. d.* whiles thou so continuest thou wilt see as I did, and do as I did, but after God had entered into combate with him and spoken dreadfully to his soul see, he is another man, and of another mind; he destroyed the churches, *now takes care of them;* he that hated the name and Gospel of Jesus *counts al things dung and dross for the excellent knowledg of Jesus,* the world is well amended but its mervailously altered, and therfore *we have found this man a pestilent fellow* Acts, 17. 16. he hath subdued the state of the world.

TERROR, *this shewes the dreadful and miserable condition of al those who after al the light that hath been let into their minds, conviction into their* consciences, horror into their hearts touching the evils that have been committed and come now to be discovered unto them, they lath the light that hath layd open their evils, distast those persons and preachers and Christians most, that have dealt most plainly to descover the loathsomness of their distempers, it shewes the irrecoverable corruption of the mind and heart that grows worst under the best means, and cleaves most to its sins under al the choycest means that would pluck their sins from their heart, and their heart from them, they are either fools or mad men that cannot endure the presence of the Physitian without whose help they could not be cured. This is made an evidence of the estrangment of Gods heart from a people, and an immediate fore-runner of their ruin. Isa. 9. 13. 14. 17. *For this people turneth not unto him that smote them, neither do they seek the Lord, therefore the Lord wil cut off from Israel head & tail, branch & rush, one day therfore the Lord shal have no pity on their young men nor mercy on their fatherless, for every one is an hipocrite.* It takes away al pity in God, al hopes in themselves of any good. After *Pharoah* had many qualmes & recoylings of spirit by *Moses* dealing with him, & the miracles which he had wrought for his repentance, & at last sides it with the hellish stiffness of his own stubborn heart, so that he cannot endure the speech or presence of *Moses* any more, Exod. 10. 28. *get thee from me, see my face no more, for the day thou seest my face thou shalt die,* God sends *Moses* no more, but sends his plagues to destroy his first born he wil not see the face of *Moses* he shal feel the fierceness of the wrath of the Lord.

# John Winthrop
## (1588–1649)

# A MODELL OF CHRISTIAN CHARITY

*Written*
*On Boarde the Arrabella,*
*On the Attlantick Ocean.*
*By the Honorable John Winthrop Esquire.*

*In His passage, (with the great Company of*
*Religious people, of which Christian Tribes he was*
*the Brave Leader and famous Governor;) from the Island*
*of Great Brittaine, to New-England in the North America.*
*Anno 1630.*

———

*Christian Charitie.*

### A MODELL HEREOF.

GOD ALMIGHTIE in his most holy and wise providence hath soe disposed of the condicion of mankinde, as in all times some must be rich some poore, some highe and eminent in power and dignitie; others meane and in subjeccion.

### THE REASON HEREOF.

1. REAS. *First,* to hold conformity with the rest of his workes, béing delighted to shewe forthe the glory of his wisdome in the variety and differance of the creatures and the glory of his power, in ordering all these differences for the preservacion and good of the whole, and the glory of his greatnes that as it is the glory of princes to have many officers, soe this great king will have many stewards counting himselfe

more honoured in dispenceing his guifts to man by man, then if three did it by his owne immediate hand.

2. REAS. *Secondly,* That he might have the more occasion to manifest the worke of his Spirit: first, upon the wicked in moderateing and restraineing them: soe that the riche and mighty should not eate upp the poore, nor the poore, and dispised rise upp against theire superiours, and shake off theire yoake; 2ly in the regenerate in exerciseing his graces in them, as in the greate ones, theire love mercy, gentlenes, temperance etc., in the poore and inferiour sorte, theire faithe patience, obedience, etc:

3. REAS. *Thirdly,* That every man might have need of other, and from hence they might be all knitt more nearly together in the bond of brotherly affeccion: from hence it appeares plainely that noe man is made more honourable then another or more wealthy etc., out of any perticuler and singuler respect to himselfe but for the glory of his creator and the common good of the creature, man; therefore God still reserves the propperty of these guifts to himselfe as Ezek: 16.17. he there calls wealthe his gold and his silver, tc. Prov: 3.9 he claimes theire service as his due honour the Lord with thy riches etc. All men being thus (by divine providence) rancked into two sortes, riche and poore; under the first, are comprehended all such as are able to live comfortably by theire owne meanes duely improved; and all others are poore according to the former distribution. There are two rules whereby wee are to walke one towards another: JUSTICE and MERCY. These are allwayes distinguished in theire act and in theire object, yet may they both concurre in the same subject in eache respect; as sometimes there may be an occasion of shewing mercy to a rich man, in some sudden danger of distresse, and allsoe doeing of meere justice to a poor man in regard of some perticuler contract etc. There is likewise a double lawe by which wee are regulated in our conversacion one towardes another: in both the former respects, the lawe of nature and the lawe of grace, or the morrall lawe or the lawe of the gospell, to omitt the rule of justice as not propperly belonging to this purpose otherwise then it may fall into consideracion in some perticuler cases: by the first of these lawes man as he was enabled soe withall is commanded to love his neighbour as himselfe, upon this ground stands all the precepts of the morrall lawe, which concernes our dealings with men. To apply this to the works of mercy this lawe requires two things first that every man afford his help to another in every want or distresse. Secondly, That hee performe this out of the same affeccion, which makes him carefull of his owne good according to that of our Saviour Math: 7.12 *Whatsoever ye would that men should doe to you.* This was practised by Abraham and Lott in entertaineing the angells and the old man of Gibea.

The lawe of grace or the Gospell hath some differance from the

former as in these respectes first the lawe of nature was given to man in
the estate of innocency; this of the gospell in the estate of regeneracy:
2ly, the former propounds one man to another, as the same fleshe and
image of god, this as a brother in Christ allsoe, and in the communion of
the same spirit and soe teacheth us to put a difference betweene
Christians and others. Doe good to all especially to the household of
faith; upon this ground the Israelites were to putt a difference betweene
the brethren of such as were strangers though not of the Canaanites. 3ly.
the lawe of nature could give noe rules for dealeing with enemies for all
are to be considered as freinds in the estate of innocency, but the Gospell
commaunds love to an enemy proofe. if thine enemie hunger feede him;
*love your enemies doe good to them that hate you* Math: 5. 44.

This lawe of the Gospell propoundes likewise a difference of seasons
and occasions, there is a time when a christian must sell all and give to
the poore as they did in the Apostles times. There is a tyme allsoe when
a christian (though they give not all yet) must give beyond theire abillity,
as they of Macedonia. Cor: 2.6. likewise community of perills calls for
extraordinary liberallity and soe doth community in some speciall service
for the churche. Lastly, when there is noe other meanes whereby our
Christian brother may be releived in this distresse, wee must help him
beyond our ability, rather then tempt God, in putting him upon help by
miraculous or extraordinary meanes.

This duty of mercy is exercised in the kindes, giveing, lending, and
forgiveing.

QUEST. What rule shall a man observe in giveing in respect of the
measure?

ANS. If the time and occasion be ordinary he is to give out of his
aboundance—let him lay aside, as god hath blessed him. If the time and
occasion be extraordinary he must be ruled by them; takeing this withall
that then a man cannot likely doe too much especially, if he may leave
himselfe and his family under probable meanes of comfortable
subsistance.

OBJECTION. A man must lay upp for posterity, the fathers lay upp for
posterity and children and he is worse then an Infidell that prouideth not
for his owne.

ANS. For the first, it is plaine, that it being spoken by way of
Comparison it must be meant of the ordinary and usuall course of
fathers and cannot extend to times and occasions extraordinary; for the
other place the Apostle speakes against such as walked inordinately, and
it is without question, that he is worse then an Infidell whoe throughe
his owne sloathe and voluptuousnes shall neglect to provide for his
family.

OBJECTION. The wise mans Eies are in his head (saith Salomon) and foreseeth the plague, therefore wee must forecast and lay upp against evill times when hee or his may stand in need of all he can gather.

ANS. This very argument Salomon useth to perswade to liberallity. Eccle: 11. 1. *cast thy bread upon the waters etc.: for thou knowest not what evill may come upon the land* Luke 16. make you freinds of the riches of iniquity; you will aske how this shall be? very well. for first he that gives to the poore lends to the lord, and he will repay him even in this life an hundred fold to him or his. The righteous is ever mercifull and lendeth and his seed enjoyeth the blessing; and besides wee know what advantage it will be to us in the day of account, when many such witnesses shall stand forthe for us to witnesse the improvement of our Tallent. And I would knowe of those whoe pleade soe much for layeing up for time to come, whether they hold that to be Gospell Math: 16. 19. Lay not upp for yourselves treasures upon earth etc. if they acknowledge it what extent will they allowe it; if onely to those primitive times lett them consider the reason whereupon our Saviour groundes it, the first is that they are subject to the moathe, the rust the Theife. Secondly, they will steale away the hearte, where the treasure is there will the heart be allsoe. The reasons are of like force at all times therefore the exhortacion must be generall and perpetuall which applies allwayes in respect of the love and affeccion to riches and in regard of the things themselves when any speciall service for the churche or perticular distresse of our brother doe call for the use of them; otherwise it is not onely lawfull but necessary to lay upp as Joseph did to have ready uppon such occasions, as the Lord (whose stewards wee are of them) shall call for them from us: Christ gives us an Instance of the first, when hee sent his disciples for the asse, and bidds them answer the owner thus, the Lord hath need of him; soe when the tabernacle was to be builte his servant sends to his people to call for their silver and gold etc.; and yeilds them noe other reason but that it was for his worke, when Elisha comes to the widowe of Sareptah and findes her prepareing to make ready her pittance for herselfe and family, he bids her first provide for him, he challengeth first gods parte which shee must first give before shee must serve her owne family, all these teache us that the lord lookes that when hee is pleased to call for his right in any thing wee have, our owne Interest wee have must stand aside, till his turne be served, for the other wee need looke noe further then to that of John 1. *He whoe hath this worlds goodes and seeth his brother to neede, and shutts upp his compassion from him, how dwelleth the love of God in him,* which comes punctually to this conclusion: *if thy brother be in want and thou canst help him, thou needst not make doubt, what thou shouldst doe,* if thou lovest God thou must help him.

QUEST. What rule must wee observe in lending?

ANS. Thou must observe whether thy brother hath present or probable or possible meanes of repayeing thee, if ther be none of these, thou must give him according to his necessity, rather then lend him as hee requires; if he hath present meanes of repayeing thee, thou art to looke at him, not as an act of mercy, but by way of commerce, wherein thou arte to walke by the rule of justice, but, if his meanes of repayeing thee be onely probable or possible then is hee an object of thy mercy thou must lend him, though there be danger of looseing it Deut: 15. 7. If any of thy brethren be poore etc. thou shalt lend him sufficient that men might not shift off this duty by the apparant hazzard, he tells them that though the Yeare of Jubile were at hand (when he must remitt it, if hee were not able to repay it before) yet he must lend him and that chearefully: it may not greive thee to give him (saith hee) and because some might object, why soe I should soone impoverishe my selfe and my family, he adds with all thy worke etc. for our Saviour Math: 5. 42. *From him that would borrow of thee turne not away*.

QUEST. What rule must wee observe in forgiveing?

ANS. Whether thou didst lend by way of commerce or in mercy, if he have noething to pay thee thou must forgive him (except in cause where thou hast a surety or a lawfull pleadge) Deut. 15. 2. Every seaventh yeare the creditor was to quitt that which hee lent to his brother if hee were poore as appeares ver: 4: save when there shall be noe poore with thee. In all these and like cases Christ was a generall rule Math: 7. 22. *Whatsoever ye would that men should doe to you doe yee the same to them allsoe.*

QUEST. What rule must wee observe and walke by in cause of community of perill?

ANS. The same as before, but with more enlargement towardes others and lesse respect towards our selves, and our owne right hence it was that in the primitive churche they sold all had all things in common, neither did any man say that that which he possessed was his owne likewise in theire returne out of the captivity, because the worke was greate for the restoreing of the church and the danger of enemies was common to all Nehemiah exhortes the Jewes to liberallity and readines in remitting theire debtes to theire brethren, and disposeth liberally of his owne to such as wanted and stands not upon his owne due, which hee might have demaunded of them, thus did some of our forefathers in times of persecucion here in England, and soe did many of the faithfull in other churches whereof wee keepe an honourable remembrance of them, and it is to be observed that both in Scriptures and latter stories of the churches that such as have beene most bountifull to the poore saintes especially in these extraordinary times and occasions god hath left them highly commended to posterity, as Zacheus, Cornelius, Dorcas, Bishop Hooper, the Cuttler of Brussells and divers others observe againe that the scripture gives noe causion to restraine any from being over liberall this way; but all men to the liberall and cherefull practise hereof by the sweetest promises as to instance one for many, Isaiah 58. 6: *Is not this the fast that I have chosen to loose the bonds of wickednes, to take off the heavy burdens to lett the oppressed goe free and to breake every yoake, to deale thy bread to the hungry and to bring the poore that wander into thy house, when thou seest the naked to cover them etc. then shall thy light breake forthe as the morneing, and thy healthe shall growe speedily, thy righteousness shall goe before thee, and the glory of the Lord shall embrace thee, then thou shalt call and the Lord shall answer thee etc.* 2. 10: if thou power out thy soule to the hungry, then shall thy light spring out in darknes, and the Lord shall guide thee continually, and satisfie thy soule in draught, and make fatt thy bones, thou shalt be like a watered garden, and they shall be of thee that shall build the old wast places etc. on the contrary most heavy cursses are layd upon such as are straightened towards the Lord and his people Judg: 5. 23. *Cursse ye Meroshe because they came not to help the Lord etc.* Pro: 21. 13. *Hee whoe shutteth his eares from hearing the cry of the poore, he shall cry and shall not be heard:* Math: 25. 41. *Goe ye curssed into everlasting fire etc.* 42. *I was hungry and ye fedd mee not.* Cor: 2. 9. 6. *He that soweth spareingly shall reape spareingly.*

Haveing allready sett forth the practise of mercy according to the rule of gods lawe, it will be usefull to lay open the groundes of it allsoe being the other parte of the Commaundement and that is the affeccion from which this exercise of mercy must arise, the Apostle tells us that this love is the fulfilling of the lawe, not that it is enough to love our brother and soe noe further but in regard of the excellency of his partes giveing any motion to the other as the soule to the body and the power it hath to sett all the faculties on worke in the outward exercise of this duty as when wee bid one make the clocke strike he doth not lay hand on the hammer which is the immediate instrument of the sound but setts on worke the first mover or maine wheele, knoweing that will certainely produce the sound which hee intends; soe the way to drawe men to the workes of mercy is not by force of argument from the goodnes or necessity of the worke, for though this course may enforce a rationall minde to some present act of mercy as is frequent in experience, yet it cannot worke such a habit in a soule as shall make it prompt upon all occasions to produce the same effect but by frameing these affeccions of love in the hearte which will as natively bring forthe the other, as any cause doth produce the effect.

The diffinition which the Scripture gives us of love is this love is the bond of perfection. First, it is a bond, or ligament. 2ly, it makes the worke perfect. There is noe body but consistes of partes and that which knitts

these partes together gives the body its perfeccion, because it makes
eache parte soe contiguous to other as thereby they doe mutually
participate with eache other, both in strengthe and infirmity in pleasure
and paine, to instance in the most perfect of all bodies, Christ and his
church make one body: the severall partes of this body considered aparte
before they were united were as disproportionate and as much
disordering as soe many contrary qualities or elements but when Christ
comes and by his spirit and love knitts all these partes to himselfe and
each to other, it is become the most perfect and best proportioned body
in the world Eph: 4. 16. Christ by whome all the body being knitt
together by every joynt for the furniture thereof according to the
effectuall power which is in the measure of every perfection of partes a
glorious body without spott or wrinckle the ligaments hereof being
Christ or his love for Christ is love 1 John: 4. 8. Soe this definition is
right love is the bond of perfeccion.

From hence wee may frame these conclusions.

1 first all true Christians are of one body in Christ 1. Cor. 12. 12. 13.
27. Ye are the body of Christ and members of your parte.

2ly. The ligamentes of this body which knitt together are love.

3ly. Noe body can be perfect which wants its propper ligamentes.

4ly. All the partes of this body being thus united are made soe
contiguous in a speciall relacion as they must needes partake of each
others strength and infirmity, joy, and sorrowe, weale and woe. 1 Cor: 12.
26. If one member suffers all suffer with it, if one be in honour, all
rejoyce with it.

5ly. This sensiblenes and sympathy of each others condicions will
necessarily infuse into each parte a native desire and endeavour, to
strengthen defend preserve and comfort the other.

To insist a little on this conclusion being the product of all the former
the truthe hereof will appeare both by precept and patterne 1. John. 3.
10. Yee ought to lay downe your lives for the brethren Gal: 6. 2. Beare
ye one anothers burthens and soe fulfill the lawe of Christ.

For patterns wee have that first of our Saviour whoe out of his good
will in obedience to his father, becomeing a parte of this body, and being
knitt with it in the bond of love, found such a native sensiblenes of our
infirmities and sorrowes as hee willingly yeilded himselfe to deathe to
ease the infirmities of the rest of his body and soe heale theire sorrowes:
from the like Sympathy of partes did the Apostles and many thousands
of the Saintes lay downe theire lives for Christ againe, the like wee may
see in the members of this body among themselves. 1. Rom. 9. Paule
could have beene contented to have beene seperated from Christ that the
Jewes might not be cutt off from the body: It is very observable which

hee professeth of his affectionate partakeing with every member: whoe is weake (saith hee) and I am not weake? whoe is offended and I burne not; and againe. 2 Cor: 7. 13. *Therefore wee are comforted because yee were comforted.* Of Epaphroditus he speaketh Phil: 2. 30. *That he regarded not his owne life to do him service soe Phebe.* And others are called the servantes of the Churche, now it is apparant that they served not for wages or by constrainte but out of love, the like wee shall finde in the histories of the churche in all ages the sweete sympathie of affeccions which was in the members of this body one towardes another, theire chearfullnes in serveing and suffering together how liberall they were without repineing harbourers without grudgeing and helpfull without reproacheing and all from hence they had fervent love amongst them which onely makes the practise of mercy constant and easie.

The next consideracion is how this love comes to be wrought; Adam in his first estate was a perfect modell of mankinde in all theire generacions, and in him this love was perfected in regard of the habit, but Adam rent in himselfe from his Creator, rent all his posterity allsoe one from another, whence it comes that every man is borne with this principle in him, to love and seeke himselfe onely and thus a man continueth till Christ comes and takes possession of the soule, and infuseth another principle love to God and our brother. And this latter haveing continuall supply from Christ, as the head and roote by which hee is united get the predominency in the soule, soe by little and little expells the former 1 John 4. 7. *Love cometh of God and every one that loveth is borne of God,* soe that this love is the fruite of the new birthe, and none can have it but the new creature, now when this quality is thus formed in the soules of men it workes like the spirit upon the drie bones Ezek. 37. 7. Bone came to bone, it gathers together the scattered bones or perfect old man Adam and knitts them into one body againe in Christ whereby a man is become againe a liveing soule.

The third consideracion is concerning the exercise of this love, which is twofold, inward or outward, the outward hath beene handled in the former preface of this discourse, for unfolding the other wee must take in our way that maxime of philosophy, simile simili gaudet or like will to like; for as it is things which are carved with disafeccion to eache other, the ground of it is from a dissimilitude or ariseing from the contrary or different nature of the things themselves, soe the ground of love is an apprehension of some resemblance in the things loved to that which affectes it, this is the cause why the Lord loves the creature, soe farre as it hath any of his image in it, he loves his elect because they are like himselfe, he beholds them in his beloved sonne: soe a mother loves her childe, because shee throughly conceives a resemblance of herselfe in it. Thus it is betweene the members of Christ, each discernes by the worke of the spirit his owne image and resemblance in another, and therefore cannot but love him as he loves himselfe: Now when the soule which is of a sociable nature findes any thing like to it selfe. It is like Adam when Eve was brought to him, shee must have it one with herselfe this is fleshe of my fleshe (saith shee) and bone of my bone shee conceives a greate delighte in it, therefore shee desires nearenes and familiarity with it: shee hath a greate propensity to doe it good and receives such content in it, as feareing the miscarriage of her beloved shee bestowes it in the inmost closett of her heart, shee will not endure that it shall want any good which shee can give it, if by occasion shee be withdrawne from the company of it, shee is still lookeing towardes the place where shee left her beloved, if shee heare it groane shee is with it presently, if shee finde it sadd and disconsolate shee sighes and mournes with it, shee hath noe such joy, as to see her beloved merry and thriveing, if shee see it wronged, shee cannot beare it without passion, shee setts noe boundes of her affeccions, nor hath any thought of reward, shee findes recompence enoughe in the exercise of her love towardes it, wee may see this Acted to life in Jonathan and David. Jonathan a valiant man endued with the spirit of Christ, soe soone as hee discovers the same spirit in David had presently his hearte knitt to him by this linement of love, soe that it is said he loved him as his owne soule, he takes soe great pleasure in him that hee stripps himselfe to adorne his beloved, his fathers kingdome was not soe precious to him as his beloved David, David shall have it with all his hearte, himselfe desires noe more but that hee may be neare to him to rejoyce in his good hee chooseth to converse with him in the wildernesse even to the hazzard of his owne life, rather then with the greate courtiers in his fathers pallace; when hee sees danger towardes him, hee spares neither care paines, nor perill to divert it, when injury was offered his beloved David, hee could not beare it, though from his owne father, and when they must parte for a season onely, they thought theire heartes would have broake for sorrowe, had not theire affeccions found vent by aboundance of teares: other instances might be brought to shewe the nature of this affeccion as of Ruthe and Naomi and many others, but this truthe is cleared enough. If any shall object that it is not possible that love should be bred or upheld without hope of requitall, it is graunted but that is not our cause, for this love is allwayes under reward it never gives, but it allwayes receives with advantage: first, in regard that among the members of the same body, love and affection are reciprocall in a most equall and sweete kinde of commerce. 3ly, in regard of the pleasure and content that the exercise of love carries with it as wee may see in the naturall body the mouth is at all the paines to receive, and mince the foode which serves for the nourishment of all the other partes of the body, yet it hath noe cause to complaine; for first, the other partes send backe by secret passages a due proporcion of the same nourishment in a better forme for the strengthening and comforteing the mouthe. 2ly the labour of the mouthe is accompanied with such pleasure and content as farre exceedes the paines it takes: soe is it in all the labour of love, among Christians, the partie loveing, reapes love againe as was shewed before, which the soule covetts more then all the wealthe in the world. 4ly. Noething yeildes more pleasure and content to the soule then when it findes that which it may love fervently, for to love and live beloved is the soules paradice, both heare and in heaven: In the state of wedlock there be many comfortes to beare out the troubles of that condicion; but let such as have tryed the most, say if there be any sweetnes in that condicion comparable to the exercise of mutuall love.

From the former consideracions ariseth these conclusions.

1 First, This love among Christians is a reall thing not imaginarie.

2ly. This love is as absolutely necessary to the being of the body of Christ, as the sinewes and other ligaments of a naturall body are to the being of that body.

3ly. This love is a divine spirituall nature free, active strong couragious permanent under valueing all things beneathe its propper object, and of all the graces this makes us nearer to resemble the virtues of our heavenly father.

4ly, It restes in the love and wellfare of its beloved, for the full and certaine knowledge of these truthes concerning the nature use, and excellency of this grace, that which the holy ghost hath left recorded 1. Cor. 13. May give full satisfaccion which is needfull for every true member of this lovely body of the Lord Jesus, to worke upon theire heartes, by prayer meditacion continuall exercise at least of the speciall power of this grace till Christ be formed in them and they in him all in eache other knitt together by this bond of love.

It rests now to make some applicacion of this discourse by the present designe which gave the occasion of writeing of it. Herein are 4 things to be propounded: first the persons, 2ly, the worke, 3ly, the end, 4ly the meanes.

1. For the persons, wee are a company professing our selves fellow members of Christ, In which respect onely though wee were absent from eache other many miles, and had our imploymentes as farre distant, yet wee ought to account our selves knitt together by this bond of love, and live in the exercise of it, if wee would have comforte of our being in Christ, this was notorious in the practise of the Christians in former times, as is testified of the Waldenses from the mouth of one of the adversaries Aeneas Sylvius, *mutuo solent amare penè antequam norint*, they used to love any of theire owne religion even before they were acquainted with them.

2ly. For the worke wee have in hand, it is by a mutuall consent through a speciall overruleing providence, and a more then an ordinary approbation of the churches of Christ to seeke out a place of cohabitation and consorteshipp under a due forme of government both civill and ecclesiasticall. In such cases as this the care of the publique must oversway all private respects, by which not onely conscience, but meare civill pollicy doth binde us; for it is a true rule that perticuler estates cannott subsist in the ruine of the publique.

3ly. The end is to improve our lives to doe more service to the Lord the comforte and encrease of the body of christe whereof wee are members that our selves and posterity may be the better preserved from the common corrupcions of this evill world to serve the Lord and worke out our salvacion under the power and purity of his holy ordinances.

4ly for the meanes whereby this must bee effected, they are 2fold, a conformity with the worke and end wee aime at, these wee see are extraordinary, therefore wee must not content our selves with usuall ordinary meanes whatsoever wee did or ought to have done when wee lived in England, the same must wee doe and more allsoe where wee goe: that which the most in theire churches maineteine as a truthe in profession onely, wee must bring into familiar and constant practise, as in this duty of love wee must love brotherly without dissimulation, wee must love one another with a pure hearte fervently wee must beare one anothers burthens, wee must not looke onely on our owne things, but allsoe on the things of our brethren, neither must wee think that the lord will beare with such faileings at our hands as hee dothe from those among whome wee have lived, and that for 3 Reasons.

1. In regard of the more neare bond of marriage, betweene him and us, wherein he hath taken us to be his after a most strickt and peculiar manner which will make him the more jealous of our love and obedience soe he tells the people of Israell, you onely have I knowne of all the families of the earthe therefore will I punishe you for your Transgressions.

2ly, because the Lord will be sanctified in them that come neare him. Wee know that there were many that corrupted the service of the Lord some setting upp alters before his owne, others offering both strange fire and strange sacrifices allsoe; yet there came noe fire from heaven, or other sudden judgement upon them as did upon Nadab and Abihu whoe yet wee may thinke did not sinne presumptuously.

3ly When God gives a speciall commission he lookes to have it strickly observed in every article, when hee gave Saule a commission to destroy Amaleck hee indented with him upon certaine articles and because hee failed in one of the least, and that upon a faire pretence, it lost him the kingdome, which should have beene his reward, if hee had observed his commission: thus stands the cause betweene God and us, wee are entered into covenant with him for this worke, wee have taken out a commission, the Lord hath given us leave to drawe our owne articles wee have professed to enterprise these accions upon these and these ends, wee have hereupon besought him of favour and blessing: now if the Lord shall please to heare us, and bring us in peace to the place wee desire, then hath hee ratified this covenant and sealed our commission, and will expect a strickt performance of the articles contained in it, but if wee shall neglect the observacion of these articles which are the ends wee have propounded, and dissembling with our God, shall fall to embrace this present world and prosecute our carnall intencions, seekeing great things for our selves and our posterity, the Lord will surely breake out in wrathe against us be revenged of such a perjured people and make us knowe the price of the breache of such a covenant.

Now the onely way to avoyde this shipwracke and to provide for our posterity is to followe the counsell of Micah, to doe justly, to love mercy, to walke humbly with our God, for this end, wee must be knitt together in this worke as one man, wee must entertaine each other in brotherly affeccion, wee must be willing to abridge our selves of our superfluities, for the supply of others necessities, wee must uphold a familiar commerce together in all meekenes, gentlenes, patience and liberallity, wee must delight in eache other, make others condicions and our owne rejoyce together, mourne together, labour, and suffer together, allwayes haveing before our eyes our commission and community in the worke, our community as members of the same body, soe shall wee keepe the unitie of the spirit in the bond of peace, the Lord will be our God and delight to dwell among us, as his owne people and will commaund a blessing upon us in all our wayes, soe that wee shall see much more of his wisdome power goodnes and truthe then formerly wee have beene acquainted with, wee shall finde that the God of Israell is among us, when tenn of us shall be able to resist a thousand of our enemies, when hee shall make us a prayse and glory, that men shall say of succeeding plantacions: the lord make it like that of New England: for wee must consider that wee shall be as a citty upon a hill, the eies of all people are uppon us; soe that if wee shall deale falsely with our god in this worke wee have undertaken and soe cause him to withdrawe his present help from us, wee shall be made a story and a by-word through the world, wee shall open the mouthes of enemies to speake evill of the wayes of god and all professours for Gods sake; wee shall shame the faces of many of gods worthy servants, and cause theire prayers to be turned into cursses upon us till wee be consumed out of the good land whether wee are goeing: and to shutt upp this discourse with that exhortacion of moses that faithfull servant of the Lord in his last farewell to Israell Deut. 30. beloved there is now sett before us life, and good, deathe and evill in that wee are commaunded this day to love the Lord our God, and to love one another to walke in his wayes and to keepe his Commaundements and his ordinance, and his lawes, and the articles of our covenant with him that wee may live and be multiplyed, and that the Lord our God may blesse us in the land whether wee goe to possesse it: but if our heartes shall turne away soe that wee will not obey, but shall be seduced and worshipp other Gods our pleasures, and proffitts, and serve them; it is propounded unto this day, wee shall surely perishe out of the good Land whether wee passe over this vast sea to possesse it;

Therefore lett us choose life,
that wee, and our seede,
may live; by obeyeing his
voyce, and cleaveing to him,
for hee is our life, and
our prosperity.

# THOMAS SHEPARD
## (1605–1649)

## OF CARNAL SECURITY IN VIRGIN CHURCHES

From *The Parable of the Ten Virgins Opened & Applied*
(London, 1660)

———

### SECT. I.

MATTH. 25. 5. *Whilst the Bridegroom tarried, they all
slumbered and slept.*

IN THIS parable were noted two things;

First, The churches preparation to meet Christ from vers. 1. to 5.

Secondly, The bridegrooms coming out to meet them, from vers. 5. to 12.

In this second part, which now we are to open, three things are to be attended unto;

1. The delay of Christs coming, or the long-suffering of Christ before he come, vers. 5.

2. The preparation he makes for his coming, a little before it, from verse 6. to vers. 10. by an awakening cry, which makes all the virgins look about them.

3. The coming it self; where those that were ready, were with joy let in; and those that were unready were with shame shut out.

### I. *The delay of Christs coming.*

Whence note first, what happened in the interim of his delay, and that is *carnal security*, expressed and set out from the lowest and highest degree of it. 1. They *slumbered; i.e.* fell a nodding or winking, as the word most properly signifies. 2. They *slept; i.e.* now they were buried in their sleep, overcome by it.

Secondly, upon whom these sleeps and slumbers fell; and that is, *they all slumbered and slept; i.e.* though for a time they were both awake, yet good and bad, wise and foolish fell into this senceless and stupid, dull and dead, sluggish and sleepy condition.

Observ. I. *That in the last days carnal security either is or will be the universal sin of virgin churches.*

Observ. II. *That carnal security falls by degrees upon the hearts of men.*

Observ. III. *That the spirit of sloath and security is the last sin that befals the people of God.*

Observ. IV. *That Christs tarrying from the churches, is the general occasion of all security in the churches; or the not coming of the bridegroom when the saints expect him, is the general cause of that security which doth befall them.*

## SECT. II.

OBSERV. 1. *That in the last days carnal security either is or will be the universal sin of virgin churches:* when the churches are purged from the gross pollutions of the world, and antichristian fornications and bondage, then either there is or will be general security: for these virgins, when they first made profession of their virginity by their burning lamps, were for a time all awakened, but at last they all slumbered and slept: this is the temper of the body of the churches.

Matth. 24. 38. *As it was in the days of Noah, so shall it be in the days of the coming of the son of man.*

Luk. 18. 8. *When the Son of man cometh, shall he find faith in the earth? i.e.* an awakening faith.

Hence the Lord forewarns his people of this, *Deut.* 6. 12. *When thou comest to such a land, beware lest thou forget the Lord thy God.*

QUEST. *But what is this their general security?*

ANSW. Look as it is in our ordinary sleep, so it is in this general security: there are these six things in it.

1. A man forgets his business, his work he was about, or is to be exercised about; so in a carnal security, men forget the Lord, his works, and his will; that which we most think of while we be awake, we least think of indeed when we be asleep: take a man awakened indeed, O then the worst remember the Lord and his covenant, Psal. 78. 47. But when asleep, the Lord and his errand is least thought of; and hence security is exprest by *forgetting God*, Psal. 50. 21. And hence *Jerusalems* security was in this, *they remembred not their latter end.*

2. A man in sleep fears no evill until it be upon him, awakening of him; so this is another ingredient into carnal security, though sin lies upon them, they fear not till evil comes; as *Josephs* brethren, though

warning is given them, they fear not: Like them in the days of *Noah* and
*Lot*. And hence Job 21. 9. *Their houses are free from fear,* the misery for the
same sin is lighted upon another; yet the secure soul fears not, as in
*Belshazar,* Dan. 5. 22.

3. In sleep all the sences are bound up, the outward sences especially,
the eye watcheth not, the ear hears not, the tongue tastes not, the body
feels not; so this is an ingredient of carnal security, it binds up all the
sences, as it did the Prophet *Jonah* his in the storm; when misery was
upon him, he heard not, he saw not, he felt not; so when misery, outward
or spiritual, is upon a man, he that had quick sences before, his eye sees
not, watcheth not; Christians neglect their watchfulness for their friends,
the Lord, and his spirit, and coming; nor watch against their enemies that
daily besiege them; the ear hears not the voice of the ministry, the voyce
of Providences, the voyce of the spirit within; the soul smels not, tastes
not the sweet of any promise, any ordinance, no! or of the grace of the
Lord himself; hence it commends them not; nay the soul feels nothing,
no evil, no good the Lord doth him; that look as the Lord there said, Isa.
29. 9, 10. *The Lord hath poured upon you a spirit of sleep, and hath closed your
eyes;* so the Lord closeth up all the sences, that a man is now stupid, when
he is fallen asleep in security.

4. In sleep there is a cessation from speaking and motion: there a man
keeps silence and lies still; so in carnal security, the spirit of prayer is
silent, Isa. 64. 7. Psal. 32. 1, 2, 3. *David* calls it a keeping of silence; *up, why
sleepest thou? seek to thy God,* say the mariners; indeed men may talk in
their sleep, so men may pray in their deep security, yet not throughly
awakened: and there is a lying still, no progress; so in carnal security the
soul stands at a stay, goes not backward, grows not worse, but goes not
forward; such a one is compared to the door on the hinge.

5. In sleep the sences being stupefied, and motion ceased, a man falls a
dreaming; some dreams he forgets, some he remembers, and in his sleep
fully and firmly believes them; so in carnal security, now a mans mind
dreams of that which is not, and of that which never shall be; a mans
mind is grown vain, and full of fancies and dreams; those things which
never entered into Gods thoughts, something a man dreams of the Lord
that this is his will and mind, which is not; of the world, that it is a goodly
thing; of things to come which shall never be.

6. In deep sleep, though a man be awakened, yet he presently is
overcome by his sleep again; so that is another ingredient into spiritual
slumber; sleepiness is predominant over his watchfulness; and thus it was
with the disciples in the garden, they slept; the Lord came once and
twice, and awakens them, yet they slept till temptation surprized them;
scarce any Christian so secure in the chambers of Christ, but he hath

some knocks of conscience, some cries of the ministry, some woundings from the Lord, and they do awake him, but yet he falls to sleep again.

SECT. III.

We shall now shew the reasons why virgin churches in the last days are or will be overcome by security.

REASON 1. First, because that in virgin churches there are the strongest provocations to this sin: which are chiefly three.

1. Rest and places of peace, and freedom from hard bondage; *Jacob* may sleep with his stone under his head, but much more easily under his own vine and figtrees. A man may be secure in the times of trouble, but much more in times of peace, when we have our beds made soft for us, and easie pillows. Friends can boldly desire us to rest, where there is lodgings for us: the world thrusts us out of lodging: While the prick is at the brest the nightingale awakes and sings, but when that is taken away it sleeps in the day. In times of persecution *Paul* is preaching till midnight, and the Lord is remembred in the songs, and sighs, and prayers of the night-season; but in times of peace, peace like *Jaels* milk and butter stupifies all the sences, though destruction be near; Hence Deut. 6. 12. *Then forget not the Lord*. Do you think that *Noah* in the Ark, when the waters swelled above the mountains, was secure? no, but when the waters ceased, and he had his vineyard planted, now he sleeps in his drunkenness, because he knew not the strength of wine. In the virgin-church, where this sleep is, we suppose this freedom from evil.

2. Because there men are most free from inward pain; for where there is much grief and pain, there's no rest, though all the house about be still; but when the house is still, and the body well, now tis hard but there may be rest; Whiles the Christian doth live under Antichristian pollution, his conscience hath no rest, and hence 'tis awake there; here (saith the soul) I want the ordinances of God, Oh that I had them! Here I see sin and wickedness abounding, that my childe is like to be poisoned therewith; here are such and such superstitions that my conscience cannot bear: Hence conscience is kept waking. But in virgin-churches, where the house is swept of these, now conscience is quiet and at rest; now I have got a Levite into my house, God is now blessing me, &c. Now conscience hath laid down its burthen, it falls down to sleep; now they cry, *The temple of the Lord, &c.*

3. Because in such churches there is most aptitude in men to spiritual fulness, *viz.* plenty of the means; there is all the ordinances; in this mountain, Isa. 25. 1. Gods feast is made, and fulness of spiritual gifts and graces, because they have now escaped the pollutions of the world, conquered the enmity of the world; now have come to a good measure

of grace, and conquered the way of their enemies, got the better of them; hence, as the *Israelites* made peace with the *Canaanites,* not when they were too strong but too weak for them: so now the soul comes to be at rest, to lay down its warfare, and to yield to a truce, to a league to his lusts and distempers for a time. When men are kept short of food, now they awake, so when the word of the Lord and his ordinances be rare and precious, and hard to finde, now a Christian can trudge after them; but when men are full, now they desire rest; so 'tis here.

4. Because in virgin-churches, there men are most apt to be overtaken with weariness; A man that never walkt on in a holy way, may at first setting out delight in Christ; but after he hath done walking in it, now he is apt to faint; especially, if he sows much, and reaps for the present but little. And hence Gal. 6. 9. *You shall reap in due season, if you faint not:* Now in virgin-churches, these virgins are such persons as have begun to make a profession, and have made a fair progress; O how difficult now is it not to be weary! it's strange to see what short spirits after the Lord, what large after the creatures we have.

REASON 2. Because they are the more easily overcome by this sin, than by any other.

1. Because it's a sin which a man least foresees or fears: the Apostle saith, *They that are drunk, and that sleep, sleep in the night;* and yet here men sleep in the open light; Why so? Men see it not, men know it not; sleep steals upon a man: it's lawful to sleep; carnal security arises chiefly from the use of lawful things, on which a mans heart and thoughts are spent; they eate, drank, gave in marriage, they could see no hurt therein. When a man is had before councels, now a man fears to sin, he knows he shall be tempted unto sin; but when the Lord brings the shoulder from under such burdens, now to fear our tables, our beds, our wives, our children, our callings, our professions and the snares of these, oh it is exceeding hard!

2. Because security is so sweet a sin; O sleep is sweet; meat is sweet, but men may be soon full of that; but when sleep comes, many hours are little enough to entertain that: some sins are sweet for a time, as a short meal and away; but sloth is a sweeter sin than any else besides. Let a Christian ask his heart, when he can take no content in pots, or loose company, or queans, and can find none in the Lord, yet this will give him ease, *viz.* his sloth; When he is weary of the world, and of walking with God also, yet sloth is his delight; and hence he crys, *A little more slumber and sleep, untill destruction comes as an armed man:* When a man delights not in his wife, children, riches, honors, yet is he sometimes contentedly swallowed up with his sleep and rest.

3. Because Satan doth make his strongest forces ready alway to bring a man first into this sin; because this makes way for the entrance of all sin

and misery; no people so happy as the *Israelites,* while they were awakened and up with God; no misery could hurt them, Jer. 2. 1, 2, 3. but when they forgot him, all misery came in; *While the strong man keeps the palace, his goods be at peace;* it's his care to keep men secure and still.

SECT. IV.

USE 1. Let us therefore now examine whether this sin be not our sin in this country, if it be not begun among us; if we be not sleeping, yet are we not slumbering? if we are not virgin-churches, why have we the name of it? if we be virgin-churches, then make search if this be not our sin; we have all our beds and lodgings provided, the Lord hath made them easie to us; we never looked for such days in *New-England,* the Lord hath freed us from the pain and anguish of our consciences; we have ordinances to the full, sermons too long, and Lectures too many, and private meetings too frequent, a large profession many have made, but are you not yet weary? if weary, not sleepy, not slumbering? it may be on you before you are aware, and you not know it; and when so it is, it may be so sweet that you may be loth to see it, that so you may forsake it. Let me knock again, is it not so? Let me come to every mans bed side, and ask your consciences.

1. Have you not forgot your God, and forgot your work also? the business for which you made this great undertaking? Psal. 106. 12. When they were saved from the sea they soon forgat the Lord: Hath not the Lord by a stretched-out arm brought thee and thine through seas and dangers, and delivered you wonderfully? are not all his kindnesses forgotten? all your promises forgotten? When the Lord had brought the *Israelites* out of their captivity, and some hopeful beginnings were, they came for the temple; the dust was precious, but Gods house did lie waste, Hag. 1. 5, 6. *Consider your ways;* no man prospered scarce in his estate; God did blow upon their corn because they forgat their end. What was your end of coming hither? the ordinances of God, the presence of God; and oh one day there better than a thousand elsewhere; hath it been so? No, but as it is vers. 9. *Every man turns to his own house:* Every man for himself, to their own house, lot, accommodation, provision for children; and in the mean while the Lords house lies waste, you build not up that; the souls of thy brethren in church-fellowship, yea, of thy family are not built up; the Lords house is despised now; and it's like the Schools of the Prophets, and much more. Oh thought we, if we had such priviledges, how would we improve them! but when we have them, have we the same thoughts? do we not forget them, like men that come to a place for gold, and find it not without digging, they fall to lade their ship with wood or coal, that which it will bear.

2. Have we not shaken off all fear almost of sin and misery? *Go to the Ant thou sluggard, she fears and provides against a winter:* Do not men think that we have fled too far for the cross to finde us, or as if the temple of the Lord was such a den as no foxes or wolves could follow us into? especially when there are causes of fear, when war is proclaimed, and the causes known, and yet they are never feared: How many men have the hand-writing of death in their consciences against them! this they confess is naught, they have lived careless, sluggish, and have had some sence of it, yet no awakening fear of the terror of the Lord; when a prince is nigh us, now to commit a little lewdness is great wickedness: where is the man that trembles at the nearness of God to us? when a breach is made, then fear enemies. Divisions and breaches go before falls of churches; where is that spirit of *Jehosaphat,* that feared and proclaimed a fast? When God hath begun to smite, what cause is there to fear! we have been hurt, and yet not laid it to heart; the lion roars, shall not the people fear? I believe we should not have had those Pequot furies upon us, but God saw we began to sleep: Where is the man that, with *Paul,* knows the terror of the Lord, and hence perswades men? when the enemy is ever about us, there is always cause of fear, and yet we fear but now and then.

3. Are not our sences bound up? look upon men in their fields and conversings, buyings and sellings; where is a daily, weekly watchfulness over our thoughts and tongues? Look to mens closets, do men there call themselves to account? can they finde leisure or need of it? are not mens eyes closed up, that the glory of God in the Scripture is a sealed thing? Men have eyes but see not; are not mens ears sealed up? Some sermons men can sleep them out; mans voyce is heard, but not the voyce of the Son of God: Oh how many men are there that become quite sermon-proof now adays! Are not men blockish, dull, senceless, heavy under all means! they taste not, smell not, whereas elsewhere, O how lively and spiritual are they!

4. Is not the spirit of prayer, that lamp going out in the church of God? the blessedness of all flourishing plantations in the world began by means of that, and shall not continue but as it continues; and if ever cause to seek for prosperity of plantations, these have need. If God should take away this generation of magistracy and ministery, what would this despised country do? and what would become of your children? then no schools for them, when no Gospel left among them; then every mans sword shall be against his brother, and God spreading the place with darkness, which through his presence is made light; what little hope of a happy generation after us, when many among us scarce know how to teach their children manners? How apt are we, like to those *Asian* churches, to fall into those very sins which overwhelmed them, and ruined them? how many fall off, and in time break forth, that it would make men sick to hear of their pranks? what place more open to temptations of persecution and worldly delusion? go up and down

the plantations, where is the man that lays things to heart? who hath the condition of the country written upon his heart, and presenting it before the Lord, rather than his own good? Oh men are silent because asleep! How do sins run thorough men as water thorough a mill, and men regard it not? what means, what deliverances have we had! but oh what little thankfulness? 2. Do we make progress; nay, is not our shadow gone back? *I sleep, but my heart waketh;* it should be so, but it is not so indeed.

5. Have we not fallen a dreaming here? what meaneth else the delusions of mens brains? what a swarm of strange opinions, which (like flies) have gone to the sores of mens heads and hearts, and these are believed also? and more dreams men have that are never spoken; every man hath some drunken conceit that rocks him asleep; dreams are quite contrary to the truths. What meaneth these, if men are not sleeping? First, drunken dreams of the world. Secondly, golden dreams of grace; that these things advance grace which indeed destroy grace; that there is no grace in the saints, no grace in Christ, no humane nature, no promise to evidence grace; no law to be a rule to them that have received grace: Who would think that ever any should so fall by a simple woman? But if this be not general; yet look how do men begin to dream concerning the world? scarce a man but finds want, or is well; if he wants, Oh then, if I had such a lot about me, such an estate, how well then were I? and *è contra,* They that have it, and now they take their rest: *Take heed,* saith the Lord, *your hearts be not overcome with cares;* So say I to you.

6. Doth not the Lord oft awaken us, yet we fall to sleep again? the Lord awakened us by the Pequot hornet, yet what use is there made of that? doth not the Lord oft meet us in an ordinance, but he is soon lost and gone again? Is there a man that hath not had his cross since he came hither, as loss in cattel and estate, a dear husband, Childe, wife dead? a sore and sharp sickness, &c. he hath been exercised with, &c. but do we not sleep still? if it be not thus, it will come; fear it for time to come; but if it be thus, then I say no more, but know it, you are in your enemies hand; and in such an enemies hand, that if you mourn not under it, will open the door either to the entrance of some gross sin and temptation, or for some heavy and sudden wrath. It's sufficient for me this day to shew you where your hurt lyeth.

## Sect. V.

Use 2. Hence see the reason why men are worse in virgin-churches, than in polluted places, and why it is so generally; because here are more temptations to make them all slumber and sleep; here their beds are made soft, here the storms are past, here they are under the shadow, and out of the sun, and security opens the door for an enemy: No wonder if the city be taken though never so strong, if it grow once secure: no wonder if the world be entred, and men are grown more worldly; and if Satan be entred, and men grow more passionate than ever before; no wonder a mans work be neglected, if he be asleep, ordinances more slighted than ever before: Never shall you see security fall upon a man alone, but it brings its train with it; when the husbandmen sleep, tares will be sown, and when the disciples sleep, temptations will enter; this is that which the Lord testifies of his people, Jer. 2. 2, 3, 4. I remember what thou didst in times of streights, in a land not sown; every one that touched you did offend; but in the seventh and eighth verses, when brought to a plentiful country, they did not so much as say, where is the Lord that hath done this for us! But yet the Lord questions his people for this, *What iniquity have you found in me?* which question you cannot answer without grief here, or confusion another day. You that are the Lords, often have heard this complaint (for this may be your condition as well as *Noah's* and *Lot's*) but now see the cause of it, how hard to awake on hour? how hard to walk with God one day? short awakenings you have, but long sleeps (this may be your condition for a time) but you cannot continue so for ever if you are the Lords. But if you do continue so, especially without bemoaning this unto the Lord, 'tis a question whether ever there was that oyl in your vessel, which others have, when not only a mans acts grow worse, but the very spirit of a man degenerates; when not only the leaves of the vine fall, but the vine it self groweth degenerate, and hence continueth so; this is a sore evidence of a woful state, Jer. 2. 20, 21. *When the yoke was upon thy neck, thou saidst, thou wouldst not transgress; but the Lord hath broken thy bands; and now thou art becom a strange vine:* Remember, it will be an heavy indictment against thee, to be good in *Mesheck,* but base in *Sion;* to be then worst when the Lord is best.

USE 3. Hence see one reason why the Lord pursueth many a soul with inward terrors and outward sorrows. Those that are fast asleep, because soft speechs cannot awaken them, hence we lay our hands upon them, and sometimes knock them, because this is the way to awaken them, and then they hear; so the word and spirit speak to a man, but such soft still winds rock them asleep rather than awaken them; hence the Lord layeth his iron hands upon a man, and knocks by blows, and now when affliction is upon you, now you can hear; When as the winds and water were ready to tear the ship in pieces, now they enquire, Why were they sent? *And the lot fell upon Jonah,* who was then sleeping; it is easie to awaken out of natural sleep, but very hard out of spiritual security: All the terrors of God on *Jonah* within and without are little enough; but at last he could hear, and run on his errand. Psal. 30. 6, 7. Why did God hide his face from *David?* he said in prosperity he *should not be moved;* this was the reason of it; the Lord sees you have need of it; seldom shall one see an awakening Christian without inward temptations and terrors, or outward sorrows: Oh consider then if the Lord do meet with thee! consider thy own security thou hast been in, or art apt to fall into! This is the sin you must enquire after and finde out; and do not account it hard, though long, though bitter; for never greater misery than for the Lord to say *Sleep on;* it is one of the heaviest judgements, for the Lord to let a man go on in a secure condition without blows; mark therefore unto the end of those blows, to be throughly awakened by them: For sometimes when the Lord sends them, a man (if they be not very bitter, if he hath any rest) lays them not to heart, Isa. 42. 25. *Fire burnt about him;* and in this country I know not what curse befalls men; peace makes men secure, and sorrow makes men discontented, and sunk, and discouraged, which may be for a fit in a saint; but to continue so, this that *Ahab:* Oh when as thou feelest the blow, look now that thou dost awaken, and be thankfull for it, that you met with that you did never reckon upon, *viz.* to be frightened out of security thereby.

### SECT. VI.

USE 4. To watch over one another, by *exhortating one another while it is called to day,* Heb. 3. 13. Let both the watchmen and members of churches do this; for this is one means appointed by the Lord to preserve the soul from sleeping, 1 Thes. 5. 1, 5, 6. *Exhorting one another;* as it is in cities, when the watch is apt to sleep, they have their companies that are passing up and down the walls the greatest part of the night, and so they are kept waking; and we shall finde, that as it is in a town where men are all asleep, one bell-man, one waking Christian will keep life, and spirit, and the power of godliness in many; and when he sleeps, all are fast. Nothing in the world brings security sooner upon men than sleepy company: officers of churches watch not over members, nor they one over another, exhorting and crying one unto another to their work, while it is called to day: Oh then let every man get up, and fall to this work of mutual exhorting! go and visit one another, go and speak oft to one another; and if thou be a childe of the light, see that thou endure not thy fellow servants to sleep in the open day in one duty or another. Know, if God stirs thee, thou wilt awaken others, 2 Cor. 5. 10. *We knowing the terrors of the Lord perswade men.*

2. Consider thy labor cannot be in vain here; the best metalled horse needs spurs; others are asleep.

You will say if I knew such a sin I would speak, but I dare not.

ANSW. It is the case of all the virgins, they have need of it, Jude 23. *Some save with fear, pulling them out of the fire,* Matth. 3.

3. Consider this is one part of your warfare, to keep your watch

whereby you may be made conquerors; You complain you have many sins and temptations arising and prevailing; never do they usually prevail, but when you are secure; first the watch is taken, and then the city is suddenly taken; now look as *Paul,* 2 Tim. 4. 6, 7. *he hath finished his course, and fought his fight, and now expects the crown;* how can you end your days in peace, that cannot in some measure finde and feel this? The church is the city of the living God, this is taken, and every man in it, unless you be watchful, and *exhort one another daily, while it is called to day:* And that I may not speak in the clouds,

4. Their sin will be yours.

First, labor to know the state of thy brethren whom thou art to exhort; what their sleepy neglects be, and sins are; it may be thou hast known one hath been very humble, tender, affected under ordinances, made many fair shews and promises of growing, and thriving, and sensibly complaining of his own vileness, and now he is in a silent sleep; dost thou know this, and wilt not speak a word to awaken him, for whom Christ shed his blood, who it may be will do thee as good a turn, and make many a prayer for thee? *Barnabas when he saw the grace of God, exhorted them with full purpose of heart to cleave unto him;* much more should you when you see grace dying, 2 Thes. 3. 11. *Paul* heard that some were idle, them he exhorts to work; what good might one word do?

Secondly, if you do not know, enquire with a spirit of much love, how it is with them; as *David* of his brethren when they were gone into the fields; do you not decline, do you not stand still? how have you found your heart since last sermon, sabbath, fast, affliction? have you got any ground against that sin you complained of last year? *&c.* Suppose you cannot do this to all, yet why not to some? Suppose you have no other place than when you meet them in the fields, do it there, Jude 20. *Build up your selves, &c.* Now here a man must know the height, how high they are built already, how can they lay their stones else? It is one of the heavy curses of God upon the Idol shepherd, *He shall not visit the hidden, nor seek the young,* Zach. 11. 16.

Thirdly, if thou knowest nothing from them, then relate thy own condition, this is a most lovely provocation, and exhortation unto another frame; for one great cause that hardeneth men in their security, is because they see no such living Christianity in the world: But when they do, *now* (Zach. 8) *many shall take hold of the skirt of a Jew, for they shall say God is with you; Agrippa* was almost perswaded and awakened when he heard *Paul* relate his conversion; although there be many impostors in the world that do so. Tell me, are all things in peace with you? the devil is in you then: what? hast no temptations? yet many; dost not observe how they prevail? yes; dost never get strength against them? yes; hast no good days after them? yes, much peace and life, and presence of God!

Hath the Lord given these talents to thee to be hid in a napkin, this treasure to keep and not to spend? who knows but that the speaking of these may awaken others? these temptations, and this condition is mine, these sins I find he makes a great matter of them; Lord what will become of me that am hardned under them? this peace they finde, my soul is a stranger to it; conscience will work thus: women should speak thus to women, and men to men; others were provoked by the example of the *Corinthians,* to help others; so there is a provoking power here.

Fourthly, If this prevail not, speak often to them, of the sins of others; in condemning others you condemn them; and this will make them look about them; view the fields, and shew them the tares that are grown up by security; and laying down these sins you strike at the root of theirs; it may be, you cannot tell certainly, Acts 2. 40. The Lord made this one means to awaken a *Belshazzar,* Dan 5. 22. God turned thy father into a beast, &c. to live in the woods, yet thou humbledst not thy self, &c. How many Professors doth God deal so withal?

Fifthly, enter into covenant and brotherly promise to exhort one another, as *David,* and *Jonathan*; if any hurt be toward *David, Jonathan* will speak of it, 1 Sam. 20. Some may in church-fellowship be more nearly knit than others, to call one another to account, to tell one another their fears, to know of one another their progress. Canst not give an account to man? how wilt thou give an account to God of it? I am perswaded many a man lies smoothered to death by means of this. Canst not come to the light of a candle? Oh how then canst thou appear before the light of the Sun.

Sixthly, provoke one another to frequency in ordinances, Heb. 10. 23, 24. and therein consider one another; dost see thy brother in doubts or complaints? call him to pray with thee; dost see things go ill in churches, and men bite the bit? call to fasting and prayer, three or four together, as *Paul,* when he saw the ship sinking, then he exhorted them, Act. 27. 22. Especially when you see danger near mens hearts, ready to be lost in the world: In these times suppose only two, or three, or four should go and pray one half hour together, and tell one another their wants, now help here; in our times it hath been so, one living Christian helps others dying.

But yet how is this neglected, as if men were resolved not only to dye sleeping themselves but to let others sleep also? No, you will say, not my self; yet it may be in your family it is so, and before the Lord.

What art alive to God and family, where thou canst do but little common good, and art dead to thy brother? it is made a sad sign of a man forsaken of God, if when he thinks he shall sleep his last, and be damned himself, yet he would have others damned also. Tell me, would you have all *New England* lye in security as well as your selves? No! do you not desire it when you use not the means that prevent it; and that is mutual exhortation; oh therefore do it; ministers may preach, and every man sleep still, unless some awake and rouse up the rest (as some, when others are abed and fast asleep) that lye a dreaming: some there be, that though doomsday were to morrow, they would sleep; oh therefore let me perswade some one or two to fall to his work, lest their security prove your undoing; therefore speak oft one to another, forsake not your assembling, visit one another, pray one for another, warning one another, that you may awake with the Lord one hour.

## SECT. VII.

USE 5. Let every man not only exhort his brother, but fear this himself; You have a race to run, many enemies to conquer, sleep not lest you fall short, sleep not lest you be taken captive: lest in exhorting others, your selves proves reprobates: I will not tell you what I fear, but Luk. 21. take heed lest your hearts be overcome; be not drunk with some delight, be not filled with vain cares; Hence, prevent it, as *Noah moved with fear made an Ark.*

First, set a high price upon those awakenings and revivings of heart that God sometimes giveth you; I am sure you finde these sometimes. A man that hath nothing to lose, will sleep with his doors open in the night; when a man hath a treasure he will be watchful to keep it; all security comes from an undervaluing of the spirit of grace, and its presence among us, Prov. 4. 13. *keep her, for it is thy life*; and when it is lost, what are you but dead?

Secondly, consider thy continual danger; if enemies be at the gates, all the town is watching; one would not think the depth of security that is in a careless heart, Psal. 30. 6. *I said I should never be moved*; he had good days and a thankful heart; then God did hide his face: a man would think *Sampson* should awake when the Philistines are upon him; but here devils be upon thee, 1 Pet. 5. 10. If all be well now, yet remember evil days; would you know when? even then when men say peace.

Thirdly, know the work you have to do, and make it your main business; when men have weighty business of the world in hand, they cannot sleep in their beds; and as the wicked, Prov. 14. 16. *They sleep not without doing mischief*; and so 'tis their main work.

Fourthly, call thy self to account daily, let not thy soul long go on without reflecting, What do I do? Harts and hawks kept from sleep lose their wildeness, but they must be constantly tended and kept watching: so consider the account you must give to God, 2 Cor. 5. 9. with 11. Hence Hag. 1. 5. Sins were upon them, and they repented not; miseries, and those were not removed; because they considered not their ways, especially before the great tribunal of God. I am perswaded the reason why men walk in their sleep, and go dreaming up and down the world, is this, they consider not, nor reflect upon themselves to any purpose; what do I? whether go I? no sermons awaken, you consider not of them.

## OF INEFFECTUAL HEARING THE WORD-SUBJECTION TO CHRIST IN ALL HIS ORDINANCES, AND APPOINTMENTS, THE BEST MEANS TO PRESERVE OUR LIBERTY.

(London, 1652)

*How we may know whether we have heard the same effectually: and by what means it may be come effectual unto us*

———

### JOHN 5. 37.

*Ye have neither heard his voice at any time, nor seen his shape.*

FROM THE 31. *Vers.* to the end of this *chapter.* Our Saviour proves that he was the *Messiah* to come, from four testimonies.

1. From the testimony of *John*; the first, yet the least, yet very strong and full, *vers.* 32. 33.

2. From the testimony of his works, greater then that of John, *vers.* 35.

3. From the testimony of the father, by his voice from heaven, *vers.* 37.

4. From the voice of the Scriptures, the highest of all, and surer then a voice from heaven. (2 Pet. 1. 19.) *v.* 39, 46.

Now these words are annexed to the third testimony, which I told you is the voice of God from heaven, set down Mat. 3. 17. For this testimony of the Father is not the inward testimony of the spirit only; because Christ speaks of publick, and evident testimonies in this place; nor is it meant of the testimony of the Father in the Scripture; for that is a distinct testimony: and though the Father doth testifie of Christ in the Scriptures; yet 'tis not as his testimony, no more then the testimony of *John,* and of his works, whereby the Father did testifie also: nor is it probable that our Saviour would at this time, omit that famous testimony of the Father at his Baptisme; which if it be not here, is no where in this *chapter.* Beside, how is this testimony the Fathers more then the Spirits; but then, being called his Son, he did evidently declare himself to be the father that spake. Lastly, the Spirits testimony is spoken of, as the testimony of *Moses* and the Prophets. *Vers.* 46, 47. *For had ye beleeved* Moses, *ye would have beleeved me, for he wrote of me,* vers. 47. *For if ye beleeve not his writings how shall he beleeve my words.*

Now our Saviour in these words answers an *objection,* which the Jewes (ever conceited of their own knowledge) might make. We know the Father as well as you; and yet we know no such testimony that he gives. Christ answers, You do not know him; for the certain knowledge of a thing, is either by seeing or hearing; now you never saw him nor heard him; you have therefore no acquaintance with him.

So that the words contain 1. Christs fearful accusation of the Jews to be ignorant of God. 2. The aggravation and extent of it, at no time, *i.e.* not only at Baptisme, but at no other time, in any ministery, or in any Scripture, &c.

QUEST. 1. *What is it not to see his shape nor hear his voice?*

ANSW. Some think they are metaphorical speeches, to expresse their ignorance of God; now though this be the scope, and the general truth, yet I conceive, the Lord speaking particularly, and knowing what he spake, intends something particularly: and it is a rule, never to flie to metaphors, where there can be a plain sense given. There is therefore two degrees of true knowledge of God in this life, or 'tis attained unto by a double meanes.

1. By hearing of him, for hence our faith comes by the Word.

2. By hearing thus from him, the mind also comes to have a true *Idea* of God, as he reveals himself in the Word and means by the Spirit, Job 42. 5. *I have heard of thee by the hearing of the ear, but now mine eye seeth thee;* and this is the *shape* here spoken of, not bodily and carnal. Now Christ doth professe that they did want both. Carnal and unregenerate hearts, neither hear Gods voice, nor have a right *Idea* of God in their mindes but become vain in their mindes, though they have meanes of knowing, and their foolish hearts are darkned; the wiser they be, the more foolish they grow.

2. *At no time, i.e.* neither at baptism, nor else in any mans ministery, nor in any of the Scriptures which you read, and where the Lord speaks.

3. But did they not hear the voice of God at Christs baptism, and at the Mount when Christ preach't, when the Scriptures were opened every Lords day and at other times amongst them?

ANSW. No, they never heard it. It's a strange thing, that such men that read, heard, preach't, remembred the Scriptures and could tell you mysteries in titles, never heard the voice of God; and yet it is most true.

OBSERVAT. *That many men may a long time together know and heare the Word of God written and spoken, yet never hear the Lord speaking that Word, no not so much as one word, title or syllable; no not so much as once, at any time.* This was the estate of the Jewes, and this is the estate of all unregenerate men. Hence Christ, Luke 19. 41. laments and weeps over *Jerusalem,* saying, *Oh that thou hadst known in this thy day, &c.*

1. QUEST. *How did the Jewes heare, and yet not heare God speaking?*

ANSW. There is a twofold word, or rather a double declaration of the same word. 1. There is Gods external or outward word, containing letters and syllables, and this is his external voice. 2. There is Gods internal word and voice, which secretly speaks to the heart, even by the external word, when that only speaks to the eare. The first the Jewes did hear at Christs Baptism, in Christs ministery, and in reading the Scriptures, and when they did hear it, it was Gods word they heard, full of glory, and so they heard the word spoken, but only man speaking it: the other comes to few, who hear not only the word spoken, but God speaking the word, Rom. 10. 18, 19. *Israel did hear,* but *Israel did not know.* Christ speaks in parables; Hence *in seeing they did not see,* Luke 8. 10. And this is one way, how 'tis true that Christ sayes, *They never heard his voice.* As 'tis with a painted sun on the wall, you see the sun and stars, but there is a difference between seeing this and the sun and starres themselves, wherein is an admirable glory: go to a painted sun, it gives you no heat, nor cherisheth you not; so it is here, &c.

2. This inward word is double. 1. Ineffectual, (though inward.) 2. Effectual. 1. Ineffectual, is that which hath some inward operation upon the heart, but it attaines not Gods end to bring a man into a state of life; and thus, Heb. 6. 2, 5. *Many tasted of the good word of God, yet fell away.* And such a heart is compared to a field which a man plowes and sowes, and raine falls on it, and yet the end is not attained, *it brings forth thistles*; and this many Jewes did hear, and hence had some kinde of faith in Christ. 2. Effectual, is that which hath such an inward efficacy upon mens hearts, as that God attaines his end thereby, Isa. 55. 11. and brings men to a state of life, of which Christ speaks, John. 6. 45. and this voice none but the elect hear; and of this Christ speaks here, as appears, *verse 38. Him whom he sent, ye beleeve not.* Hence it is you have heard God at no time. Hence he speaks of such a hearing and knowing, such a hearing outwardly, as is accompanied with such a hearing inwardly, Job. 14. 17. so that many men may hear the word spoken outwardly, but never inwardly: they may hear it inwardly, but never effectually, translating them from state to state, from death to life, from life to life and glory. No sense of the majesty of God speaking, nor effectual hearing of the word spoken. When the sun is down the moon may arise, but yet a man is cold and dark; but when the sun ariseth, on it warmes, nourisheth and cherisheth, &c. *nothing is hid from it*; so it is here, when the Lord speaks inwardly and effectually to the heart.

REAS. 1. From that great distance and infinite separation of mens soules from God, that though God cals, yet they can't hear no more then men a 1000 mile off. Eph. 2. 1. *Men are dead in sin.* Now what is spiritual death, but separation of the soul from God, & God from it. A dead man cannot hear one word at no one time, he was not dead if he could. Mens minds are far from God, & hearts also, that they are neither stricken with the sight of his glory, nor sense and savour of his goodnesse, but must be vaine, and have worldly hearts in the church, nay adulterous eyes, or if they listen, God is gone from them, and from his Word also, Hos. 5. 6.

REAS. 2. From the mighty and wonderful strange power of Satan, which blindes their eyes they cannot see nor hear, 2 Cor. 4. 4. Never such clear light, never such an effectuall word, as that of the Apostles, yet it was *hid*; why? *The God of this world blinded them,* either he will keep such a noise and lumber in their heads, that they cannot hear God speaking for the noise, or else turn himself into an angel of light, and speak, and by their light will blinde them, that the light in them shall be darknesse. Rom. 1. 22. When men with natural light began to be most wise, then they became the greatest fooles: so 'tis with other knowledge of Scripture, and things they heare. Happy were it for many a man if he had never heard nor seen; for that which he hath heard and seen keeps him from hearing. *Tyre* and *Sidon* would hear sooner then *Capernaum* that heard most.

REAS. 3. From the righteous judgment of God, in leaving men to be blinded and made deaf, from and by the means whereby they should hear and know; that as it is with the Saints, all evil things are for their good, so all good things are for their hurt, Isa. 6. 10. The meriting cause is unbelief and sin, but the deep and hidden rise of all is Gods eternal dereliction of them, God never intended love, special love to them, hence he never speaks one word to them, 2 Cor. 4. 3. John 6. 65. *Many were offended at his words and forsook him.* Now to take off this offence, I said, *None can come to me, except it be given him of the father,* what is that? see *vers. 45 and 37.*

USE 1. Hence see the reason, why the Word is so wonderfully ineffectual to the soules of many men, that it never stirs them, that it's a strange thing to them; it's Heb. 12. 19. like the law, *a voice of words,* a sound of words, so they hear men spake but understand no more then if they speak in a strange language, or if they do, it concernes not them; or if it stirs, 'tis but as the blowing of the winde upon a rock, which blusters for a time; but when the winde is down they are still. Truly they hear the word spoken, but they do not hear God speaking. They heard *Latimer* speak, but not God speaking, they hear a sound, which every one sayes, and they think is the word, but they hear not God speaking it.

One would wonder that those Jewes that heard *John* and his disciples, *Moses* and the Prophets, nay Gods voice from heaven, saying, *This is my sonne,* that they should not hear this, and receive him with all their hearts, but they did not hear his voice. One would wonder to see, that such things which a gracious heart thinks, this would draw every heart, yet remaine not stir'd, things which the devils tremble at, and others which

Angels wonder at, yet they hear not. Oh they hear not God speak, they are dead in their graves, farre from God; and there they are kept by the mighty power of Satan, like one in a deep dark cave, kept by fiery dragons under the ground, and the tombstone is laid upon them. If Christ spake he would make the dead to heare, and the blinde to see.

USE 2. Hence see why the Saints finde such changes and alterations in themselves when they come to heare; sometimes their hearts are quickned, fed and cherished, healed and comforted, relieved and visited; sometime again dead and senseless, heavy and hardned. Mark 8. 17, 18, 21. *How is it ye do not understand?* Nay which is more, that the same truth which they hear at one time, should affect them, and at another time doth not; the same thing which they have heard a hundred times, and never stir'd them, at last should. The reason is, they heard the Word of God spoken at one time, but not God speaking; and they heard the Lord speaking that same Word at another time; the Lord is in his Word at one time, the Word goes alone at another time; as in *Eliah,* the Lord was not in the whirlwinde, but he spake in the *still voice,* and hence there he was to *Elijah,* Luke 24. 25. *with* 32. Not that you are to lay blame on the Lord; for he blows where he listeth; but to make us see 'tis not in outward meanes, nor 'tis not in our own spirits to quicken our selves; and to make us ashamed of our own darknesse, that when he speaks, yet we cannot hear, there is so much power of spiritual death and Satan yet within us, only out of his pity he speaks sometimes; not that you should despise the outward word; no, no, the Lord is there shining in perfection of glory, and that which doth thee no good, the Lord makes powerful to some others. But prize the spirit of God in that Word, which alone can speak to thee.

USE 3. Of dread and terrour to all unregenerate men. Hence see the heavy wrath of God against them: they have indeed the Scriptures, and the precious Word of God dispensed to them; but the Lord never speaks one word unto them. If any one from whom we expect and look for love, passe by us and never speak; What not speak a word? and we call to him and he will not speak, we conclude he is angry and displeased with us. You look for love, do you not? you that heare every Sabbath, and come to lectures, and you must out; tis well: yes, you will say, *His love is better then life,* and frownes more bitter then death; Love? wo to me if the Lord do not love me, better never been born. I hope he loves me. Happy I if the mountains might fall on me, to crush me in pieces if he loves me not, &c. but consider if he loves, he will then speak peace unspeakable to thy conscience when humbled, life to thy heart, joy in the Holy Ghost, Isa. 57. 19. John 6. 63. 1. Thes. 1. 6. But look upon thy soul, and see this day in the sight of God, whether ever the Lord spake one word to thee: outwardly indeed he hath, but not inwardly; inwardly also, but not effectually, *to turn them from darknesse to light, and the power of Satan to God, &c.* The voice of God is full of majesty, it shakes the heart; 'tis full of life, it quickens the dead, and light, and peace, and gives wisdom to the simple. Ps. 119. *Opening of thy word gives light to the eyes.* How many women, ever learning and never knowing, and many men learning and knowing what is said, but never heare God speak? Then know the wrath of the Lord, see and go home mourning under it. There is a fourefold wrath in this.

1. 'Tis the Lords sore wrath and displeasure, Zach. 1. 2. with *ver.* 4. If one should expect love from another to do much for him, and he did not, it may be he would not take it as a signe of displeasure: but if he will not do a small thing, not speak a word to him, oh this is bitter; what will not the Lord speak a word, not one word, especially when thy life lies on it, thy soule lies on it, eternity lies on it, especially the Lord that is so merciful and pitiful? this is a signe of sore anger.

2. 'Tis a token of Gods old displeasure, eternal displeasure; I know you cannot heare; hence though God speaks, you hear him not: but why doth not the Lord remove that deafnesse? you old hearers, that have eares fat with hearing, but heavy, he never intended love, else he would speak there would be some time of love. Rom. 11. 7, 8. *The elect have had it, others are blinded, as 'tis written, God hath given them the spirit of slumber, eyes that they should not see, and eares that they should not hear to this day.*

3. 'Tis the Lords present displeasure. When a man looks for love and speech, and he doth not speak at those times he is not wont to speak; one may take it as no signe of anger: but when the Lord shall speak usually, and then he speaks not, this is a sad signe. 1 Sam. 28. 6, 15. He cries out of this, *He answers me not by* Urim *nor dreames,* nor thee by the Gospel nor Law, neither where he useth to answer. If this anger were to come, it were some comfort: but when 'tis now upon thee, even that very sermon and Word whereby he speaks to others, but not a word to thee.

4. 'Tis his insensible anger: for a fat heart and an heavy eare ever go together; for you will say, I feel no hurt in this, I have heard and been never the better, but yet that hath made me never the worse. Oh poor creature! 'tis because you feel it not; but when the time of misery shall come, you will say, This is wo and load enough, for the Lord to give no answer. Psal. 74. 9. *We see not our Prophets, nor any to tell us how long:* so you that despise meanes you shall then lament and say, none can tell how long. Oh therefore, lament this thy condition now, that the Lord may hear some of your cries, &c.

USE 4. Hence examine whether ever you heard the Lords voice or no: not only outwardly (for that you know you have often done) but inwardly; and not only so, for so ye may do, and yet our eares heavy; but effectually, that if it be not so, you may be humble and say, Lord how have

I spent my time in vaine? and if it be so, you may be thankful, and say, Lord, what am I that the infinite God should speak to me?

There is great need of trial of this, for a man may reade, hear and understand externally, whatever another may; and yet the whole Scripture a sealed book.

There are therefore these three degrees, by which you shall discern the effectual voice of God, you must take them joyntly.

1. The voice of God singles a man out, and (though it be generally written or spoken) speaks particularly to the very heart of a man, with a marvellous kinde of majesty and glory of God stamp't upon it; and shining in it.

When a man heares things generally delivered, the blessed estate of the Saints, the cursed estate of the wicked, consolations to the one, curses to the other, exhortations to faith and obedience, to both, and a man sits by, and never thinks the Lord is now speaking, and means me. Or if it doth so, yet thinks he intends me no more then others, he heares not the Lord speaking; for when he speaks, he speaks particularly to the very heart of a man: he doth so fit the word to him, whether it be the Word of the law to humble him, or of Gospel to comfort, or of command to guide, as if the Lord meant none but them.

The word is like an exact picture, it looks every man in the face that looks on it, if God speaks in it, Heb. 4. 12, 13. *It searcheth the heart, verse* 12. but *verse* 13. He speaks of God, how comes that in? because God, the majesty of God comes with it when God speaks it; *With whom we have to do,* why is that put in? because when the Lord speaks, a man thinks now I have to do with God, if I resist I oppose a God. Before this a man thinks he hath nothing to do with God, they are such strangers. Hence it is one man is wrought on in a Sermon, another not. God hath singled out one, not the other that day. Hence take a man unhumbled, he hears many things, and it may be understands not; if so, yet they concern not him; if they do, and conscience is stir'd, yet they think man means them, and speaks by hap, and others are as bad as they, and and his trouble is not much. At last he heares his secret thoughts and sins discovered, all his life is made known, and thinks 'tis the Lord verily that hath done this; now God speaks, 1 Cor. 14. 25. Those things he did neither believe nor imagine; &c. John 4. 29. *See the man that hath told me all that ever I did.* Hence take a soul that is humbled, he heares of the free offer of grace, he refuseth it; why, this is to all and to hypocrites as well as to me. Apply any promise to it, it casts by all, it looks upon them as things generally spoken, and applied by man, but they hear not God speaking; but when the Lord comes, he doth so meet with their objections, and speaks what they have been thinking may be true; that they think this is the Lord, this is to me. Hosea 2. 14. *I'le speak to her heart:* and hence 'tis called *the ingraffed word,* James 1. 21. like one branch of many, applied to the stock, Job 33. 14, 16.

2. The voice of the Lord doth not only speak particularly, but it goes further; it comes not only with an almighty power, but with a certain everlasting efficacy and power on the soul. Thus 'tis here, *verse* 38. *Ye have not his word in you,* they had it out of them; and not only in you, but abiding in you, 1 Pet. 1. 23. *Born of incorruptible seed,* the Apostle seems to speak a kinde of birth by corruptible seed, and such are like goodly flowers which soon wither, but you are born of incorruptible seed, which hath an eternal savour, sweetnesse and power. Mat. 13. Of the foure grounds three of them fall away. John 15. 16. Their fruit does not remain: they have some living affection at the present, but they go away and it dies. Look but upon particulars, doth the Lord once speak by the word, and humble the heart? it never lifts up its head more; doth he reveal the glory of Christ? that light never goes out more. Isa. 60. 19. 2 Cor. 4. 4, 5. As at the first Creation, there was light, and so continues to this day; so doth he give life, John 11. 26. You shall never die more; doth he give peace and joy? no man shall take their joy from them. Isa. 32. 17. *Fruit of Righteousnesse and Peace, and assurance for ever.* Doth he give the spirit of all these, which Gal. 3. comes by hearing of faith? it shall abide for ever, John 14. 17.

That look as Gods love is everlasting, so his words have an everlasting excellency and efficacy in them, and goodnes in them, the sweetest token of his love: and as Christs purchase is only of eternal good things; so the application of this purchase by the Word, 'tis of eternal worth: peace, but peace eternal, life, light, favour, joy, but joy eternal; like mustard seed, though very little, yet mighty in increase, and never subdued again; so that though it be but little, yet 'tis eternal: and hence observe where God hath spoken effectually, the longer the man lives, the more he growes in the vertue and power of the word; another though wonderfully ravished for a time, yet dies, most commonly outwardly in external profession, but ever in inward savour; so that when you hear the word, and it moves you, affects you, and *John is a burning light, and you rejoyce therein, but 'tis but for a season.* The evil spirit comes on you, and *David* playes upon his harp, and ministers preach sweet things, but as soon as the Musick is done, the evil spirit returns, I say you never heard the Lords voice. The peace and joy of the Lord enters into eternity, and the Apostle expresly calls him an unfruitful hearer, James 1. 24. *that sees his face and forgets himself.* A gracious heart can say, this peace shall go to heaven; and joy, and love, and fear, it's part of eternal glory.

3. The voice of the Lord comes not only thus particularly, and with eternal efficacy, but with such efficacy as carries unto, and centers in Christ; so 'tis here: *For him whom God hath sent you believe not.* John 6. 41.

*They shall be taught of God:* wherein doth that appear? *they shall hear and learn so as to come to me;* if the law humbles them, it's such a humbling as drives them unto Christ, poor and undone, Rom. 10. 4. If the word gives peace to them, 'tis such a peace which at the last they finde in Christ, Eph. 2. 17, 18. with 14. If it live holily, it lives unto Christ, not meerly as to God, and to quiet conscience, unto a Creator as *Adam,* but for Christs sake. 2 Cor. 5. 14, 15. *We judge that if we were dead, and Christ died for us, we should then live unto him;* if they grow up by the word, 'tis in Christ, Eph. 4. 14. Though Christ be not mentioned, yet it is strange to see, let the word speak what it will, whether terrour; Oh my need of Christ! mercy and grace; oh the love of Christ! oh the blood of Christ! command; Oh that I may live to honour Christ, and wrong him no more! Duties; Oh the easie yoke of Christ! They look upon the whole Word rightly dispensed as the Bridegrooms voice, and truly his words are sweet.

For a man may have some such feare, reformation, affection, as may continue, but never carry him out of himself unto Christ. The Pharisees knew the law, were very exact even til their death, profited as *Paul* said he did; yet they had not the word abiding in them; because not driven out of themselves to Christ, to rest there.

Hence when men shall hear many things, but to what end do you heare, or what vertue have the things you hear? Do they only please fancy for a time? or do you hear to increase your knowledge and parts? or do you hear for custome and company, and to quiet conscience? or are you affected and sunk, but not driven by all to lay thy head on Christ? the Lord never spake yet to thee; when the word hath laid you on this foundation, truly it's office is done and ended, Gods end is now attained, &c.

Oh try your selves here, have you heard, but never heard the voice of the Lord, rushing upon thee with majesty, speaking to thy heart, and the very secrets of it, but have said, This is for others, and when you have thought the man hath spoken to you, your hearts have then swollen against him? or have you thus heard, but all dies and withers like flowers, the same heart still? or have you had some powerful stroke which remaines, but it forceth you not out of your selves to Christ, there to rest, there to joy, there to live, there to die? truly your time hath been spent in vain, you never yet heard the Lord speak. Oh mourn for it, thou art still in thy blood, if he never said Live; in thy bondage, if the Lord never said, Come forth. This is the condition of many to be lamented with teares. But if thou hast thus heard particularly, and though but little light, life and peace, yet it is of eternal efficacy, and all to draw thee to Christ; then blesse the Lord: *For blessed are our eares that hear,* and I say as *Moses* said, Deut. 4. 32. *Ask if ever people heard God speaking and live.* The Apostle, Heb. 12. 24. makes it a greater matter to come to hear God on *Mount Sion,* and yet live; Blessed be God I live.

OBJECT. But may not many of the Saints hear, and hear the Lord speak; but not feel this everlasting power and efficacy?

ANSW. I would not lay a foundation of unthankfulnesse, nor discourage any; and therefore, note for answer these particulars.

1. There may be an eternal efficacy of the Word, and yet ly hid, and not felt for a time. The Word is compared, you know, to seed, and that in this respect; the seed it is cast under the clod in the winter-time, and it hath a vertue in it to grow; but it is hid, and comes not to blade of a good while; and when it doth blade, yet it beares not fruit of a long time: so here, the Lord may cast the seed of his Word into the heart; but it is hidden for a time, it is not felt as yet, but there it is; a word of threatening, a word of promise, a word of command; a man may cast it by, and say, It belongs not to me; a man may slight the command for a time: Yet notwithstanding, the Lord having cast his seed into the heart; it shall spring up. As many a childe, the father speaks to it, and applies the word home to it, when it is of some years; the childe regardes it not: but now stay some time, till the Lord do bring it into some sad affliction; now a man begins to think, I remember what my father spake to me once, & I regarded it not then: Now this seed which was cast when the childe was young, it shall spring up twenty years after. John 2. 22. Christ had said, *He would destroy the temple, and raise it againe in three dayes:* Now *when he was risen from the dead, his disciples remembred that which he had spoken to them,* but they regarded it not before; *These things,* saith Christ, *have I spoken to you whiles I was with you; but when the comforter is come, he shall bring all these words to your remembrance that I have said unto you.* One sentence it may be that hath discovered a mans sin, it lyes hid; but when the time of ripening drawes near, you shall see the word will have marvelous increase; and that sin it may be will bring to minde twenty sins; and that promise of God which gives but a little consolation, consider'd in it self, it shall give marvelous consolation. One would wonder to see what one word will do, when the Lords time of blessing it is come.

2. After that a Christian hath had the feeling of the efficacy of the word, he may lose the feeling of it again, and yet the being of it may remain; and the reason is this, partly because there is not alwayes need of feeling the like efficacy in the word. A man may have by the word a marvelous deal of assurance of Gods love, and sense of mercy and joy in the Holy Ghost, he may have this in the feeling of it: this word, it did ly hid for a time; afterward it springs up and gives him peace. But he loses his peace again, his sun do's set, and it is midnight with him within twenty four hours, and he is as much in the dark as before; Now the being of this peace is there, but he hath no need of the feeling of it at all times; the Lord he will reserve that till some time of tentation, that he

shall meet withall. As *Paul*, he had marvelous Revelations; but *Paul* had more need of humiliation, then exaltation; and there was not that use of *Pauls* having those glorious manifestations to him; *I will glory in my infirmities:* There was need for *Paul* to know the evils of his heart, that he might walk humbly; and it did not make so much for the glory of the Lord, as this that *Paul* should say; I have this misery and darknesse, and sins, and yet Jesus Christ he will take away all: There was not need for *Paul* to have those joyes at all times, that he had at one time. So the Lord he gives a Christian joy and peace, now there is no need for a Christian to have it alwayes. *I will pour floods of water on dry ground:* Beloved, if there should be nothing but raine, raine every day and night, the ground would be glutted with raine, and so turned into a puddle; but when the land is dry and thirsty, now the ground hath need of raine: Let the earth make use of that raine it hath: and when it is dry and thirsty, I will give more, saith the Lord. So the Lord he gives the soul joy and peace; Now, if it should continue, the very peace and joy of God, would not be pleasant to the soul; or at least, not so pleasant as it will be, when the Lord takes it away, and gives it the soul again. A Christian comes to the meeting-house, and the Lord fills the sailes of a poor soul, that he wonders the Lord should meet him, and speak so suitably to him: But as soone as he is gone out again, this is the complaint of the soul, all is lost again; now the soul it falls a mourning again. It is not for the glory of God to give the soul such peace out of his ordinances, as he doth in them; the soul it would not prize the ordinances of the Lord so much; yet there it is; and when they come again, the Lord, he either gives them the same refreshings again, or else there is a new spring.

3. The eternall efficacy of the word and voice of God; it may be preserved in an internall spirit of prayer, for the continuance of it while a man hath it, and for the return of it when it is lost. Ps. 119. 4, 5. *Thou hast commanded us to keep thy precepts diligently. David* he knew his own weaknesse; yet he intimates with what power it came on his heart: *Oh that my soul were directed to keep thy statues;* when the soul sees the beauty of a command, and the good will of God, how sweet it is, and how amiable the way and work of God is; *Oh that my heart were directed to keep thy statutes.* And so when it is gone, Psal. 63. 3. *My soul thirsteth after thee, Lord,* saith *David, that I may see thy glory and power, as I have seen thee in thy sanctuary.* He doth not say, that I may see thy glory and power in thy sanctuary, though that might be too; no, but *that I may see thy glory and power, as I have seen thee in thy sanctuary. David* he did finde a want of seeing him as he had done; yet the vertue of it did remaine in a spirit of thirsting, and desire: *My soul thirsteth for thee, as in a dry land where no water is, that I may see thee.* A Christian may have at sometime such a glimpse (in hearing the word) of Gods grace, of the exceeding riches of Gods

grace, and the love of God to him, that he may be in a little heaven at that time; ravished in the admiration of that mercy, that ever God should look to him. It is so, and the word sayes so, and the soul is ravished with wonderment at it; yet God is gone again, and the soul loses it. Now the soul thinks, I have lost the efficacy of Gods word, but it is not so; for thus it may be preserved. Oh that I may see this God as I have done: And all his life-time the soul may finde the want of this, and yet it may be preserved in a spirit of prayer. For whom the Lord hath given once a glimpse of his glory; the soul it cannot be at rest, but it breatheth for more of that mercy and presence; a Christian may finde his spirit marvelously refreshed at the word, he may taste how good the Lord is, and he may lose it again: but this may be preserved in a spirit of longing after this God, and presence again. And I will say this, brethren, A Christian may finde no good by the word to his apprehension; he sees the admirable blessed estate of the Saints, and exceeding riches of God in Christ, sees the sweetnesse of the wayes of God; goes home and thinks within himself, happy they that are in this condition: Blessed are they that can walk thus with God; but I cannot, saith the soul. I say it may finde it thus, when he cannot finde the reall efficacy of the word as he would do; he may receive the benefit of that word, if the Lord do but only give him a heart to desire it. Oh that the Lord would but thus manifest himself to me; the soul may go away poor and hungry from the word, and the Lord may yet reserve a spirit of thirsting after that good which a man desires to finde; and there is the efficacy of the word there.

As now there are two golden vessels; one a man fills, and it is every day dropping, and he preserves it; another vessel he do's not fil, but with something that he hath, he is every day widening of it. So some Christians, the Lord he's a filling of them; others, the Lord he do's not fill them with such peace and joy; ay, but though the Lord is not filling of them, he is a widening of them: there is such a vertue that the Lord do's enlarge the heart; with secret desires and longings after more of Gods grace, and Christs: The Lord he saith, I intend to make this man a vessel of glory; and I intend he shall have a great deal of glory and peace at the last. The Lord he leaves such an impression of the word upon him, as that thereby he enlargeth the heart; *Open thy mouth wide, and I will fill it.*

4. A Christian may have the everlasting efficacy of the word and voice of God preserved in a spirit of thankfulnesse and love to the Lord, for those joyes and good that it findes by the word sometimes. When it feels that the sweet and savour of the word is gone, a spirit of thankfulnesse and love to the word that doth remaine; the Lord he preserves the efficacy of the word in this way. Psal. 119. 7. *I shall*, saith *David, then praise thee with uprightnesse of heart, when I shall have learned thy righteous judgements.* The Lord he may teach his people his righteous judgements;

and the savour and feeling, and strength of them to their feeling may be gone, and yet it is preserved in a spirit of thankfulnesse and praise, that ever the Lord should shew it such mercy. When the spirit is gone, the spirit of love and thankfulnesse remaines. As now a man hath heard the word, the Lord he hath effectually wrought on him, and changed his heart, and drawn him to himself; a Christian it may be he may lose those sorrowes and humiliations, and the remembrance of those things; yet there remaineth to his dying day this spirit, he blesseth God, and wondereth at God, that ever he should make the word effectual; that he should leave so many thousands in the world, and cast his skirt over him, and say to him, Live; this do's remain still.

Brethren, the Lord do's sometimes let light into a mans minde to discover his sin: now this light it do's not sensibly overcome the power of sinne: but now the soul blesseth God for that word which hath convinced it; had I never seen my sinne, saith the soul, I should never a sought for power against it, and pardon of it; and this continues now, and cannot but continue; here is the efficacy of the word, the word of Gods grace; though the flower of it be gone, yet there is an eternal power of the word; that the soul can say, It hath come to me, and helped me against these sins; and the soul wonders at the Lord, it should be so much as it is. So again, a Christian he findes marvelous refreshings and affection whiles he is a hearing; when he is gone away, he findes not the same, but he blesseth God for those affections he findes, and there remains an eternall efficacy of the word.

5. The eternall efficacy of the word, it may be and is preserved, by nourishing, increasing and restoring the new man that is eternall. There is a double efficacy that the word hath; the first is to beget a Christian to life, and this new man is eternall. I conceive all the actions of the new man may be suspended, and the increasings of the new creature may be decayed, though God doth renew it again: but this never do's decay, it never dies: *He that is born of God cannot sin, because he is borne of God; and because the seed of God remaines in him.*

2. There is efficacy in the word when it hath begotten a man to nourish him up; and so the word it is food to him, that was seed to him to beget him, which food is eternal. How is it eternal? Is it in this, that now the sweetnesse, savour and remembrance of every thing that doth refresh him, shall last in it self? No, but in this respect it is eternall, in that it leaveth its secret vertue in the nourishing of that which is eternall. As now *Adam* when he was in innocency, and had an immortall body, his food it should have been an immortal food to him; but how should that have been? should he alwayes have had the same strength, from the same diet, which he ate long before? No, but in this respect it should have been an immortall food to him, in that it was to nourish that which was to be

eternal: so it is here, the word of Gods grace it begets a man, it humbles a man, and drawes the soul to Christ; but afterwards, there are many things that God speaks to the soul in the word, that hath an eternall vertue, in that it doth nourish up the new creature; the word hath a secret vertue in it for this end. I will shew it you thus; Isa. 58. 11. The Lord he professes to his people, *Thy soul shall be as a watered garden:* The Lord will make the souls of his people like watered gardens, in peace, and joy, and life. Now look as if so be trees by water or by some springs that run by it, and slide away, and ye cannot tell, which it is that makes them to grow; yet ye know this, there is in all of them joyned together, a secret insensible vertue; that every one of them addes something to the flourishing of the tree: so it is here, the Saints of God, the word of God it comes to them, and passes by them; and ye cannot tell whether this part or that part of the word leave any vertue, but many times a man feels no vertue; yet it is manifest, here is a flourishing Christian, here is heart, and life, and peace that it hath with God, and the soul it remains flourishing; there is a secret vertue, all the words that run by and passe by the souls of Gods people, they do leave a marvellous vertue, to make the soules of Gods people like watered gardens, and to increase in grace. Note it by the way you that live under the means of grace, *your soules shall be like watered gardens*; if God have spoken to you first or last, the Lord speaks many times to you, sometimes affecting, and sometimes warning, sometimes convincing and humbling, and speaking peace, and there is a vertue that remaines, and if ye finde it not, know that God hath not spoken to you.

6. The eternal efficacy of the Word may be preserved in a power of conflict against the power of sin: for therein the Lords power of the Word does principally appear in this life, though not in a power of victory, I mean a compleat victory, yet an imperfect and incompleat victory, there ever is first or last, whereever there is a power of conflict. I mean thus, the Word it singles a man out, and speaks to his heart, and sets him at variance with his sin, and with himself for his sin, and he joynes side with God in the use of all meanes, that his unbelieving heart and proud spirit may be subdued; it sets him at variance with his sin; now there is many a Christian thinks there is no power of the Word; oh my unbelief continues still, and my vain minde, and I can finde little strength; no, ye must not look for a power of compleat victory, but yet there is a power of conflict; God he sets the soul at an everlasting distance with his sin, never to be reconciled, and looks to the Lord, that by his Word and spirit he would subdue them, that so he may see the death of them, and he sides with the Lord in the use of all means, comes to the Word, and comes to prayer, and sayes, Speak against my sin, Lord; Lord, waste these distempers: and so the soul is thus at variance with his sin, although his

temptations do get winde and hill of him, he goes again, and to them again: and though he perisheth, and never have mercy from the Lord; yet, Lord, that I may never sin against thee more, help therefore, Lord, by this promise, and mercy and meanes; and here he keeps him, and here he holds. Truly, brethren, here is an eternal vertue, and such a vertue as no hypocrites have, that have some sting of conscience, and after they have some peace, they are at truce with their sins. No, there is an everlasting conflict and warfare, and I do assure you there is an everlasting power gone forth. Mat. 12. 20. *Christ will not break the bruised reed, nor quench the smoaking flax, till judgement come to victory*; therefore there may be judgement, but it may not come to victory, there may be smoak and fire, and it may almost go out, and the Lord he blowes it up again, and at the last, though it be weak and little, and he think with himself he shall never get strength again, yet the Lord will give victory in his time.

Only be cautious here; I told you there is an incompleat victory, the Lord never sets his people at variance with their sin, but they have victory, but it is an incompleat victory, Saith the Lord, *I will drive out the Hittites, and Canaanites, and Perizzites before you, but I will do it by little and little.* There is many a Christian that findes within himself a spirit of warfare against his sin, and did he examine himself, he should finde a spirit of victory; but he thinks he hath none because his victory is not compleat. If he had a heart so to believe as never to doubt more, and such quickning as never to be dead more, never to depart from God more, now I should think the Word comes with power; but I finde that these evils prevaile against me. There is many a one does scorn the kindnesse of Christ, because he findes not compleat victory, but darknesse remaines still, and sinful lusts remaine still, therefore the Word doth me no good at all, saith he. The Lord he hath given thee a spirit of conflict, and hath set thee at an everlasting distance with thy sin, and he doth give thee some victory. beloved, a Christian may decay in the power of the grace of Christ, which he hath received from the word, and voice of God in the Word, and he may decay and grow to a very low estate; yet he shall finde this, the Word of the Lord hath come with power to him, it will recover his soul again, and so the efficacy of the Word is eternal. Psal. 72. Its said of Christ, that *his people shall feare him so long as sun and moon shall endure,* that is, continually, all their life-time. It may be said, there may be many that finde decay of their service and obedience, and they lose their feare of the Lord, and their dread, and their humble walking before him, *He shall come as the raine on the mowen grasse:* many times a Christian hath his flourishing time as the grasse, but when the grasse is mowen, it is as a dry chip; so the soul it may grow dry, as dry as a chip. Now where is your sap and savour? but I tell you, if you belong to the Lord Jesus, the raine it will fall again, the Word of God set on by the spirit of Christ, it shall fall upon you as the raine on the mowen grasse, and you know that it recovers little by little, and puts on a green coat again. Here is the eternal love of the Lord Jesus to his people, and thus the eternal efficacy of the word does continue.

3. USE is of exhortation. Oh brethren and beloved in the Lord Jesus, may a Christian heare the Word of God spoken, and yet never hear God speak? may he hear it externally and not internally? then rest not in external hearing, and with some little movings, and affections, and stirrings of the Word of Gods grace in hearing. Let not the Word be to you as the sound of many waters, and a noise, no efficacy of the Word that do remaine on your soules. Brethren and beloved in Christ, I lay my finger on the sore in these times. Oh the contempt of the Gospel of Christ, though I believe it hath its efficacy in the heart of the Elect: that is the thing I presse, never be content with external hearing, though thou mayest have some affection, and know new things, unlesse thou finde the Lord speaking with an eternal efficacy to thy soul. I conceive two things are to be done, that the word may come with an everlasting efficacy; although something is to be done by ministers; that is, to preach truth, and Gospel-truth, fetch't from heaven with many prayers, and soaked truth with many teares. *Ye shall know the truth, and that truth shall make you free.* Convicting truth. *We preach,* saith the Apostle, *in the demonstration of the Spirit. The Spirit of God when he cometh, he convinceth the world of sin.* Let ministers do so. Preach convincing truth and Gospel-truth, fetch'd from heaven, and bathed in teares. Oh brethren, let the fire burn clear, let there not be more smoake then fire, it will never come with power then; convincing Gospel-truth, set on by the demonstration of the Spirit of the Lord, and this will set a Christian at liberty; there is never such a Sermon that the faithful ones of God preach to you; if it come not with a power to loosen you and call you home; it comes with a power to blinde you: it is *an axe at the root of the trees;* but I leave this. What means ought the people to use, that the Word of God may come with efficacy?

Them that are in their unregenerate estate, the Lord only knowes how to work on their hearts; they must come to the outward meanes. I speak to the Saints of God, I leave others to the infinite mercy of the Lord; *It is not in him that willeth or runneth, but in the Lord that sheweth mercy.* In the use of meanes.

1. Meanes. Do not only see they infirmities and weaknesse, but pray to God to give thee a heart bleeding under the sense of thy many infirmities. Many times men slight them, and are not sensible of them; I do not say wickednesses and wilfulnesses, but thy infirmities and weaknesses, get a heart mourning under them. A Christian is made up of infirmities and weaknesses, a man would not think there is that in another, which he knowes by himself. Oh brethren, labour for a broken

heart in the sense of your many infirmities and weaknesses, darknesse and enmity, vanity and unsavourinesse, the Lord will have his time to speak to such a soul. *Break up the fallow ground of your hearts,—lest my wrath break out with fire:* the Lord hath promised *to dwell with the poor and contrite.* Look as it was with our Saviour Christ, they brought the sick and the lame ones to him, and vertue went out from Christ to heal them all. Bring thy sick and blinde heart to Christ, and vertue shall go forth from Christ to heal it.

2. Draw near to God in the Word, by looking on it as God speaking to thee. We are far from God, and therefore we cannot hear him: draw near to him when you come to the external Word, when you come to heare the Word, heare it as the voice of God; *You heard the Word as the Word of God,* which you felt in you. I do not speak that the soule should take every thing that ministers speak as the Word of God, but that which is the Word of God, take it as God speaking. I am not able to expresse the infinite unknown sweetnesse, and mercy, and presence of God, that you shall finde thus coming. I know it is a common truth, but I am not ashamed to tell you, I have not for many a year understood this truth, and I see but little of it yet; ye have heard of it, but ye do not understand what it is to hear God speaking. When God hath an intent to harden a mans heart and to damn him, either he shall have a prejudice against the man, or else if he hath not a prejudice against the man, there is a secret loathing of the truth, in regard of the commands of it, and that is all, and the Lord he hardens, and blindes, and prepares for eternal ruine, all the men in the world by this meanes, that live under the meanes. When the Lord spake to *Samuel, Samuel* heard a voice, but he heard it is not as spoken by God, but when he took *Elies* counsel, and saw it was the Lord that spoke; now he listens to the voice of the Lord, and now the Lord opens all his minde to him.

3. Do not trust to the external word. It is a heaven on earth to hear the Word exalted, a glorious thing to hear the Word of God as Gods Word; but trust to the free grace of God in it, and the spirit of God in Christ to set on that Word. When they brought the lame, and blinde, and halt to Christ, they looked for the Word and the power of it; *Speak the Word, Lord, and thy servants shall be whole*; so bring your blinde, lame, and halt soules to Christ, and trust to the free grace of the Lord Jesus Christ. *The Work of the Lord it shall prosper in his hand*; so the Word of the Lord it shall prosper in his hand also.

Lastly, so seek the Lord, and so heare the Word, to see the truth, and so heare the truth, as that you lay up your happinesse in this world, in closing with the truth and with the word. Brethren, what is a mans happinesse in heaven, but to close with God and Christ? I cannot come to God now, the most that I can have of God now is in his word; if it be happinesse in heaven to close with God in Christ, truly then it is a mans happinesse to close with God in his word on earth; and if it be your happinesse, lay up your happinesse in it. *My son*, saith Solomon, *if thou wilt hear my word, let them not depart from thine eyes; keep them in the middest of thy heart;* place thy happinesse in them. *So shall they be life to thy soul.* Neverthelesse brethren, let a mans soul be set upon any thing in the world, when he comes to hear, besides the word; if he lay not up his happinesse in closing with the word; truely, the word it will be like a song to him. The Prophet *Ezekiel* tells them, *Their hearts were gone after their covetousnesse.* When a man comes to hear a Sermon, there is a Sermon and the market, there is a Sermon and a friend to speak withall; and so marly young people will go abroad to hear Sermons; What is the end of it? It is, that ye may get wives and husbands many of you; but it is not your blessednesse to close with the Lord in his word. I have known some men that have had a distaste against the truth of the Lord; and I have known them for many a day, they have not been able to understand the truth of the Lord. When it shall be thus with a man, that a mans heart is set on something else besides the word of the Lord, that it is not my happinesse to close with the truth of the Lord; such a man shall never understand the truth of the Lord. Though the word be sweet to you sometimes, if your blessednesse do not lye in this, to enjoy God; Oh this Gospel of God, and these commands of God, that your blessednesse do not lye in cleaving to the Lord in his word; I say, it is a certain truth, you shall be blinded and hardned by the word: For here is a rule; whatsoever a mans heart is set on, as his chiefest good, the presence of that good it comes with power: so here, the precious Gospel of Christ, when the presence of it commands the heart, nothing is good enough for it, and it closeth with it, and with Christ in it.

I beseech you therefore, beloved in Christ, set upon the use of these meanes, think within your selves; what if the Lord had left me without the word? I will tell you what ye would have been. Look upon these poor *Indians,* herds of beasts; look upon others on their ale-benches, enemies to the Lord, such a one thou hadst been.

This blessed word and voice of God, every tittle of it cost the blood of Christ; written all the lines of it in the blood of Christ. Oh, make much of it, and it will make much of you; it will comfort you, and strengthen you, and revive you; and if the word come not with power, ye shall be under the power of something else; if not under the power of the word, then under the power of some lust. What is the reason that these poor creatures, that are come to the tryall for life and death, that have fallen into such sins as were never heard of? What is the reason that they are under the power of their lusts? I will tell you what *Solomon* saith, *My son, if wisdome enter into thy heart, and discretion be pleasant to thy soul, it shall keep thee from the strange woman,* & sinful companion. If it be pleasant, here is the reason, the word of Gods grace it never came with power, or if it came with power, powerless the word of Gods grace hath been to them; and because it hath not come with power, the Lord he hath given them over to the power of their lusts, and sinfull distempers. Oh brethren, truely I cannot see how any man can maintaine any evidence of Gods electing love; that shall hear and hear, and good dayes mend him not, nor bad dayes paire him: that can commend a sermon, and speak of it; but that efficacy is not known to him, neither doth he mourne for the want of it; but the eternall efficacy thereof is a stranger to it. 1 Thes. 1. 5. *Knowing,* saith the Apostle, *your election of God;* How did he know it? For, saith he, *Our Gospel came not to you in word, but in power,* ye will rejoyce the hearts of your ministers, when the word comes with power. Let me say this, and so I conclude.

I remember the Lords threatning; *I will take away the staffe of bread, and ye shall eat, and shall not be satisfied;* When the Lord shall let men have the word, when the Lord shall not take away the word, but the staffe of the word. Suppose you poor parents, fathers, and mothers; your families should have good corne, but when you come to eat it, no strength at all, but ye dye and weare away; and others that are about you, they have planted the same corne, and eat and are satisfied; What will ye do in this case? You would set apart a day of fasting and prayer; and say, good Lord, what a curse is upon me? my poor children are dying before me, others have the staffe of corne; but my family have no strength at all. Ye would mourne if it were thus with your poor cattell. Oh, for poor creatures to have the word, but the efficacy of it to be taken away; no blessing, no power at all. Oh poor creatures, go and say! Oh the curse of God that lyes on me, the wrath of God that lyes on my servants, it is a heavy plague. But oh the sweetnesse and excellency of it, when a Christian shall finde everlasting vertue and efficacy conveyed to him by the word.

All you that are before the Lord this day, ye shall see an end of all perfection; but eternall things are not they worth something? You shall see an end of all delights and contentments; but this shall comfort you when you are a dying, that the word which you attended upon the Lord in, such peace, and such consolations I have found by it; and the efficacy of that word then remaines with you; nay, goes to heaven with you. *I commend you therefore to the word of his grace, which is able to build you up unto an eternall inheritance amongst them that are sanctified,* Acts 20. 32.

# INCREASE MATHER
## (1639–1723)

## PREDESTINATION AND HUMAN EXERTIONS

From *Awakening Truths Tending to Conversion*
(Boston, 1710)

THERE are some sinners so unreasonable, and so wicked. Ask them why they don't reform their Lives, why don't you turn over a new leaf, and amend your ways and your doings, they will answer, God does not give me grace. I can't convert my self, and God does not convert me. Thus do they insinuate as if God were in fault, and the blame of their unconversion to be imputed unto him. But as Elihu speaks, *Suffer me a little, and I will shew you what I have yet to say on God's behalf.*

1. I say, God is not bound to give sinners grace: He is an absolute Sovereign, and may give grace or deny grace to whom he pleaseth. Shall the thing formed, say to him that formed it, why hast thou made me thus? has not the potter power over the clay, to make one vessel unto honour, and another to dishonour? The glorious God has a greater power over his creatures, than the potter has over the clay. Wherefore, *He has Mercy on whom He will have Mercy, and whom He will He hardens,* Rom. 9.18. If He giveth grace to any man in the world, it is from his sovereign good pleasure. Why were such poor fishermen as *Peter,* and *James,* and *John,* and others, as mean as they, made the subjects of saving grace, when many incomparably beyond them in learning and wisdom, have been left to perish in their unbelief? Even so, because so it has seemed good in the sight of him, who is the Lord of Heaven and earth, Math. 11. 25, 26. Grace is a wonderful gift of God. Sinners are enemies to him, and rebels against him: Is he bound to bestow such a gift on his enemies, when it may be too they will not so much as humbly pray unto him for it[?] Indeed he sometimes has done so. Sinners that never prayed to him, that never had one thought in their hearts of returning to him, he has miraculously prevented them with sovereign grace. So it was with the converted Gentiles. Of them the Lord sayes, *I am sought of them that asked not for me,*

*I am found of them that sought me not, I said, behold me, behold me to a Nation that was not called by my Name,* Isa. 69. 1. Nay, sometimes when sinners have been in the height of their resistance and rebellion, to shew the exceeding riches of his grace, God has then converted them. Thus it was with *Saul* afterwards *Paul,* when he was breathing out slaughters against the disciples of the Lord, then did God give him faith in Christ, without his praying for it. Thus also those converts in the second chapter of the Acts. Not many days before their conversion they had been murdering the Son of God. And just before the sermon began they were mocking of the preacher, and yet converted by that sermon. Such instances there have been known in the world, of men that have come to hear a sermon only to deride it, and yet have been savingly wrought upon by it. A credible author reports, that two profane men drinking together, knowing that Mr. *Hooker* was to preach, one of them said to the other, *Let us go hear how Hooker will baul,* yet was he converted by that very sermon, which he went to hear with a scornful spirit. And after that had such a love for Mr. *Hooker,* as to remove three thousand miles, that so he might live under his ministry. Such Examples are wonderful evidences of sovereign grace.

2. Altho' it is true, (as has been shewed) that sinners cannot convert themselves, their *Cannot* is a wilful *Cannot.* Math. 22. 2. *They will not come.* It is not said they *could not* (tho' they could not of themselves come to Christ) but that they *would not* come. If it were in the power of a sinner to convert himself, he would not do it: For he hates conversion. *It is abomination to fools to depart from evil,* Prov. 13. 19. Psal. 50. 17. *Thou hatest instruction.* If they hate to be converted they will not chuse it. Prov. 1. 29. *They hated knowledge, and did not chuse the fear of the Lord.* Their hearts are in love, and in league with their lusts, yea they hate to be *turned* from them: they love darkness rather than light, they hate the light, neither come they to the light, Joh. 3. 19, 20. Sinners are haters of God: they say and think that they love him, but the Lord knows that they hate him, and therefore they will not repent of their sins, and believe on Christ. Christ said to the Jews, *You will not come to me that you might have Life,* Joh. 5. 40. No, they would dy first. And why would they not come? The reason of their aversion is mentioned in v. 42. *I know you, that you have not the Love of God in you.* Their carnal unregenerate minds were full of enmity against God, and therefore they would not come to Jesus Christ the Son of God. They cannot convert themselves, and they are not willing that God should convert them. If sinners were willing to have grace and holiness, why do they not repair to him for it, who alone can give it to them? An hungry man is willing to have bread, therefore he will seek after it, where ever it is to be had. When the Egyptians were hunger bitten, they went to Pharaoh, crying for bread, he bid them go to Joseph, and they did so. Thus if sinners were willing to be converted, they would cry to God to turn them: whenas there are many

sinners that did never put up one earnest prayer to God in their Lives, that he would bestow converting grace on them.

3. Sinners can do more towards their own conversion than they do or will do. They should give *diligence* to make sure of their being effectually called. They should *strive* to enter in at the strait gate. Conversion is the strait gate that leadeth unto salvation. They should *labour* not for the meat that perisheth, but for that which endureth to everlasting life: but they do not give diligence, they do not strive, they do not labour to obtain grace and salvation: therefore they perish, and perish justly. Prov. 21. 25. *The desire of the slothful kills him, for his hands refuse to labor.* Men say that they desire grace, and yet their hands refuse to labour, they will be at no pains to obtain it: and this slothfulness kills them. It proves the death of their souls. *The soul of the sluggard desireth and has nothing, but the soul of the diligent shall be made fat,* Prov. 13. 4. There are several things which sinners have power to do in order to their own conversion, & which they ought to do, but they will not.

(1) They have power to avoid those things which are an hindrance of conversion. *e.g.* They can if they will forbear the outward acts of sin. By giving way to sin their hearts are hardned, and their conversion becomes the more difficult. Heb. 3. 13. *Take heed lest any of you be hardned through the deceitfulness of sin.* But sinners give way to many sins which they could abstain from, if they would. A Sabbath-breaker can forbear his profaning of the Sabbath. An ungodly swearer can forbear his profane oathes, if he will. A lyar can forbear telling such lyes. Sinners can avoid the temptations which will endanger their falling into sin. He that knows that if he goeth to such a place, or into such a company, he will probably be drawn into sin, ought to avoid the temptation. Prov. 4. 15. *Avoid it, turn from it, and pass away.* The sinner can do so if he will, but he will not keep out of the way of temptation. A drunkard will not avoid the Temptation to that his sin. Prov. 23. 31. *Look not on the wine when it giveth his colour.* He can chuse whether he will look on the wine or no: he has power to refrain, but will not. Thus men by habituating themselves to sin, do what in them is to hinder their own conversion. Jer. 13. 23. *Can the Ethiopian change his skin, or the leopard his spots? Then may you also do good that are accustomed to do evil.* Again, evil companions hinder conversion. *Alas! Alas! Alas!* these have been the eternal ruin of many a young man, that was in an hopeful way for conversion: He has fallen in with vain companions, they have given him bad counsel, so have convictions been stifled, and the motions of Gods holy Spirit quenched'in his soul. The word of the Lord sayes, *Forsake the foolish & Live,* Prov. 9. 6. The sinner has power to forsake them, but he will not tho' he dies for it.

(2) Sinners have power to wait on God in the use of means which has a tendency to promote conversion. They can if they will, not only

forsake evil companions, but associate themselves with those that are good: then are they in the way of conversion. Prov. 13. 20. *He that walketh with wise men shall be wise, but a companion of fools shall be destroyed.* That learned & holy man Dr. *Goodwin* in the account which he giveth of his conversion, declares, That when he was a young schollar in the University of *Cambridge,* there were in that *College,* which he belonged unto, a *number of holy youth's* (that's his expression) his associating himself with them was an happy means of furthering the work of conversion in his soul. This unconverted sinners have power to do. Their feet are as able to carry them to a godly Meeting as to an ungodly one. Reading the Scripture has sometimes been the means of conversion. I could tell you of several learned Jews that were converted from their Judaism by Reading the 53. Chapter of Isaiah. The famous Fr. *Junius,* was converted from his *Atheism* reading the first chapter of John's Gospel. He that can read is able to read the Scripture, and books which promote godliness in the power of it, but a sinful creature chuseth rather to mispend his time in reading vain romances, or it may be worse books. A diligent attendance to the word of God is the way to obtain converting grace. Rom. 10. 17. *Faith comes by hearing, and hearing by the word of God.* Sinners many times do not mind what they hear. Nay, it may be they will *set themselves to sleep when God is speaking to them* by his minister? And shall they then complain, that they cannot convert themselves, & that God will not convert them? Once more, serious thinking & consideration on spiritual and eternal things is oftentimes blessed unto conversion. This is what God has given men power to do, if they will use that power. They ought seriously to think what they have done, and what they are, and what their end is like to be. If they would do so, it may be repentance would be the effect of it. 1 King. 8. 47. *If they shall bethink themselves, and repent, and make supplication.* David sayes, *I thought on my wayes, and turned my feet unto thy testimonies,* Psal. 119. 59. If men would be perswaded *to think seriously,* it may be they would *turn. How long shall thy vain thoughts lodge within thee?* A sinner will suffer vain thoughts to lodge within him, but serious & holy thoughts he will give no lodging unto, he will not suffer them to abide in his heart. *Serious consideration* is a duty incumbent on sinners. Hag. 1. 5. *Thus sayes the Lord of hosts, consider your wayes.* Would the unconverted sinner, consider sadly what his sinful wayes have been, what numberless sins he has been guilty of, and what a fountain of sin his heart is, and whither he is going, it may be conversion would follow upon such serious consideration. Ezek. 18. 28 *Because he considereth and turns away from all his transgressions.* Yes, if he is set upon *considering,* there is great hopes that he will turn, and that he shall live, and not dye. If he will be perswaded to go alone, to think and consider sadly with himself, What is my present Condition? Am I in Christ, or am I not in Christ?

If I should dy this night, What would become of my soul? In what world must it be to all eternity. It may be such considerations would issue in conversion. Sinners should consider of death, that the thing is certain, and the time uncertain, and that they run an infinite hazzard if they neglect making sure of an Interest in Christ one day longer. Deut. 32. 29. *O that they were wise, that they would consider their latter end!* And they should *Consider* of the *eternity* which follows immediately upon death. If they would do that, surely it would affect their souls. A late writer (which I have formerly mentioned) speaks of a pious man, that one in company with him observing a more than ordinary fixedness and concern in his countenance, asked him, What his thoughts were upon, he then thereupon uttered that word *For-ever*, and so continued saying nothing but repeating that word, *For-ever! For-ever! For-ever!* a quarter of an hour together. His thoughts and soul was swallowed up with the consideration of ETERNITY. And truly if an unconverted sinner would be perswaded to go alone and think seriously of eternity, if it were but for one quarter of an hour, it may be it would have an everlasting impression on his heart. This sinners can do if they will: and if they will not do as much as this comes to, towards their own conversion and salvation, how inexcusable will they be? Their blood will be upon their own heads. Let them no more say, *God must do all, we can do nothing,* and so encourage themselves to live in a careless neglect of God, and of their own souls, and salvation. Most certainly, altho' we cannot say, That if men improve their natural abilities as they ought to do, that grace will infallibly follow, yet there will not one sinner in all the reprobate world, stand forth at the day of judgment, and say, Lord, thou knowest I did all that possibly I could do, for the obtaining grace, and for all that, thou didst withhold it from me.

## MAN KNOWS NOT HIS TIME

From *A Discourse Concerning the
Uncertainty of the Times of Men*
(Boston, 1697)

THE DOCTRINE at present before us, is,
   *That for the most part the miserable children of men, know not their time.*

   There are three things for us here briefly to enquire into. (1.) *What times they are which men know not?* (2.) *How it does appear that they are ignorant thereof.* (3.) The reason *why they are kept in ignorance of their time.*

   Quest. 1. *What times are they which men know not?*

Ans. 1. *Time is sometimes put for the proper season for action*. For the fittest season for a man to effect what he is undertaking. The seventy Greek interpreters translate the words *KAIRON AUTOU*. There is a *Season*, a fit time for men to go to work in. If they take hold of that nick of opportunity, they will prosper and succeed in their endeavours. It is a great part of wisdom to know that season. Hence it is said, *A wise mans heart discerneth both time and judgment*. Eccles. 8. 5. But few have that wisdom or knowledge. Therefore it is added in the next verse. *because to every purpose there is time and judgment, therefore the misery of man is great upon him*. The meaning is, because men discern not the proper time for them to effect what they purpose, their misery is great. If they would attempt such a thing just at such a time, they would make themselves and others happy, but missing that opportunity great misery comes upon them. So it is as to Civil Affairs very frequently: Men discern not the proper only season for them to obtain what they desire. Yea, and so it is as to spirituals. Men are not aware of the proper season wherein they may obtain good for their souls. There is a price put into their hands to get wisdom, but they have no heart to know and improve it. There is a day of grace in which if men seek to God for mercy they shall find it. Isa. 55. 6. *Seek ye the Lord while he may be found*. The most of them that have such a day know it not until their finding time is past. Thus it was with Israel of old. Jere. 8. 7. *The stork in the heaven knows her appointed time, the turtle, and the crane, and the swallow observe the time of their coming, but my people know not the judgment of the Lord*. They discerned not the *judgments*, that is the dispensations of God. They had a summer of prosperity but did not improve it. There was a winter of adversity coming on them, but they knew it not, nor did they use the proper only means to prevent it. So the Jews when Christ was amongst them, had a blessed time if they had known it: but they knew not the things of their peace, in the day of their peace; they knew not the Time of their visitation.

2. *A man knows not what Changes shall attend him whilest in this world*. Changes of Providence are in the Scripture called *Times*. It is said that the Acts of David, and *the times that went over him,* and over Israel, and over all the kingdoms of the countries, were written by *Samuel,* and *Nathan* the Prophet, and in the Book of *Gad* the *Seer,* meaning the changes of Providence which they were subject unto. 1 Chron. 29. 30. A man knows not whether he shall see good or evil days for the time to come: he knoweth what his past days have been; but does not know what they shall be for the time to come. It may be he is now in prosperity: he has friends, children, relations, which he takes delight in, he has health, an estate, and esteem in the world, he does not know that he shall have any of these things for the future. Indeed, men in prosperity are apt to think (as they would have it) that they shall alwayes, or for a long time be so:

but very often they find themselves greatly mistaken. The Psalmist confesseth that it was so with him. Psal. 30. 6, 7. *In my prosperity I said, I shall never be moved, Lord, by the favour, thou hast made my mountain to stand strong: thou didst hide thy face and I was troubled.* His enemies were all subdued: his mountain, that is his kingdom, especially his royal palace in mount Sion was become exceeding strong, that now he thought all dangers were over, but *Absaloms* unexpected rebellion involved him and the whole land in trouble. The good people in *Josiahs* time promised themselves great happiness for many a year under the government of such a king as he was. Lam. 4. 20. *Of whom we said under his shadow we shall Live.* But his sudden death made a sad change in all the publick affairs. A man knows not *what* afflictions shall come upon him whilest on the earth. This is true concerning particular persons: they may know in general, that afflictions shall attend them in an evil sinful world. But what those afflictions in particular shall be they know not. Thus the Apostle speaks, Act. 20. 22, 23. *I go bound in spirit to Jerusalem, not knowing what things shall befall me there, save that the holy Spirit witnesseth in every city, saying, that bonds and afflictions abide me.* So that he knew in general that he should meet with affliction, but not in special what the affliction would be. So is it true concerning a people, that they know not what *times* or *changes* may pass over them. Little was it thought that whilest *Hoshea* (who was the best of all the nineteen kings that had ruled over the Ten Tribes) was reigning, a powerful forreign enemy should invade the land and make them all slaves. Little did the Jews think that when *Josiah* was but thirty nine years old, he should dy before that year was out, and they never see good day more after his death. And as men know not *what* their changes and afflictions must be, so neither *when* they shall come upon them. Whether it will be a long or a short time before those changes overtake them. Mar. 13. 35. *You know not when the master of the house comes, at even, or at mid-night, or at the cock crowing, or in the morning.* Thus a man knoweth not whether the sharpest afflictions which are reserved for him, shall come upon him in his youth, or in his middle age, or in his old age; though for the most part mens greatest afflictions overtake them in their old age. Nor can any man know whether his afflictions will soon be over or continue for a longer time. Thus, the Lords people knew that their captivity in *Babylon* should last for seventy years and no longer; but that knowledge was by divine revelation. As for some other persecutions they knew not how long they would continue. Psal. 74. 9. *There is no more a Prophet, neither is there any that knows how long.* Those words seem to respect the persecution under *Antiochus,* when there was no Prophet.

3. *A man knows not the time of his death:* Often it is so, that when death falls upon a man, he thinks no more of it, than the fishes think of the net

before they are caught in it; or then the birds think of the snare before they are taken in it, as *Solomon* here speaks. It useth to be said, (and it is a plain, weighty known truth) that nothing is more certain then that every man shall Dy, and nothing more uncertain than the time when. Old *Isaac* said, Gen. 27. 2. *Behold, I know not the day of my death.* Though he Lived above twenty years after he spoke those words, he did not know that he should Live a day longer. A man cannot know how long himself or another shall live. It is true that *Hezekiah* was ascertained that he should not dy before fifteen years were expired. And the Prophet *Jeremy* knew that *Hananiah* should not live a year to an end. Jer. 28. 16. *This year thou shalt dy, because thou hast taught rebellion against the Lord.* But those were extraordinary cases. It is not a usual thing for a man to know before hand how many months or years he shall live in this world: Nor may he desire to know it, but he ought to leave that with God. Although *David* prayed, saying, *Lord make me to know my end, and the number of my dayes, what it is.* Psal. 39. 4. His meaning is, not that he might know just how many dayes he should live, but that he might be made duely sensible of his own frailty and mortality, and lead his life accordingly. Oftentimes death is nearest to men when they least think of it; especially it is so with ungodly men: we have an instance of it in *Agag.* He came before *Samuel, delicately, and said, surely the bitterness of death is past.* 1. Sam. 15. 32. Little did he think, that within a few hours, he should be cut to pieces. When *Haman* boasted of his being the chief favourite at court, and that the queen had invited no one but the king & himself to a banquet, he little thought of the destruction which was then preparing for him. When *Belshazzar* was in the beginning of the night drinking and making merry with his profane companions, he little thought that he should be a dead man before morning; but *that night was Belshazzar slain.* Dan. 5. 30. The rich fool in the Gospel dream'd of a long life and merry: He said to his soul, eat, drink and be merry, thou hast goods laid up for many years. But God said, *This night thy soul shall be required of thee:* He must appear immediately before the dreadful tribunal. Luk. 12. 20. Thus we see what time it is which men know not.

The second thing to be enquired into, is, *How it does appear that men know not their time.*

Answ. 1. It is evident, *In that all future contingencies are known to God only.* Hence Christ said to the Disciples, *It is not for you to know the times and the seasons which the father has put in his own power.* Act. 1. 7. Future times and contingent events, the knowledge & disposal of them has God reserved to himself. There are future things which happen necessarily, that a man may know them long before they come to pass: *God has appointed lights in the Heaven to be for signs and seasons.* Gen. 1. 14. These move regularly and unfailably according to that order which the Creator has established.

Therefore a man may know infallibly how many hours or minutes such a day or night will be long before the time comes; He may know when there will be an *eclipse* of the sun or of the moon, twenty, or an hundred years before it comes to pass: but for contingent things, which have no necessary dependence on the constituted order of nature, but upon the meer pleasure and Providence of God, they are not known except unto God, or to them unto whom he shall reveal them. The Lord challengeth this as his prerogative. The idols whom the heathen worshipped, could not make known future contingencies. Isa. 41. 22, 23. *Let them shew us what shall happen, or declare us things for to come, shew the things that are to come hereafter, that we may know they are Gods.* To do this was past their skill. The devil knows many future things which men are ignorant of; he could foretel *Sauls* ruin, and *Davids* coming to the kingdom. Nevertheless, there are many future events which he has no knowledge of. Therefore he often deludes those that enquire of him with deceitful and uncertain answers. But as for men they are ignorant of future things, which most nearly concern themselves, or their own families. No man knows so much as who shall be his heir, or enjoy the estate which he has laboured for. Psal. 39. 6. *Surely every man walks in a vain shew, he heapeth up riches, and knows not who shall gather them.* He knows not whether one of his relations, or a meer stranger shall possess that estate which he has taken so much pains, and disquieted himself so much for the obtaining of it. This meditation made *Solomon* out of Love with this world. He knew as much as any man, and yet he confesseth that he did not know whether the man that should come after him, and enjoy all that he had laboured for, would be a wise man or a fool, Eccles. 2. 18, 19. And he sayes, *A man knows not that which shall be; for who can tell him when it shall be.* Eccles. 8. 7. He knows neither what nor when it shall be. And again he saith, *A man cannot tell what shall be; and what shall be after him who can tell him!* Eccl. 10. 14. This is to be understood concerning contingent events. Such as the particular afflictions which are to befall a man, or the time, place, or manner of his death.

2. *The times of men are ordered according to the decree of God.* There is nothing comes to pass in the earth, but what was first determined by a wise decree in Heaven. Act. 15. 18. *Known unto God are all his works from the beginning of the world.* God knows what he has to do. The Apostle speaks there concerning the conversion of the Gentiles. This did God fore-know and decree from the beginning of the world, yea from all eternity. The like is to be said concerning every thing which happens in the world. Not a sparrow falls to the ground without his Providence, and therefore not without his decree, the one being an infallible effect of the other. He has decreed when and where every man that comes into the world shall be born; and where he shall live, in what country, and in what

town; yea, and in what house too. Act. 17. 26. *He has determined the times before appointed, & the bounds of their habitation.* He has decreed when every man shall dy. Eccl. 3. 2. *There is a time to be born, and a time to dy.* That is to say, a time decreed and appointed by God when every man shall be born, and when he shall dy. Eccl. 3. 2. Nor shall any man live a day longer than the time which the Lord has appointed for him. Job 14. 5. *His dayes are determined, the number of his months are with thee, thou hast appointed his bounds that he cannot pass.* All the circumstances attending every mans death, the place and the manner of it, whether he shall dy by sickness, or by any other accident, all is determined in Heaven before it comes to pass on the earth. Now the decrees of God are secret things until the event or some divine revelation shall discover them. Deut. 29. 29. *Secret things belong unto the Lord our God.* His divine decrees are those secret things, which Himself alone knows. Rom. 11. 34. *For who hath known the mind of the Lord? or, who has been his counsellor?*

3. *The conversations of men generally make it manifest, that they know not their time.* They do many things which they would not do, and they neglect many things which they would certainly practise, if they knew what times are near them. Math. 24. 43. *If the good man of the house had known in what watch the theef would come, he would have watched, and would not have suffered his house to be broken up.* Thus men live in a careless neglect of God, and of their own souls and salvation, but if they knew that death will come stealing suddenly upon them, they would watch and pray. Did they know that before the next week, they shall be in another world, they would live after another manner than now they do. Most commonly persons are light and vain in their spirits, when heavy tidings is near to them. Did they know what sad news they shall hear shortly, they would be in a more solemn frame of spirit. Isa. 5. 12. *The harp and the viol, the tabret, and the pipe, and wine are in their feasts, but they regard not the work of the Lord, neither consider the operation of his hands.* Had they known what work God intended to make with them speedily, they would have minded something else besides their sensual pleasures and delights.

We proceed to enquire 3. *Whence it is that men know not their time.*

*Answ.* It is from God. He will have them to be kept in ignorance and uncertainties about their time: and this for wise & holy ends. *e.g.*

1. That so his children might live by faith. That so they might live a life of holy dependance upon God continually. They must not know their times, that so they might trust in the Lord at all times. God would not have his children to be anxiously solicitous about future events, but to leave themselves and theirs with their Heavenly Father, to dispose of all their concernments, as he in his infinite wisdom and faithfulness shall see good.

2. That their obedience may be tried. That they may follow the Lord,

as it were blind-fold, withersoever He shall lead them, though they do not see one step of their way before them, as *Abraham* did. Heb. 11. 8. *When he was called to go out into a place which he should after receive for an inheritance, he obeyed, and went out not knowing whither he went.* We must follow God, tho' we know not what He will do with us, or how He will dispose of us, as to our temporal concerns, submitting our selves, yea, our lives and all entirely to the will of God in every thing. That saying ought to be often in our mouths, *If the Lord will,* and we shall live, and do this or that. Jam. 4. 15.

3. Men must not know their time, that so they may be ever watchful. Math. 25. 13. *Watch therefore, for you know neither the day nor the hour wherein the Son of Man comes.* The generality of men, if they had it revealed to them (as *Hezekiah*) that they should certainly live so many years, they would in the mean time be careless about their souls, and the world to come. We see that notwithstanding they are uncertain how short their time may be, they are regardless about their future eternal estate. How much more would they be so, if they knew that death and Judgment were not far off from them?

4. As to some they are kept in Ignorance of their times, that so they may with the more comfort and composure of spirit follow the work which they are called unto: that they may with diligence and chearfulness attend the duties of their general and particular calling; which they could not do, if they knew what evil times and things are appointed for them. The terror of what is coming on them, would be so dismal to them, that they could not enjoy themselves, nor take comfort in any thing they enjoy. As the Apostle speaks to the covetous Jews, Jam. 5. 1. *Go to now you rich men, weep and howl for your miseries that shall come upon you.* So there are many in the world, that would spend their days in weeping and howling, did they but know what is coming on them and theirs. When the Prophet *Elisha* had it revealed to him, that sad things were coming on the Land, by reason of a bloody neighbour nation, which would break in upon them, and exercise barbarous Cruelties; the holy man wept at the foreknowledge of it. 2 King. 8. 11. *The man of God wept.* So there would be nothing but weeping in many families, weeping in many towns, and in some whole countries, did men but know their times. Therefore they must be kept in ignorance thereof until the things come upon them. . . .

And now as I have spoken these things to all this assembly, so let me apply them in a special manner to you the *scholars* of this *colledge,* who are here present before the Lord. I am concerned in my spirit for you. All of you are my children: and do you think that I can see my children drowned, and not be troubled for it? God has come among you this last week, & lessened two of your number by a sad & awful Providence. Do you think these two were greater sinners than any amongst you. No, no, they were both of them hopeful youths. One of them (young *Eyres*) was an only Son, and a desirable dutiful Son, of a sweet amiable temper, beloved by every body. He was observed to read the Scriptures constantly every day with great alacrity. A sign that there was *some good thing in him towards the God of Israel.* As for the other *(Maxwell)* the rebuke of Heaven in taking him away is the more solemn, in that his pious relations sent him from far: to be educated in this nursery, for religion and good literature. I took special notice of him; but could never observe any thing in him, but what was commendable, he was ingenious, and industrious, and I believe truly pious; had he lived, he was like to have been a choice instrument of service to the Church of God in his time. And I am perswaded that his soul is among the Angels of God. *But if this be done to the green tree, what shall be done to the dry?* This fatal blow looks ominously on the poor *colledge.* Considering some other circumstances; there is cause to fear lest *suddenly* there will be no *colledge* in *New England*; and this as a sign that ere long there will be no churches there. I know there is a blessed day to the visible church not far off; but it is the judgment of very learned men, that in the glorious times promised to the church on earth, *America* will be Hell. And altho there is a number of the elect of God yet to be born here, I am verily afraid, that in process of time, *New England* will be the wofullest place in all *America,* as some other parts of the world once famous for religion, are now the dolefullest on the earth, perfect emblems and pictures of Hell. When you see this little *academy* fallen to the ground (as now it is shaking and most like to fall) then know it is a terrible thing which God is about to bring upon this land. In the mean time, you the *students* here, are concerned to bewail the breach which the Lord has made among you. If you slight and make light of this hand of the Lord, or do not make a due improvement of it, you may fear, that God has not done with you, but that he has more arrows to shoot amongst you, that shall suddenly strike some of you ere long. But Oh that the Lord would sanctify what has hapned to awaken you unto serious thoughts about death and eternity. Who knows but that God may make these sudden deaths, an occasion of promoting the salvation, & eternal Life of some amongst you. It is related concerning *Waldo,* (he from whom the *Waldenses* have that name given them) that the occasion of his conversion was the *sudden death* of one of his companions. The sight of that made him serious. He did not know, but that he might *dy suddenly* too, and that he was therefore concerned to be always fit to dy. So did he turn to the Lord, and became a great instrument of glory to God and good to his Church. Oh! that it might be so with you.

# SLEEPING AT SERMONS

From *Practical Truths Tending to*
*Promote the Power of Godliness*
(Boston, 1682)

INSTR. 1. *We may here take notice that the nature of man is wofully corrupted*
*and depraved,* else they would not be so apt to sleep when the precious
truths of God are dispensed in his name, yea, and men are more apt to
sleep then, than at another time. Some woful creatures, have been so
wicked as to profess they have gone to hear sermons on purpose, that so
they might sleep, finding themselves at such times much disposed that
way. This argueth as Satans malice, so the great corruption and
depravation of the nature of men, whence it is that they are inclined unto
evil, and indisposed to the thing that good is. Yea, some will sit and sleep
under the best preaching in the world. When *Paul* was alive, there was
not a better preacher upon the earth then he. *Austin* had three wishes:
one was, that (if the Lord had seen meet) he might see Christ in the flesh:
his second wish was, that he might have seen *Paul in the Pulpit*; but
notwithstanding *Pauls* being so excellent a preacher, there were some that
could sit and sleep under his ministry. When soul-melting sermons are
preached about Christ the Saviour, about the pardon of sin, about the
glory of Heaven, there are some that will sleep under them. When soul-
awakening sermons are preached, enough to make rocks to rend and to
bleed; when the word falls down from Heaven like thunder, the voice of
the Lord therein being very powerful and full of majesty, able to break
the Cedars of *Lebanon,* and to make the wilderness to shake; yet some
will sit and sleep under it: such is the woful corruption and desperate
hardness of the hearts of the children of men.

Instr. 2. *Hence see, that there is great danger in those things which men are apt*
*to look upon as little sins, yea as no sins at all.*

As for sleeping at sermons, some look upon it as no sin; others account
it a *peccadillo,* a sin not worth taking notice of, or the troubling themselves
about. But my text sheweth that danger and death is in it. We have
solemn instances in the Scripture, concerning those that have lost their
lives, because they have been guilty of such miscarriages, as carnal reason
will say are but little sins. When there was a man that gathered a few
sticks upon the Sabbath day, he was put to death for it; and yet men
would be apt to think his sin was not (though indeed it was) very great.
Men account it a small matter to add something of their own to the
worship of God: but when *Nadab* and *Abihu* did so, *there went out fire from*
*the Lord,* and consumed them to death. When *Vzzah* a good man, did
with a pious intention touch the Ark, (which he being no priest should

not have done) *God smote him for his error, that he dyed by the Ark of God.* Behold! the severity of God, and let us tremble at it. Common sins, which almost every one is guilty of, are accounted small iniquities; but there is exceeding danger in following a multitude to do evil. Sins of omission are esteemed small, but mens souls may be thrown into the fire and burned for ever, not only for bearing evil fruit, but because they do not bring forth good fruit, Mat. 3. 10. At the last day the Son of God will pronounce a sentence of eternal death upon thousands of millions, because they have omitted these and those duties which he required and expected from them. Sinful words are looked upon as small evils by many. How common is it for persons to say, *what shall we be made offenders for a word?* abusing that Scripture which reproveth those that make others offenders for speaking good and faithful words. But doth not the Scripture say, *by thy words thou shalt be condemned,* Mat. 12. 37. Corrupt communications, obscene discourses, unclean lascivious speeches, discover the persons that delight in them to be amongst the number of those that shall (without Repentance) be condemned at the day of *judgment,* yet there are some that make light of them. Thus concerning those words which some call *petty oathes;* some are so profanely ignorant as to think, that they may swear by *their faith and troth,* and that there is no great hurt or danger in it. But there is danger of no less than damnation for these seemingly little sins, if men shall allow themselves therein, notwithstanding the Commandment of God to the contrary. See the word of the Lord to this purpose, Jam. 5. 12. *But above all things swear not,* (i.e. vainly, or except duely called thereunto) *neither by Heaven, neither by the earth, neither by any other oath,* therefore not by your faith or troth, *lest you fall into condemnation.*

Again, sinful thoughts are esteemed small evils; but I must tell you, that vain thoughts, and much more vile unclean thoughts, if indulged and delighted in, may hinder the salvation of a mans soul. Witness that Scripture, Jer. 4. 14. *O Jerusalem, wash thine heart from wickedness, that thou mayest be saved; how long shall thy vain thoughts lodge within thee?* so that there is more than a little danger, in those evils, which men account little sins.

# SAMUEL WILLARD

## (1640–1707)

## SAINTS NOT KNOWN BY EXTERNALS

From *The Child's Portion*

(Boston, 1684)

1. THE REASON why the Children of God are so little regarded here in the world; it is because the world knows not who they are, nor what they are born unto: their great glory for the present is within; outwardly they look like other men, they eat, drink, labour, converse in earthly imployments, as others do; the communion which they have with God in all of these, is a secret thing: they are sick, poor, naked, distressed like other men; those inward supports which they have under all those exercises, are remote from publick view: they dy, and are buried under the clods, and their bodyes putrifie and rot like other men; and none see those joyes that their souls are entered into, nor that guard of Angels which comes as a convoy, and carryes them into *Abraham's* bosom: Nay, they have their sins, their spots, their imperfections and weaknesses here, as well as other men; but their tears, repentance, secret mournings, and renewals of faith, and restorings to peace and soul-comfort, are secret.

And hence,

Though the righteous man be indeed surpassingly more excellent than his neighbour, yet is he not thought so to be: Whereas, did the world see and understand, whose sons they are, what inheritances they are the undoubted heirs of, and what are those gloryes they shall ere long be made to possess, it would alter their opinion, and make them afraid of them, and not dare to do them any wrong. How fearful was *Abimestech* of *Abraham*, when God did but tell him he was a Prophet? Gen. 20. 7, 8.

2. Here we see the reason why the people of God are often so doubtful, disquiet, discontent, and afraid to dy (I put things together) the ground of all this is because they do not as yet see clearly what they shall be: it would be a matter of just wonderment to see the children of God

112

so easily and often shaken, so disturbed and perplexed in hours of temptation, were it not from the consideration, that they at present know so little of themselves or their happiness: sometimes their sonship it self doth not appear to them, but they are in the dark, at a loss about the evidencing of it to the satisfaction of their own minds; and from hence it is that many doubtings arise, and their souls are disquieted. Sometimes their present sufferings look bigger in their thoughts, than the conceptions or apprehensions which they entertain of their future glory, these things being near, and the other looked on at a distance, and hence they out-weigh, in their rash judgements, and now they are disquiet and discontent, and say with him, Psal. 73. 13. *I have cleansed my heart in vain, and washed my hands in innocency.* And usually in their good frames, they apprehend more of the sweetness of present communion with God in his ordinances, than of that blessed immediate communion in glory; and this makes them, with good *Hezekiah,* to turn away their faces from the messages of death and change: all these things are arguments of the weak sight and dark thoughts which we here have of the things of another world: which yet, it is the holy pleasure of God, that it shall be so a while, for the advancing of his own ends in his Saints.

3. Learn hence a reason why the present sufferings of God's Children can neither argue against, nor yet prejudice their felicity: for the time is not yet come wherein they are to appear like themselves: *Joseph's* prisoned condition, and prison robes set him never the further off from his preferment in *Pharaoh's* Court; but were indeed the very harbingers of it: When the appointed time for the manifestation of the Sons of God shall come, he can fetch them out in hast, change them in the twinkling of an eye, and cloath them upon with all that excellency and splendid glory, whereby, they who were but the other day lying among the pots, shall with their dazzling lustre outshine the sun in the firmament. It is the Almighty's good pleasure, that their life, for the present, should be hid with Christ in God: but yet he hath his time, and will take his opportunity to reveal and make it known.

4. This teacheth us that the glory of the sons of God must needs be wonderfully and astonishingly great: For why? Have they not already in hand, that which surpasses the knowledge of all the world, and which is in value transcendently more worth than all the crowns and kingdoms, and gloryes of it? Do they not live upon, and satisfie their souls with marrow and fatness here, Psal. 63. 5. Are they not here replenished with the fatness of God's house? Psal. 36. 8. Who, but he that enjoys it, can declare what an happiness it is to enjoy peace with God, and fellowship with Christ, assurance of his love, and consolation of his spirit? Who, but he that hath felt it, can tell what it is to have the love of God shed abroad

in his heart, and in his soul to hear the sweet voice of pardon, and promises of glory? to ly all night in the bosom of Christ, and have his left hand underneath his head, and his right hand imbracing of him? And yet he that knows all this doth not know what he shall be: these are but the displayes of the outward temple, or holy place; what then is to be seen in the Holy of Holies? These are but drops, and rivulets which come in pipes, and in little portions; how glorious a thing then must it needs be to dwel at the fountain, and swim for ever in those bankless, and bottomless oceans of glory? How happy then are the dead in Christ, who are now seeing, tasting, knowing and experiencing these things?

## THE DEATH OF A SAINT

From *The High Esteem Which God*
*Hath of the Death of His Saints*
(Boston, 1683)

1. *When the Saints die let us mourn:* And there is no greater argument to be found that we should excite our selves to mourn by, then the remembrance that they were *Saints:* it should more effect our hearts at the thoughts of this that they were *Saints,* then that they were our father, or mother, or brethren, or nearest or dearest friends, for this is that which makes their loss to be greater than any other relation doth or can; others are natural, but these are pious tears that are shed upon this account: another man may be a private loss when he is gone, his family or his Neighbours, or Consorts may miss him; but a *Saint,* though he be a private Christian, is yet, when he dies a, publick loss, and deserves the *tears of Israel;* how much more than when he hath been a Saint providentially put into a capacity of being, and by grace helpt and enabled to be a publick benefit by the Orb he moved in? when a Saint *dies* there is manifold ground of mourning; there is then a pillar pluckt out of the building, a foundation stone taken out of the wall, a man removed out of the gap; and now it is to be greatly feared that God is departing, and *calamities* are coming, and are not these *things* to be lamented?

2. *When the Saints die beware of irregular mourning:* though we are to lament their death, yet we must beware that it be after the right manner: a dying Saint may say to his weeping friends that stand round about, wringing their hands, after the same language that Christ did to those weeping women, Luk. 23. 27, 28, 29. *Daughters of Jerusalem, weep not for me, but for your selves, and your children,* &c. It is we and not they that are indangered and endamaged by it: we may therefore weep for our selves, and there is good reason for it, but to mourn for them is superfluous.

Is their death precious in Gods? let it not be miserable in our esteem: and tell me you whose hearts throb, and eyes run over with sorrow, is it not a precious thing to be asleep in Jesus? to ly in the lap of his providence, and rest from the labours and sorrows of a troublesome world? to be laid out of the noise of the whistling winds, and feel none of the impetuosity of those storms and tempests that are blowing abroad? to be out of the sight and hearing of the rolling and dashing waves of the roaring sea? to sleep out the rest of the tempestuous night of this world, standing in the inner chamber of Gods Providence, in answer to that sweet invitation? Isai. 26. 22. *Come my people, enter into thy chambers, and shut thy doors about thee*, &c. . . .

3. *Is the death of the Saints precious in Gods sight? let it be so in ours too.* They are not to be accounted for contemptible things which God sets an high value upon; and it is our wisdom to think and speak of persons and things as God doth: we ought not to slight the death of the righteous, and speak meanly of it, as of a thing that is little momentous: I am sure their arrival at Heaven is there taken notice of as a thing worthy of observation; and shall not their departure be regarded? they are welcomed into the palace of delight with *panegyricks*; and shall then be hence dismissed with no more but a sorry saying, there is now a good man gone, and he will be missed in the family, or the church to which he once belonged? We should embalm the memory of the Saints with the sweet smelling spices that grew in their own gardens, and pick the chiefest flowers out of those beds to strew their graves withal; we should remember and make mention of them with honourable thoughts and words: and though it be now grown a nickname of contempt among wicked and prophane men, yet count it the most orient jewel in their crown, the most odoriferous and pleasant flower in their garland, that we can say of them that they lived and died Saints; all other eschutcheons will either wear away, or be taken down, every other monument will become old, and grow over with the moss of time, and their titles, though cut in brass, will be canker-eaten and illegible: this onely will endure and be fresh and flourishing, when marble it self shall be turned into common dust.

Such an one it is whom we have now lost; and Oh that we knew how great a loss we have sustained in him! they are little things to be put into the account, and weigh but light in the commendations we have to give him; to say, this government hath lost a magistrate; this town hath lost a good benefactor; this church hath lost an honourable member; his company hath lost a worthy captain; his family hath lost a loving and kind husband, father, master; the poor have lost a liberal and merciful friend; that nature had furnished him with a sweet and affable disposition, and even temper; that Providence had given him a prosperous and flourishing portion of this worlds goods; that the love and respect of the people had lifted him up to places of honour and preferment; this, this outshines them all; that he was a Saint upon earth; that he lived like a Saint here, and died the precious death of a Saint, and now is gone to rest with the Saints in glory: this hath raised those relicks of his above common dust, and made them precious dust. When conscience of duty stimulated me to perform my part of his exequies, and put me upon it to do him honour at his death; methoughts justice required, and envy it self would not nibble at this character: and if the tree be to be known by its fruits, his works shall praise him in the gates: For his constant and close secret communion with God (which none but hypocrites are wont to do with the sound of a trumpet) such as were most intimate with him, have known and can testifie: the care which he had to keep up constant family worship, in reading of the Scriptures, and praying in his family (from which no business publick or private could divert him) was almost now unparalleld; the honourable respect he bore to God's holy ordinances, by diligently attending upon them, and esteeming highly of God's servants for their work sake, and care that he used to live the truths which he heard from time to time, was very singular: the exemplariness of his life and converse among men, and the endeavours which he used to shew forth the graces of the spirit, not being ashamed of Christ, nor being willing to be a shame unto him; let all that knew him bear witness of: his meek boldness in reproving sin, and gentle faithfulness in endeavouring to win sinners as he had opportunity, is known to such as lay in his way: His constancy in all these whiles times have changed, and many professors have degenerated, when he strove to grow better as the times grew worse, will speak the sincerity of his profession: his living above the world, and keeping his heart disentangled, and his mind in Heaven, in the midst of all outward occasions and urgency of business, bespake him not to be of this world, but a pilgrim on the earth, a citizen of Heaven: in a word, he was a true *Nathaniel*.

But God hath taken him from us, and by this stroak given us one more sad prognostick of misery a coming: when there are but a few Saints in the world, and those die apace too, what is to be thought to be at the door? I dare say his death was precious in Gods sight, and he had some holy end in taking him away just now, who might probably have lived many years, and done much more service for God in his generation: i shall not make it my work to prophesie; the Lord grant we do not all know it too soon to our cost. Mean time let us have such in remembrance, and labour to be followers of them who through faith and patience do now inherit the promises, and that will be the best way to divert the omen: let us account the *Saints* precious whiles they live, and God will not begrutch them to us: but if we by contempt, obloquy, and wickedly grieving their *righteous souls,* make their lives a burden to them; if they cannot live in honour among men, they shall die in favour with God, and he will make their death a precious gain to them, though it be a direful presage of a great inundation of sad calamities coming upon those whom they leave behind them.

# THE CHARACTER OF A GOOD RULER
## (Boston, 1694)

WHETHER THE Ordination of *Civil Government* be an *article of the law of nature,* and it should accordingly have been established upon the multiplication of mankind, although they had retained their primitive Integrity: Or whether it have only a *positive right,* and was introduced upon man's *apostacy;* is a question about which all are not agreed. The equity of it, to be sure, is founded in the law natural, and is to be discovered by the light of nature, being accordingly acknowledged by such as are strangers to Scripture revelation; and by Christians it is reducible to the first command in the second table of the decalogue; which is supposed to be a transcript of the law given to *Adam* at the first, and written upon the tables of his heart. For tho', had man kept his first state, the moral image concreated in him, consisting in, *knowledg, righteousness, and true holiness,* would have maintained him in a perfect understanding of, and spontaneous obedience to the whole duty incumbent on him, without the need of civil laws to direct him, or a civil sword to lay compulsion on him; and it would have been the true golden age, which the heathen *mythologists* are to fabulous about. Yet even then did the all-wise God ordain orders of superiority and inferiority among men, and required all *honour* to be paid accordingly. But since the unhappy fall hath robbed man of that perfection, and filled his heart with perverse and rebellious principles, tending to the subversion of all order and the reducing of the world to a *chaos;* necessity requires, and the political happiness of a people is concerned in the establishment of civil government. The want of it hath ever been pernicious, and attended on with miserable circumstances. When there was no governour in Israel, but every man did what he would, what horrible outrages, were then perpetrated, though holy and zealous *Phinehas* was at that time the high-priest? and we ourselves have had a specimen of this in the short *anarchy* accompanying our late *revolution.* Gods Wisdom therefore, and his goodness is to be adored in that he hath laid in such a relief for the children of men, against the mischief which would otherwise devour them; and engraven an inclination on their hearts, generally to comply with it. But this nowithstanding, mens sins may put a curse into their blessings, & render their remedy to be not better, possibly worse than the malady. Government is to prevent and cure the disorders that are apt to break forth among the societies of men; and to promote the civil peace and prosperity of such a people, as well as to suppress impiety, and nourish religion. For this end there are to be both rulers, and such as are to be *ruled* by them: and the weal or wo of a people mainly depends on the qualifications of those *rulers*, by whom we are to be governed. . . .

## DOCTRINE

*It is of highest consequence, that civil rulers should be just men, and such as rule in the fear of God.* . . .

*Civil rulers* are all such as are in the exercise of a rightful authority over others. These do not all of them stand in one equal rank, nor are alike influential into government. There are supreme and subordinate powers: and of these also there are some who have a *legislative*, others an *executive* power in their hands; which two, though they may sometimes meet in the same persons, yet are in themselves things of a different nature. There are *superiour magistrates* in *provinces*, and such as are of *council* with them, and *assembly men*, the *representatives* of the people. There are *judges* in courts, *superiour* and *inferiour; justices* of the peace in their several precincts: and in each of these orders there resides a measure of authority.

Now, that all these may be just, it is firstly required, that they have a principle of mo*ral honesty* in them, and swaying of them: that they *love righteousness, and hate iniquity*: that they be *men of truth*, Exod. 18. 21. for every man will act in his relation, according to the principle that rules in him: so that an unrighteous man will be an unrighteous ruler, so far as he hath an opportunity.

They must also be acquainted with the rules of righteousness; they must know what is just, and what is unjust, be *able men*, Exod. 18. 21. For, though men may know and not do, yet *without knowledge the mind cannot be good*. Ignorance is a foundation for error, and will likely produce it, when the man applies himself to act: and if he do right at any time, it is but by guess, which is a very poor commendation.

Again, he must be one that respects the cause, and not the persons in all his administrations, Deut. 1. 17. *Ye shall not respect persons in judgment,* &c. if his affections oversway his judgment at any time, they will be a crooked biais, that will turn him out of the way, and that shall be justice in one mans case, which will not be so in another.

Farthermore, he must be one whom neither flattery nor bribery may be able to remove out of his way, Deut. 16. 19. *Thou shalt not wrest judgment, thou shalt not respect persons, neither take a gift*; and hence he must be one who hates both ambition and covetousness, Exod. 18. 21 *Hating covetousness*; which word signifies, a *greedy desire,* and is applicable to both the fore cited vices: for if these rule him, he will never be a just ruler.

Finally, he must be one who prefers the publick benefit above all private and separate interests whatsoever. Every man in his place, owes himself to the good of the whole; and if he doth not so devote himself, he is unjust: and he who either to advance himself, or to be revenged on another, will push on injurious laws, or pervert the true intention of such as are in force, is an unjust man: and he who is under the influence of a *narrow spirit,* will be ready to do so, as occasion offers. . . .

Nor is this *justice* to be lookt upon as separate from the *fear of God,* but as influenced and maintained by it. He therefore that rule*th in the fear of God,* is one who acknowledgeth God to be his soveraign, and carries in his heart an awful fear of him: who owns his commission to be from him, and expects ere long to be called to give in an account of his managing of it: which maketh him to study in all things to please him, and to be afraid of doing any thing that will provoke him.

And accordingly, he is a student in the law of God, and *meditates in it day and night*; making it the rule into which he ultimately resolves all that he doth in his place. We find that in the old law, the king was to *write* a copy of it with his own hand, and to make use of it at all times: Deut. 17. 18, 19.

If he hath any thing to do in the making of laws, he will consult a good conscience, and what may be pleasing to God, and will be far from *framing mischief by a law.* And if he be to execute any laws of men, he will not dare to give a judgment for such an one as directly crosseth the command of God, but counts it *ipso facto* void, and his conscience acquitted of his oath.

Yea the *fear of God* will make him not to think himself lawless; nor dare to bear witness, by laws and penalties, against sins in others, which he countenanceth and encourageth by living in the practise of himself: but to use utmost endeavours that his own life may be an exemplification of obedience, and others may learn by him, what a veneration he hath for the laws that are enacted for the good of man-kind.

In a word, he is one that will take care to promote *piety* as well as *honesty* among men; and do his utmost that the true religion may be countenanced and established, and that all ungodliness, as well as unrighteousness, may have a due testimony born against it at all times. So he resolves Psal. 75. 10. *All the horns of the wicked also will I cut off; but the horns of the righteous shall be exalted.*

It then follows that we enquire of what great moment or consequence it is that these should be such: and there is a three-fold respect in which the high importance of it is to be discovered by us.

1. In respect to the glory of God.

Civil rulers are Gods vicegerents here upon earth; hence they are sometimes honoured with the title of Gods, Psal. 82 6. *I have said ye are Gods.* Government is Gods ordinance; and those that are vested with it, however *mediately* introduced into it, have their rightful authority from him, Prov. 8. 15, 16. *By me kings reign, and princes decree justice. By me princes rule, and nobles, even all the judges of the earth,* and they that are from him, should be for him, and ought to seek the honour of him who is *King of Kings, and Lord of Lords:* which they only then do, when they manage their whole interest and power with a design for his glory; & accordingly manage themselves in all their ministrations by the statutes of his kingdom; which none will ever do, but they that are *just, Ruling in the fear of God.* Righteousness and religion flourishing in these, will be as a torch on an hill, whose light and influence will be vastly extensive: every one will be advantaged to see their good works, and to glorifie God for and in them. Their very example will have the force of a law in it, and win many by a powerful attraction, to the avoiding of sin, and practising of righteousness. They will be a good copy, that many will be ambitious to write after: and their faithful administrations will render them a *terror to evil doers, and an encouragement to them that do well*; which will advance the very end of government. Whereas the evil deportment, and ill management of rule*rs,* who are unjust, and void of the fear of God, is an open scandal, and of a more pernicious tendency than the wickedness of others; inasmuch as their example is a discouragement to them that are well disposed, and animates those that are set in their hearts for iniquity, and they are thereby emboldened to shew their heads, and to declare their sin as *Sodom*: hence that remark of the Psalmist, Psal. 12. 8. *The wicked walk on every side, when the vilest men are exalted.* Those that would bear their testimony against impiety and debauchery, are frowned on and neglected; and such as would nourish them are countenanced: and either good laws to suppress them are not provided, or they are laid by as things obsolete, and of no service: and thus all abominations come in upon a people as a flood, and the name of God is wofully dishonoured by this means: and hereupon the last and most excellent end of government comes to be frustrated, and what is there that we can conceive to be of greater weight than this? if this be lost, the glory of such a people is gone.

2. In regard to the weal of the people over whom they rule.

A people are not made for rulers, but rulers for a people. It is indeed an honour which God puts upon some above others, when he takes them from among the people, and sets them up to rule over them, but it is for the peoples sake, and the civil felicity of them is the next end of civil policy; and the happiness of rulers is bound up with theirs in it. Nor can any wise men in authority think themselves happy in the misery of their subjects, to whom they either are or should be as children are to their fathers: we have the benefit of government expressed, 1. Tim. 2 : 2. *a quiet Life and a peaceable, in all godliness and honesty.* And it lies especialy with rulers, under God, to make a people happy or miserable. When men can injoy their liberties and rights without molestation or oppression; when they can live without fear of being born down by their more potent neighbours; when they are secured against violence, and may be righted against them that offer them any injury, without fraud; and are encouraged to serve God in their own way, with freedom, and without being imposed upon contrary to the Gospel precepts; now are they an happy people. But this is to be expected from none other but men just and pious: they that are otherwise, will themselves be oppressours, and they that are influenced by them, and dependent on them, will adde to the grievance. They that should look after them will do it fast enough: yea every one will usurp a License to do so to his neighbour upon an advantage: and such a people must needs groan under an intollerable burden. Besides, it is a great truth, that the mercies and judgments of God come upon a people, according as their rulers carry themselves in managing of the trust which God hath committed to them. Just and zealous rulers, are men that *stand in the gap,* and keep off judgments from a sinning people; God *sought* for *one* such, Ezek. 22. 30. they *turn away wrath,* when it hath made an inroad, so it is recorded of Phinehas that he did, Ps. 106. 30. And God is wont to bless such a people, as He did *Israel* and *Judah* in the days of *David, Solomon, Jehoshaphat, Hezekiah,* and *Josiah:* whereas when these fall into such sins as God is Provoked at, the people are like to smart for it. There is such an influence with the prevarications of these men, that, in the righteous judgment of God, those under them suffer grievously by it. This the heathen observed in the course of Providence, and made that remark upon it, *Delirant reges, plectuntur Achivi.* Thus *David* numbers the people, and seventy thousand of the men of Israel die for it, 2Sa. 24. Yea such may be the influence of the male-administration of rulers, though done without malice, and in an heat of misguided *zeal* for the people of GOD; as *Sauls* act in slaying the *Gibeonites* is recorded to have been 2 Sam. 21 .2. That the guilt may ly long upon a land, and break out in terrible judgments a great while after, and not be expiated till the sin be openly confessed, and the atonement sought unto.

3. With reference to *rulers* themselves.

It is, as we before observed, a dignity put upon them, to be preferred to government over their brethren; to have the oversight, not of beasts, but of men. But as there is a great trust devolved on them, so there is an answerable reckoning which they must be called unto: and however they are setled in Authority by men, yet GOD, who rules over all, hath put them in only *durante bene plecito:* they are upon their good behaviour; they are *stewards,* and whensoever GOD pleaseth, He will call for a reckoning, and put them out. *God sets up, and he pulls down*; and he hath a respect to mens carriages in his dealings with them. Godly and zealous *Phinehas* got a blessing for himself and his posterity, Numb. 25. 11. &c. Whereas *Saul* procured for himself a rejection, and the laying aside and almost extirpation of his family. We have this also instanced in *Shebna* and *Eliakim* Isa. 22. 15. &c. Yea, what did *Jeroboam,* what did *Ahab,* and many others procure for themselves, by their ill government, but the utter rooting out of their names, and posterity? The *fourth generation* may rue that ever they derived from such progenitors. The only sure way for rulers to build up their own houses, is to be such in their places as *David* was, of whom we have that testimony, Psal. 78. 71, 72. *He brought him to feed* Jacob *his people, and* Israel *his inheritance. So he fed them according to the integrity of his heart, and guided them by the skilfulness of his hands.* And although GOD doth not always peculiarly put a brand in this world upon impious and unjust rulers, yet there is a tribunal before which they must stand e're long as other men; only their account will be so much the more fearful, and condemnation more tremendous, by how much they have neglected to take their greater advantages to glorify GOD, and abused their power to His dishonour, by which they had a fairer opportunity than other men.

# DEGENERATING NEW ENGLAND

From *The Peril of the Times Displayed*
(Boston, 1700)

I CONFESS THAT it must be granted, that in the best times, and in places where the power of Godliness is most flourishing, there have been, and will be those that have not the fear of God before their eyes: there were so in the times of the greatest *reformation* that we read of in the Book of God. In this world we must expect that *wicked men will be mixed with the Godly,* and such as will dare to shew their wickedness in their lives, and not be afraid *to transgress in a land of uprightness.* But when such are not countenanced, but due testimony is born against them; when they are contemned in the places where they live, and a note of infamy and scandal is put upon them; this will not be charged on such a people for *apostasy:* But when such sins grow frequent, and those that have taken on themselves a name of being religious, begin to indulge themselves herein; and men that allow themselves in such things are not *reproached* for it, but are in as good credit as the best, it then becomes a bad symptom, and saith that the times are declining and perilous. Much more when such as these will undertake to justify, and patronize such things: and are there not sad complaints made on this account? I shall here instance only in some that are more notorious. Are not Gods *Sabbaths* wofully neglected? How wofully can such as would be esteemed Godly, encroach upon holy time, and be engaged, either in secular business, or in vain company, and possibly in publick houses, when they should be at home, in their closets, or with their families, sanctifying of Gods day, and shewing of the *honourable esteem* they have for it? And I am well satisfyed, that *where the strict observation of Gods Sabbath is lost, there the power of Godliness is gone.* How much complaint is there made of woful *dishonesty* in their dealings, practised by such as can talk high of their religion? How many fallacious tricks they can use in their commerce? How deceitful in their labour? How false to their words and promises? as if dissembling and lying were no reproach to the name of Christians. How many *intemperate church members* are there reported to be, who spend their precious time in frequenting publick houses, and keeping of loose and lewd company? who can come to the *Lords table* on the Sabbath, and wrong themselves by excessive drinking on the week days? How much *animosity, contention,* and implacable bitterness of spirit, breaking forth in indecent words and carriages, between such as are bound in the strongest evangelical ties to *love one another, and meekly to bear with each others infirmities?* How much raising, spreading, and receiving of *slanders* and *defamations* one of another; contrary to that charity which ought to *cover a multitude of sins?* These, and a great many more of like nature, . . . so far as they spread and prevail, and begin to grow common, are an ill omen; for, they are indisputable denials of the power of Godliness, at least in the vigour of it, in those who are guilty of them, for *that teacheth men to live Soberly, Righteously and Godly.*

# COTTON MATHER
## (1663–1728)

## THE WONDERS OF THE INVISIBLE WORLD
### (Boston, 1693)

Observations as well Historical as Theological, upon the
Nature, the Number, and the Operations of the DEVILS

An Hortatory and Necessary ADDRESS. To a Country now
Extraordinarily Alarum'd by the Wrath of the Devil. Tis this,

Let us now make a good and a right use, of the prodigious descent, which the Devil, in great wrath, is at this day making upon our land. Upon the death of a great man once, an orator call'd the town together, crying out, *concurrite cives, dilapla sunt vestra mania!* that is, come together, neighbours, your town-walls, are fallen down! But such is the descent of the Devil at this day upon ourselves, that I may truly tell you, the walls of the whole world are broken down! The usual walls of defence about mankind have such a gap made in them, that the very Devils are broke in upon us, to seduce the souls, torment the bodies, sully the credits, and consume the estates of our neighbours, with impressions both as real and as furious, as if the invisible world were becoming incarnate, on purpose for the vexing of us. And what use ought now to be made of so tremendous a dispensation? we are engaged in a fast this day; but shall we try to fetch, meat out of the eater, and make the lion to afford some hony for our souls?

That the Devil, is come down unto us with great wrath, we find, we feel, we now deplore. In many wayes, for many years, hat the Devil been assaying to extirpate the kingdom of our Lord Jesus here. New-England may complain of the Devil, as in Psal. 129. 1, 2. *Many a time have they afflicted me, from my youth, may,* New-England now say; many a time have they afflicted me from my youth; yet they have not prevailed against me. But now there is a more than ordinary affliction, with which the Devil is galling of us: and such an one as is indeed unparallelable. The things confessed by witches and the things endured by others, laid together, amount unto this account of our affliction. The Devil, exhibiting himself ordinarily as a small black man, has decoy'd a fearful knot of proud, froward, ignorant, envious, and malicious creatures, to list themselves in his horrid service, by entring their names in a book by him tendred unto them. These witches, whereof above a score have now confessed, and shown their deeds, and some are now tormented by the Devils, for confessing, have met in hellish randezvouzes, wherein the confessors do say, they have had their diabolical sacraments, imitating the baptism and the supper of our Lord. In these hellish meetings, these monsters have associated themselves to do no less a thing than, to destroy the kingdom of our Lord Jesus Christ, in these parts of the world; and in order hereunto, first, they each of them have their spectres, or Devils, commission'd by them, and representing of them, to be the engines of their malice. By these wicked spectres, they seize poor people about the country, with various and bloody torments; and of those evidently preternatural torments there are some have dy'd. They have bewitched some, even so far as to make them self-destroyers: and others are in many towns here and there languishing under their Evil hands. The people thus afflicted, are miserably scratched and bitten, so that the marks are most visible to all the world, but the causes utterly invisible; and the same invisible furies do most visibly stick pins into the bodies of the afflicted, and scaled them, & hideously distort, and disjoint all their members, besides a thousand other sorts of plagues beyond these of any natural diseases which they give unto them. Yea, they sometimes drag the poor people out of their chambers, and carry them over trees and hills, for diverse miles together. A large part of the persons tortured by these diabolical spectres, are horribly tempted by them, sometime, with fair promises, and sometimes with hard threatnings, but alwayes with felt miseries, to sign the Devils laws in a spectral book laid before them; which two or three of these poor sufferers, being by their tiresome sufferings overcome to do, they have immediately been released from all their miseries, & they appear'd in spectre then to torture those that were before their fellow-sufferers. The witches which by their covenant with the Devil, are become owners of spectres, are oftentimes by their own spectres required and compelled to give their consent, for the molestation of some, which they had no mind otherwise to fall upon; and cruel depredations are then made upon the vicinage. In the prosecution of these witchcrafts, among a thousand other unaccountable things, the spectres have an odd faculty of cloathing the most substantial and corporeal Instruments of torture, with invisibility, while the wounds thereby given have been the most palpable things in the world; so that the sufferers assaulted with Instruments of iron wholly unseen to the standers-by, tho, to their cost seen by themselves, have upon snatching, wrested the instruments out of the spectres hands, and every one has then immediately not only beheld, but handled, an Iron instrument taken by a Devil from a neighbour. These wicked spectres have proceeded so far, as to steal several quantities of mony from divers people, part of which money has before sufficient spectators been dropt out of the air into the hands of the sufferers, while the spectres have been urging them to subscribe their covenant with death. In such extravagant wayes, have these wretches propounded, the dragooning of as many as they can, into their own combination, and the destroying of others, with lingring, spreading, deadly diseases; till our country should at last become too hot for us. Among the ghastly Instances of the success which those bloody witches have had, we have seen even some of their own children, so dedicated unto the Devil, that in their Infancy, it is found, the imps have sucked them, and rendred them venemous to a prodigy. We have also seen the Devils first batteries, upon the town, where the first church of our Lord in this colony was gathered, producing those distractions, which have almost ruined the town. We have seen likewise the plague reaching afterwards into other towns far and near, where the houses of good men have the Devils, filling of them with terrible vexations!

This is the descent, which, as it seems, the Devil has now made upon us. But that which makes this descent the more formidable is; the multitude and quality of persons accused of an interest in this witchcraft, by the Efficacy of the spectres which take their name and shape upon them; causing very many good and wise men to fear, that many innocent, yea, and some vertuous persons, are by the Devils in this matter, imposed upon; that the Devils have obtain'd the power, to take on them the likeness of harmless people, and in that likeness to afflict other people, and be so abused by præstigious dœmons, that upon their look or touch, the afflicted shall be oddly affected. Arguments from the providence of God, on the one side, and from our charity towards man on the other side, have made this now to become a most agitated controversy among us. There is an agony produced in the minds of men, lest the Devil should sham us with devices, of perhaps a finer thred, than was ever yet practised upon the world. The whole business is become hereupon so snarled, and the determination of the question one way or another, so dismal, that our honourable judges have a room for Jehoshaphats exclamation, we know not what to do! they have used, as judges have heretofore done, the spectral evidences, to introduce their further enquiries into the lives of the persons accused; and they have thereupon, by the wonderful providence of God, been so strengthened with other evidences, that some of the witch gang have been fairly executed. But what shall be done, as to those against whom the evidence is chiefly founded in the dark world? here they do solemnly demand our addresses to the, father of lights, on their behalf. But in the mean time, the Devil improves the darkness of this affair, to push us into a blind mans buffet, and we are even ready to be sinfully, yea, hotly, and madly, mauling one another, in the dark.

The consequence of these things, every considerate man trembles at; and the more, because the frequent cheats of passion, and rumour, do precipitate so many, that I wish I could say, the most were considerate.

But that which carries on the formidableness of our trialls, unto that which may be called, a wrath unto the uttermost, is this: it is not without the wrath of the Almighty God himself, that the Devil is permitted thus to come down upon us in wrath. It was said, in Isa. 9. 19. *Thro the wrath of the Lord of hosts, the land is darkened.* Our land is darkned indeed; since the powers of darkness are turned in upon us, tis a dark time, yea a black night indeed, now the tty-dogs of the pit, are abroad among us: but, It is thro the wrath of the Lord of hosts! Inasmuch as the fire-brands of hell it self are used for the scorching of us, with cause enough may we cry out, what means the heat of this anger? blessed Lord! are all the other Instruments of thy vengeance, too good for the chastisement of such transgressors as we are? must the very Devils be sent out of their own place, to be our troublers?: must we be lash'd with scorpions, fetch'd from the place of torment? must this wilderness be made a receptacle for the dragons of the wilderness? If a lapland should nourish in it vast numbers, the successors of the old biarmi, who can with looks or words bewitch other people, or sell winds to marriners, and have their familiar spirits which they bequeath to their children when they dy, and by their enchanted kettle-drums can learn things done a thousand leagues off; If a swedeland should afford a village, where some scores of haggs, may not only have their meetings with familiar spirits, but also by their enchantments drag many scores of poor children out of their bed-chambers, to be spoiled at those meetings; this, were not altogether a matter of so much wonder! But that New-England should this way be harassed! they are not Chaldeans, that bitter and hasty nation, but they are, bitter and burning Devils; they are not swarthy Indians, but they are sooty Devils; that are let loose upon us. Ah, poor New-England! must the plague of Old Egypt come upon thee? whereof we read in Psal. 78. 49. *He cast upon them the fierceness of his anger, wrath, and indignation, and trouble, by sending evil angels among them.* What? o what must next be looked for. must that which is there next mentioned, be next encountered? He spared not their soul from death, but gave their life over to the pestilence. For my part, when I consider what Melancthon saies, in one of his Epistles, that these diabolical spectacles are often prodigies;

and when I consider, how often people have been by spectres called upon, just before their deaths; I am verily afraid, lest some wasting mortality, be among the things, which this plague is the forerunner of. I pray God, prevent it!

But now, what shall we do?

I. Let the Devils coming down in great wrath upon us, cause us to come down in great grief before the Lord. We may truly and sadly say, we are brought very low! Low, indeed when the serpents of the dust, are crawling and coyling about us, and Insulting over us. May we not say, we are in the very belly of hell, when hell it self is feeding upon us? But how low is that! o let us then most penitently lay our selves very low before the God of heaven, who has thus abased us. When a truculent nero, a Devil of a man, was turned in upon the world, it was said in, 1 Pet. 5. 6. *Humble yourselves under the mighty hand of God.* How much more now ought we to humble ourselves, under that mighty hand of that God who indeed has the Devil in a chain, but has horribly lengthened out the chain! when the old people of God, heard any blasphemies tearing of his ever-blessed name to pieces, they were to rend their cloaths at what they heard. I am sure that we have cause to rend our hearts this day, when we see what an high treason has been committed against the most high God, by the witchcrafts in our neighbourhood. We may say; and shall we not be humbled when we say it? We have seen an horrible thing done in our land! O 'tis a most humbling thing, to think, that ever there should be such an abomination among us, as for a crue of humane race, to renounce their maker, and to unite with the Devil, for the troubling of mankind, and for people to be, (as is by some confess'd) baptized by a fiend using this form upon them, *Thou art mine, and I have a full power over thee!* afterwards communicating in an hellish bread and wine, by that fiend admnistred unto them. It was said in Deut. 18. 10, 11, 12. *There shall not be found among you an Inchanter, or a witch, or a charmer, or a consulter with familiar spirits, or a wizzard, or a necromancer; for all that do these things are an abomination to the Lord, and because of these abominations, the Lord thy God doth drive them out before thee.* That New-England now should have these abominations in it, yea, that some of no mean profession, should be found guilty of them: alas, what humiliations are we all hereby oblig'd unto? O 'tis a defiled land, wherein we live; let us be humbled for these defiling abominations, lest we be driven out of our land. It's a very humbling thing to think, what reproaches will be cast upon us, for this matter, among, the daughters of the Philistines. Indeed, enough might easily be said for the vindication of this country from the singularity of this matter, by ripping up, what has been discovered in others. Great Britain alone, and this also in our dayes of greatest light, has had that in it, which may divert the calumnies of an ill-natured world, from centring here. They are the words of the devout Bishop Hall, Satans prevalency in this age, is most clear in the marvellous number of witches, abounding in all places. Now hundreds are discovered in one shire; and, if fame deceive us not, in a village of fourteen houses in the north, are found so many of this damned brood. Yea, and these of both sexes, who have professed much knowledge, holiness, and devotion, are drawn into this damnable practice. I suppose the doctor in the first of those passages, may refer to what happened in the year 1645. When so many vassals of the Devil were detected, that there were thirty try'd at one time, whereas about fourteen were hang'd, and an hundred more detained in the prisons of Suffolk and Essex. Among other things which many of these acknowledged, one was, that they were to undergo certain punishments, if they did not such and such hurts, as were appointed them. And, among the rest that were then executed, there was an old parson, called, Lowis, who confessed, that he had a couple of imps, whereof one was alwayes putting him upon the doing of mischief; once particularly, that imp calling for his consent so to do, went immediately and sunk a ship, there under sail. I pray, let not New-England become of an unsavoury and a sulphurous resentment in the opinion of the world abroad for the doleful things which are now fallen out among us, while there are such histories of other places abroad in the world. Nevertheless, I am sure that *one,* the people of New-England, have cause enough to humble our selves under our most humbling circumstances. We must no more, be, haughty, because of the Lords Holy Mountain among us; no, it becomes us rather to be, humble, because we have been such an habitation of Unholy Devils!

II. Since the Devil is come down in great wrath upon us, let not us in our great wrath against one another provide a lodging for him. It was a more wholesome caution, in Eph. 4. 26, 27. *Let not the sun go down upon your wrath: neither give place to the Devil.* The Devil is come down to see what quarter he shall find among us: and if, his coming down, do now fill us with wrath against one another; and if between the cause of the sufferers on one hand, and the cause of the suspected on t' other, we carry things to such extreams of passion as are now gaining upon us, the Devil will bless himself to find such a convenient lodging as we shall therein afford unto him. And it may be that the wrath which we have had against one another has had more then a little influence upon the coming down of the Devil in that wrath which now amazes us. Have not many of us been Devils one unto another for slanderings, for backbitings, for animosities? for this, among other causes, perhaps, God has permitted the Devils to be worrying, as they now are, among us. But it is high time to leave off all devilism, when the Devil himself is falling upon us: and it is no time for us to be censuring and reviling one another, with a

Devilish wrath, when the wrath of the Devil is annoying of us. The way for us to out-wit the Devil, in the wiles with which he now vexes us, would be for us, to join as one man in our cries to God, for the directing, and Issuing of this thorny business; but if we do not lift up our hands to heaven, without wrath, we cannot then do it without doubt, of speeding in it. I am ashamed when I read French authors giving this character of Englishmen [*Ils se haissent les uns les autres, et sont en division continuelle.*] they hate one another, and are always quarrelling one with another. And I shall be much more ashamed, if it become the character of New-Englanders; which is indeed, what the Devil would have. Satan would make us bruise one another, by breaking of the peace among us; but O let us disappoint him. We read of a thing that sometimes happens to the Devil when he is foaming with his wrath, in Mat. 12. 43. *The unclean spirit seeks rest, and finds none.* But we give rest unto the Devil, by wrath one against another. If we would lay aside all fierceness, and keeness, in the disputes which the Devil has raised among us; and if we would use to one another none but the, soft answers, which turn away wrath, i should hope that we might light upon such counsels, as would quickly Extricate us out of our labyrinths. But the old Incendiary of the world, is come from hell, with sparks of hell-Fire flashing on every side of him; and we make ourselves tynder to the sparks. When the Emperour Henry III. kept the feast of Pentecost, at the City Mentz, there arose dissension among some of the people there, which came from words to blows, and at last it passed on to the shedding of blood. After the tumult was over, when they came to that clause in their devotions, *Thou hast made this day glorious*; the Devil to the unexpressible terrour of that vast assembly, made the temple ring with the outcry but I have made this day quarrelsome! we are truly come into a day, which by being well managed might be very glorious, for the exterminating of those, accursed things, which have hitherto been the clogs of our prosperity; but if we make this day quarrelsome, thro' any raging confidences, alas, O Lord, my flesh trembles for fear of thee, and I am afraid of thy judgments. Erasmus, among other historians, tells us, that at a town in Germany, a Witch or Devil, appear'd on the top of a chimney, threatning to set the town on fire: and at length, scattering a pot of ashes abroad, the town was presently and horribly burn't unto the ground. Methinks, I see the spectres, from the tops of the chimneys to the north ward, threatning to scatter fire, about the countrey; but let us quench that fire by the most amicable correspondencies: lest, as the spectres, have, they say, already most literally burn't some of our dwellings, there do come forth a further fire from the brambles of hell, which may more terribly devour us. Let us not be like a troubled house, altho' we are so much haunted by the Devils. Let our long suffering be a well-placed piece of armour, about us, against the fiery darts of the wicked ones. History informs us, that so long ago, as the year, 858. a certain pestilent and malignant sort of a dæmon, molested caumont in germany with all sorts of methods to stir up strife among the citizens. He uttered prophecies, he detected villanies, he branded people with all kind of infamies. He incensed the neighbourhood against one man particularly, as the cause of all the mischiefs: who yet proved himself innocent. He threw stones at the inhabitants, and at length burn't their habitations, till the commission of the dæmon could go no further. I say, let us be well aware lest such dæmons do, come hither also!

III. Inasmuch as the Devil is come down in great wrath, we had need labour, with all the care and speed we can to divert the great wrath of heaven from coming at the same time upon us. The God of heaven has with long and loud admonitions, been calling us to, a reformation of our provoking evils, as the only way to avoid that wrath of his, which does not only threaten, but consume us. 'Tis because we have been deaf to those calls, that we are now by a provoked God, laid open to the wrath of the Devil himself. It is said in Prov. 16. 17. *When a mans ways please the Lord, he maketh even his enemies to be at peace with him.* The Devil is our grand enemy; and tho' we would not be at peace with him, yet we would be at peace from him; that is, we would have him unable to disquiet our peace. But inasmuch as the wrath which we endure from this enemy, will allow us no peace, we may be sure, our ways have not pleased the Lord. It is because we have broken the hedge of Gods precepts, that the hedge of Gods provodence is not so entire as it uses to be about us; but serpents are biting of us. O let us then set our selves to make our peace with our God, whom we have displeased by our iniquities: and let us not imagine that we can encounter the wrath of the Devil while there is the wrath of God almighty to set that mastiff upon us. *Reformation! Reformation!* has been the repeated cry, of all the judgments, that have hitherto been upon us; because we have been as deaf adders thereunto, the adders of the Infernal pit are now hissing about us. At length, as it was of old said, in Luke 16. 30. *If one went unto them, from the dead, they will repent;* even so, there are some come unto us from the damned. The great God has loosed the bars of the pit, so that many damned spirits are come in among us, to make us repent of our misdemeanours. The means which the Lord had formerly employ'd for our awakening, were such, that he might well have said, what could I have done more? and yet after all, he has done more, in some regards, than was ever done for the awakening of any people in the world. The things now done to awaken our enquiries after our provoking Evils, and our endeavours to reform those evils; are most extraordinary things; for which cause I would freely speak it, if we now do not some extraordinary things in returning to God, we are the most incurable, and I wish it be not quickly said, the most miserable, people under the sun. Believe me, 'tis a time for all people to do something extraordinary, in searching and trying of their ways, and in turning to the Lord. It is at an extraordinary rate of circumspection and spiritual mindedness, that we should all now maintain a walk with God. At such a time as this, ought magistrates to do something extraordinary in promoting of what is laudable, and in restraining and chastising of evil doers. At such a time as this, ought ministers to do something extraordinary in pulling the souls of men out of the snares of the Devil, not only by publick Preaching, but by personal visits and counsels, from house to house. At such a time as this, ought churches to do something extraordinary, in renewing of their covenants, and in remembring, and reviving the obligations of what they have renewed. Some admirable designs about the reformation of manners, have lately been on foot in the English nation, in pursuance of the most excellent admonitions, which have been given for it, by the letters of their majesties. Besides the vigorous agreements of the justices here and there in the Kingdom; assisted by Godly gentlemen and informers, to execute the laws upon profane offenders: there has been started, a proposal, for the well-affected people in every parish, to enter into orderly societies, whereof every member shall bind himself, not only to avoid profaneness in himself, but also according unto to their place, to do their utmost in first reproving, and, if it must be so, then exposing, and so punishing, as the law directs, for, others that shall be guilty. It has been observed, that the English nation has had some of its greatest successes, upon some special, and signal actions this way; and a discouragement given unto legal proceedings of this kind, must needs be very exercising to the, wise that observe these things. But, O why should not New-England be the most forward part of the English nation in such reformations? methinks I hear the Lord from heaven saying over us, *O that my people had hearkened unto me; then I should soon have subdued the Devils, as well as their other enemies!* there have been some feeble essays towards reformation, of late in our churches; but, I pray, what comes of them? do we stay till the storm of his wrath be over? nay, let us be doing what we can as fast as we can, to divert the storm. The Devil, having broke in upon our world, there is great asking, who is it that have brought them in? and many do by spectral exhibitions come to be cry'd out upon. I hope in Gods time, it will be found, that among those that are thus cry'd out upon, there are persons yet clear from the great transgression; but indeed, all the unreformed among us, may justly be cry'd out upon, as having too much of an hand in letting of the Devils in to our borders; 'tis our worldliness, our formality, our sensuality, and our iniquity, that has help'd this letting of the Devils in. O let us then at last, consider our wayes. 'Tis a strange passage recorded by Mr. Clark, in the life of his father, that the people of his parish refusing to be reclaimed from their sabbath breaking, by all the zealous testimonies which that good man bore against it; at last, on a night after the people had retired home from a revelling profanation of the Lords Day, there was heard a great noise, with rattling of chains, up and down the town, and the horrid scent of brimstone fill'd the neighbourhood. Upon which the guilty consciences of the wretches, told them, the Devil was come to fetch them away: and it so terrify'd them, that an eminent reformation follow'd the sermons which that man of God preached thereupon. Behold, sinners, behold, and wonder, lest you perish; the very Devils are walking about our streets, with lengthened chains, making a dreadful noise in our ears, and brimstone even without a metaphor, is making an hellish and horrid stench in our nostrils. I pray, leave off all those things, whereof your guilty consciences may now accuse you, lest these Devils do yet more direfully fall upon you. Reformation is at this time, our only preservation.

IV. When the Devil is come down in great wrath, let every great vice which may have a more particular tendency to make us a prey unto that wrath, come into a due discredit with us. It is the general concession of all men, who are not become too unreasonable for common conversation, that the Invitation of witchcrafts is the thing that ha's now introduced the Devil into the midst of us. I say then, let not only all witchcrafts be duely abominated with us, but also let us be duely watchful against all the steps leading thereunto. There are lesser sorceries which, they say, are too frequent in our land. As it was said in 2 King. 17. 9. The children of Israel did secretly those things that were not right against the Lord their God. So tis to be feared, the children of New-England have secretly done many things that have been pleasing to the Devil. They say, that in some towns, it ha's been an usual thing for people to cure hurts with spells, or to use detestable conjurations, with sieves, & keys, and pease, and nails, and horse-shooes, and I know not what other implements, to learn the things, for which they have a forbidden, and an impious curiositie. 'Tis in the Devils name, that such things are done; and in Gods name I do this day charge them, as vile impieties. By these courses 'tis, that people play upon the hole of the asp; till that cruelly venemous asp has pull'd many of them, into the deep hole, of witchcraft it self. It has been acknowledged by some who have sunk the deepest into this horrible pit, that they began, at these little witchcrafts; on which 'tis pitty but the laws of the English nation, whereby the incorrigible repetition of those tricks, is made felony, were severally executed. From the like sinful curiosity it is, that the prognostications of judicial astrology, are so injudiciously regarded by multitudes among us; and although the jugling astrologers do scarce ever hit right, except it be in such weighty judgments, forsooth, as that many old men will dy such a year, and that there will be many losses felt by some that venture to sea, and that there will be much lying and cheating in the world; yet their foolish admirers, will not be perswaded, but that the innocent stars have been concern'd in these events. It is a disgrace to the English nation that the phamphlets of such idle, futil, trifling star-gazers are so much considered; and the countenance hereby given to a study, wherein at last, all is done by impulse, if any thing be done to any purpose at all, is not a little perilous to the souls of men. It is, (a science, I dare not call it, but) a juggle, whereof the learned hall, well says, It is presumptuous and unwarrantable, & cry'd ever down by councils and fathers, as unlawful, as that which lies in the mid-way between magick, and imposture, and partakes not a little of both. Men consult the aspects of planets, whose northern or southern motions receive denominations from a cælestial dragon, till the Infernal dragon at length insinuate into them, with a poyson of witchcraft that can't be cured. Has there not also been a world of discontent in our borders? 'Tis no wonder, that the fiery serpents are so stinging of us; we have been a most murmuring generation. It is not irrational, to ascribe the late stupendous growth of witches among us, partly to the bitter discontents, which affliction and poverty has fill'd us with: it is inconceivable, what advantage the Devil gains over men, by discontent. Moreover, the sin of unbelief may be reckoned as perhaps the chief crime of our land. We are told, God swears in wrath, against them that believe not; and what follows then but this, that the Devil comes unto them in wrath? Never were the offers of the Gospel, more freely tendered, or more basely despised, among any people under the whole cope of heaven, than in this New-England. Seems it at all marvellous unto us, that the Devil should get such footing in our country? why, 'tis because the saviour has been slighted here, perhaps more than any where. The Blessed Lord Jesus Christ has been profering to us, grace, and glory, and every good thing, and been alluring of us to accept of him, with such terms as these; undone sinner, I am all; art thou willing that I should be thy all? but, as a proof of that contempt which this unbelief has cast upon these proffers, I would seriously ask of the so many hundreds above a thousand people within these walls; which of you all, o how few of you, can indeed say, Christ is mine, and I am his, and he is the beloved of my soul? I would only say thus much: when the precious and glorious Jesus, is Entreating of us to receive him, in all his offices, with all his benefits, the Devil minds what respect we pay unto that heavenly Lord; if we refuse him that speaks from heaven, then he that, comes from hell, does with a sort of claim set in, and cry out, Lord, since this Wretch is not willing that thou shouldst have him, I pray, let me have him. And thus, by the just vengeance of Heaven, the Devil becomes a master, a prince, a God, unto the miserable unbelievers; but O what are many of them then hurried unto! all of these evil things, do I now set before you, as branded with the mark of the Devil upon them.

V. With great regard, with great pitty, should we lay to heart the condition of those, who are cast into affliction, by the great wrath of the Devil. There is a number of our good neighbours, and some of them very particularly noted for goodness and vertue, of whom we may say, Lord, they are vexed with Devils. Their tortures being primarily Inflicted on their spirits, may indeed cause the impressions thereof upon their bodies to be the less durable, tho' rather the more sensible: but they Endure horrible things, and many have been actually murdered. Hard censures now bestow'd upon these poor sufferers, cannot but be very displeasing unto our Lord, who, as he said, about some that had been butchered by a Pilate, in Luc. 13. 2, 3. *Think ye that these were sinners above others, because they suffered such things? I tell you no, but except ye repent, ye shall all likewise perish:* Even so, he now says, think ye that they who now suffer by the Devil, have been greater sinners than their neighbours. No, do you repent of your own sins, lest the Devil come to fall foul of you, as he has done to them. And if this be so, how rash a thing would it be, if such of the poor sufferers, as carry it with a becoming piety, seriousness, and humiliation under their present suffering, should be unjustly censured; or have their very calamity imputed unto them as a crime? It is an easy thing, for us to fall into, the fault of, adding affliction to the afflicted, and of, talking to the grief of those that are already wounded. Nor can it be wisdom to slight the dangers of such a fault. In the mean time, we have no bowels in us, if we do not compassionate the distressed county of Essex, now crying to all these colonies, have pitty on me, O ye my friends, have pitty on me, for the hand of the Lord has touched me, and the wrath of the Devil has been therewithal turned upon me. But indeed, if an hearty pity be due to any, I am sure, the difficulties which attend our honourable judges, doe demand no inconsiderable share in that pitty. What a difficult, what an arduous task, have those worthy personages now upon their hands? to carry the knife so exactly, that on the one side, there may be no Innocent blood shed, by too unseeing a zeal for the children of Israel; and that on the other side, there may be no shelter given to those diabolical works of darkness, without the removal whereof we never shall have peace; or to those furies whereof several have kill'd more people perhaps than would serve to make a village: *Hic labor, hoc opus est!* O what need have we, to be concerned, that the sins of our Israel, may not provoke the God of heaven to leave his Davids, unto a wrong step, in a matter of such consequence, as is now before them! our disingenuous, uncharitable, unchristian reproaching of such faithful men, after all, the prayers and supplications, with strong crying and tears, with which we are daily plying the throne of grace, that they may be kept, from what they fear, is none of the way for our preventing of what we fear. Nor all this while, ought our pitty to forget such accused ones, as call for indeed our most compassionate pitty, till there be fuller evidences that they are less worthy of it. If Satan have any where maliciously brought upon the stage, those that have hitherto had a just and good stock of reputation, for their just and good living, among us; If the Evil one have obtained a permission to appear, in the figure of such as we have cause to think, have hitherto abstained, even from the appearance of evil: it is in truth, such an invasion upon mankind, as may well raise an horror in us all: but, O what compassions are due to such as may come under such misrepresentations, of the great accuser! who of us can say, what may be shewn in the glasses of the great lying spirit? altho' the usual providence of God [we praise him!] keeps us from such a mishap; yet where have we an absolute promise, that we shall every one always be kept from it? as long as charity is bound, to think no evil, it will not hurt us that are private persons, to forbear the judgment which belongs not unto us. Let it rather be our wish: may the Lord help them to learn the lessons, for which they are now put unto so hard a school.

VI. With a great zeal, we should lay hold on the covenant of God, that we may secure us and ours, from the great wrath, with which the Devil rages. Let us come into the covenant of grace, and then we shall not be hook'd into a covenant with the Devil, nor be altogether unfurnished with armour, against the wretches that are in the covenant. The way to come under the saving Influences of the new covenant, is, to close with the Lord Jesus Christ, who is the all-sufficient mediator of it: let us therefore do that, by resigning up ourselves unto the saving, teaching, and ruling, hands of this blessed mediator. Then we shall be, what we read in Jude 1. *Preserved in Christ Jesus: that is, as the destroying angel, could not meddle with such as had been distinguished, by the blood of the passeover on their houses, thus the blood of the Lord Jesus Christ, sprinkled on our souls, will preserve us from the Devil.* The birds of prey (and indeed the Devils most literally in the shape of great birds!) are flying about: Would we find a covert from these vultures? Let us then hear our Lord Jesus from heaven clocquing unto us, O that you would be gathered under my wings! well; when this is done, then let us own the covenant, which we are now come into, by joining ourselves to a particular church, walking in the order of the Gospel; at the doing whereof, according to that covenant of God, we give up ourselves unto the Lord, and in him unto one another. While others have had their names entred in the Devils book; let our names be found in the church book, and let us be, written among the living in Jerusalem. By no means let, church work sink and fail in the midst of us; but let the tragical accidents which now happen, exceedingly quicken that work. So many of the rising generation, utterly forgetting the errand of our fathers to build churches in this wilderness, and so many of our cottages being allow'd to live, where they do not, and perhaps can not, wait upon God with the churches of his people! 'tis as likely as any one thing to procure the swarmings of witch crafts among us. But it becomes us, with a like ardour, to bring our poor children with us, as we shall do, when we come ourselves, into the covenant of God. It would break an heart of stone, to have seen, what I have lately seen; even poor children of several ages, even from seven to twenty more or less, confessing their familiarity with Devils; but at the same time, in doleful bitter lamentations, that made a little pourtraiture of hell it self, expostulating with their execrable parents, for devoting them to the Devil in their infancy, and so entailing of Devillism upon them! now, as the Psalmist could say, *My zeal hath consumed me, because my enemies have forgotten thy words:* Even so, let the nefarious wickedness of those that have explicitly dedicated their children to the Devil, even with devi-lish symbols, of such a dedication, provoke our zeal to have our children, sincerely, signally, and openly consecrated unto God; with an education afterwards assuring and confirming that consecration.

VII. Let our prayer go up with great faith, against the Devil, that comes down in great wrath. Such is the antipathy of the Devil to our prayer, that he cannot bear to stay long where much of it is: indeed it is *Diaboli Flagellum,* as well as, *Miseriæ Remedium;* the Devil will soon be scourgd out of the Lord's temple, by a whip, made and used, with the, effectual fervent prayer of righteous men. When the Devil by afflicting of us, drives us to our prayers, he is, the fool making a whip for his own back. Our Lord said of the Devil, in Matt. 17. 21. *This kind goes not out, but by prayer and fasting.* But, prayer and fasting will soon make the Devil be gone. Here are charms indeed! sacred and blessed charms, which the Devil cannot stand before. A promise of God, being well managed in the hands of them, that are much upon their knees, will so resist the Devil, that he will flee from us. At every other weapon, the Devils will be too hard for us; the spiritual wickednesses in high places, have manifestly the upper hand of us; that old serpent will be too old for us, too cunning, too subtil; they will soon out-wit us, if we think to encounter them with any wit of our own. But when we come to prayers, incessant and vehement prayers before the Lord, there we shall be too hard for them. When well-directed prayers, that great artillery of heaven, are brought into the field, there, methinks I see, there are these workers of iniquity fallen, all of them! and who can tell, how much the most obscure Christian among you all, may do towards the deliverance of our land from the molestations which the Devil is now giving to us. I have read, that on a day of prayer kept by some good people for and with a

possessed person, the Devil at last flew out of the window, and referring
to a devout, plain, mean woman then in the room, he cry'd out, O the
woman behind the door! 'Tis that woman that forces me away! thus, the
Devil that now troubles us, may be forced within a while to forsake us:
and it shall be said, he was driven away by the prayers of some obscure
and retired souls, which the world has taken but little notice of! the great
God, is about a great work at this day among us; now there is extream
hazzard left the Devil by compulsion must submit unto that great work,
may also by permission, come to confound that work: both in the
detections of some, and in the confessions of others, whose unGodly
deeds may be brought forth, by a great work of God, there is hazzard lest
the Devil intertwist some of his delusions. 'Tis prayer, I say, 'tis prayer,
that must carry us well thro' the strange things that are now upon us.
Only that prayer must then be, the prayer of faith: o where is our faith
in him, who hath spoiled these principalities and powers, on his cross
triumphing over them!

VIII. Lastly, shake off, every soul, shake off the hard yoke of the Devil,
if you would not perish under the Great Wrath of the Devil. Where 'tis
said, the whole world lies in wickedness, 'tis by some of the ancients
rendred, the whole world lies in the Devil. The Devil is a prince, yea, the
Devil is a God unto all the unregenerate; and alas, there is, a whole world
of them. Desolate sinners, consider what an horrid Lord it is that you are
Enslav'd unto; and oh shake off your slavery to such a Lord. Instead of
him, now make your choice of the eternal God in Jesus Christ; choose
him with a most unalterable resolution; and unto him say, with Thomas,
my Lord, and my God! say with the church, Lord, other Lords have had
the dominion over us, but now thou alone shalt be our Lord for ever.
Then instead of your perishing under the wrath of the Devils, God will
fetch you to a place among those that fill up the room of the Devils, left
by their fall from the Ethereal regions. It was a most awful speech made
by the Devil, possessing a young woman, at a village in Germany, by the
command of God, I am come to torment the body of this young
woman, though I cannot hurt her soul; and it is that I may warn men, to
take heed of sinning against God. Indeed (said he) 'tis very sore against
my will that I do it; but the command of God forces me to declare what
I do; however I know that at the last day, I shall have more souls than God
himself. So spoke that horrible Devil! but o that none of our souls may
be found among the prizes of the Devil, in the day of God! O that what
the Devil has been forc'd to declare, of his kingdom among us, may
prejudice our hearts against him for ever!

My text says, the Devil is come down in great wrath, for he has but a
short time. Yea, but if you do not by a speedy and thorough conversion
to God, escape the wrath of the Devil, you will your selves go down,

where the Devil is to be, and you will there be sweltring under the Devils wrath, not for a short time, but, world without end; not for a short time, but for, Infinite millions of ages. The smoke of your torment under that wrath, will ascend for ever and ever! Indeed the Devils time for his wrath upon you in this world, can be but short, but his time for you to do his work, or, which is all one, to delay your turning to God, that is a long time. When the Devil was going to be dispossessed of a man, he roar'd out, am I to be tormented before my time. you will torment the Devil, if you rescue your souls out of his hands, by true repentance; if once you begin to look that way, hee'll cry out, o this is before my time, I must have more time, yet in the service of such a guilty soul. But, I beseech you, let us join thus to torment the Devil, in an Holy Revenge upon him, for all the injuries which he has done unto us; let us tell him, Satan, Thy time with me is but short, nay, thy time with me shall be no more; I am unutterably sorry that it has been so much; depart from me thou evil-doer, that would'st have me to be an evil-doer like thy self; I will now for ever keep the Commandments of that God, in whom I live, and move, and have my being! the Devil has plaid a fine game for himself indeed, if by his troubling of our land, the souls of many people should come to, think upon their wayes, till they turn their feet into the testimonies of the Lord. Now that the Devil may be thus outshot in his own bow, is the desire of all that love the salvation of God among us, as well as of him, who has thus addressed you. Amen.

# JONATHAN EDWARDS
## (1703–1758)

# GOD GLORIFIED IN THE WORK OF REDEMPTION, BY THE GREATNESS OF MAN'S DEPENDENCE UPON HIM, IN THE WHOLE OF IT
## (1731)

1 Cor. 1:29–31.

*That no flesh should glory in his presence. But of him are ye
in Christ Jesus, who of God is made unto us wisdom, and
righteousness, and sanctification, and redemption. That, according
as it is written, He that glorieth, let him glory in the Lord.*

THOSE CHRISTIANS to whom the Apostle directed this epistle, dwelt in a part of the world where human wisdom was in great repute; as the Apostle observes in the twenty-second verse of this chapter, "The Greeks seek after wisdom." Corinth was not far from Athens, that had been for many ages the most famous seat of philosophy and learning in the world.

The Apostle therefore observes to them how that God by the gospel destroyed, and brought to naught, their human wisdom. The learned Grecians, and their great philosophers, by all their wisdom did not know God, they were not able to find out the truth in divine things. But after they had done their utmost to no effect, it pleased God at length, to reveal himself by the gospel; which they accounted foolishness: he "chose the foolish things of the world to confound the wise, and the weak things of the world to confound the things which are mighty, and the base things of the world, and things that are despised, yea and things which are not, to bring to naught the things that are." And the Apostle informs them why he thus did in the verse of the text, "That no flesh should glory in his presence," etc. In which words may be observed,

1. What God aims at in the disposition of things in the affair of redemption, viz. that man should not glory in himself, but alone in God; "That no flesh should glory in his presence. . . . That according as it is written, He that glorieth, let him glory in the Lord."

2. How this end is attained in the work of redemption, viz. by that absolute and immediate dependence which men have upon God in that work, for all their good. Inasmuch as,

(1) All the good that they have is in and through Christ; he "is made unto us wisdom, righteousness, sanctification, and redemption." All the good of the fallen and redeemed creature is concerned in these four things, and can't be better distributed than into them; but Christ is each of them to us, and we have none of them any otherwise than in him. He "is made of God unto us wisdom": in him are all the proper good, and true excellency of the understanding. Wisdom was a thing that the Greeks admired; but Christ is the true light of the world, 'tis through him alone that true *wisdom* is imparted to the mind. 'Tis in and by Christ that we have *righteousness:* 'tis by being in him that we are justified, have our sins pardoned, and are received as righteous into God's favor. 'Tis by Christ that we have *sanctification:* we have in him true excellency of heart, as well as of understanding; and he is made unto us inherent as well as imputed righteousness. 'Tis by Christ that we have *redemption,* or the actual deliverance from all misery, and the bestowment of all happiness and glory. Thus we have all our good by Christ who is God.

(2) Another instance wherein our dependence on God for all our good appears, is this, that 'tis God that has given us Christ, that we might have these benefits through him; he "of God is made unto us wisdom, righteousness," etc.

(3) 'Tis of him that we are in Christ Jesus, and come to have an interest in him, and so do receive those blessings which he is made unto us. 'Tis God that gives us faith whereby we close with Christ.

So that in this verse is shown our dependence on each person in the Trinity for all our good. We are dependent on Christ the Son of God, as he is our wisdom, righteousness, sanctification, and redemption. We are dependent on the Father, who have given us Christ, and made him to be these things to us. We are dependent on the Holy Ghost, for 'tis "of him that we are in Christ Jesus"; 'tis the Spirit of God that gives faith in him, whereby we receive him, and close with him.

# DOCTRINE

*God is glorified in the work of redemption in this, that there
appears in it so absolute and universal a dependence of
the redeemed on him.*

Here I propose to show,

I. That there is an absolute and universal dependence of the redeemed
on God for all their good. And,

II. That God hereby is exalted and glorified in the work of redemption.

I. There is an absolute and universal dependence of the redeemed on
God. The nature and contrivance of our redemption is such, that the
redeemed are in everything directly, immediately, and entirely dependent
on God: they are dependent on him for all, and are dependent on him
every way.

The several ways wherein the dependence of one being may be upon
another for its good, and wherein the redeemed of Jesus Christ depend
on God for all their good, are these, viz. that they have all their good *of*
him, and that they have all *through* him, and that they have all *in* him: that
he be the cause and original whence all their good comes, therein it is *of*
him; and that he be the medium by which it is obtained and conveyed,
therein they have it *through* him; and that he be that good itself that is
given and conveyed, therein it is *in* him.

Now those that are redeemed by Jesus Christ do in all these respects
very directly and entirely depend on God for their all.

*First.* The redeemed have all their good *of* God. God is the great
Author of it; he is the first cause of it, and not only so but he is the only
proper cause.

'Tis *of* God that we have our Redeemer. 'Tis God that has provided a
Savior for us. Jesus Christ is not only of God in his person, as he is the
only begotten Son of God; but he is from God as we are concerned in
him, and in his office of mediator; he is the gift of God to us: God chose
and anointed him, appointed him his work, and sent him into the world.

And as it is God that gives, so 'tis God that accepts the Savior. As it is
God that provides and gives the Redeemer to buy salvation for us, so it
is *of* God that that salvation is bought: he gives the purchaser, and he
affords the thing purchased.

'Tis of God that Christ becomes ours, that we are brought to him, and
are united to him: 'tis of God that we receive faith to close with him, that
we may have an interest in him. Eph. 2:8, *For by grace ye are saved, through
faith; and that not of yourselves, it is the gift of God.* 'Tis of God that we actually
do receive all the benefits that Christ has purchased. 'Tis God that pardons

and justifies, and delivers from going down to hell, and 'tis his favor that the redeemed are received into, and are made the objects of, when they are justified. So it is God that delivers from the dominion of sin, and cleanses us from our filthiness, and changes us from our deformity. 'Tis of God that the redeemed do receive all their true excellency, wisdom and holiness; and that two ways, viz. as the Holy Ghost by whom these things are immediately wrought is from God, proceeds from him, and is sent by him; and also as the Holy Ghost himself is God, by whose operation and indwelling, the knowledge of God and divine things, and a holy disposition, and all grace are conferred and upheld.

And though means are made use of in conferring grace on men's souls, yet 'tis of God that we have these means of grace, and 'tis God that makes them effectual. 'Tis of God that we have the Holy Scriptures; they are the Word of God. 'Tis of God that we have ordinances, and their efficacy depends on the immediate influence of the Spirit of God. The ministers of the gospel are sent of God, and all their sufficiency is of him. 2. Cor. 4:7, *We have this treasure in earthen vessels, that the excellency of the power may be of God, and not of us.* Their success depends entirely and absolutely on the immediate blessing and influence of God.

1. The redeemed have all of the *grace* of God. It was of mere grace that God gave us his only begotten Son. The grace is great in proportion to the dignity and excellency of what is given: the gift was infinitely precious, because it was of a person infinitely worthy, a person of infinite glory; and also because it was of a person infinitely near and dear to God. The grace is great in proportion to the benefit we have given us in him: the benefit is doubly infinite in that in him we have deliverance from an infinite, because an eternal misery, and do also receive eternal joy and glory. The grace in bestowing this gift is great in proportion to our unworthiness to whom it is given; instead of deserving such a gift, we merited infinitely ill of God's hands. The grace is great according to the manner of giving, or in proportion to the humiliation and expense of the method and means by which way is made for our having the gift. He gave him to us dwelling amongst us; he gave him to us incarnate, or in our own nature; he gave him to us in our nature, in the like infirmities in which we have it in our fallen state, and which in us do accompany, and are occasioned by, the sinful corruption of our nature. He gave him to us in a low and afflicted state; and not only so but he gave him to us slain that he might be a feast for our souls.

The grace of God in bestowing this gift is most free. It was what God was under no obligation to bestow: he might have rejected fallen man, as he did the fallen angels. It was what we never did anything to merit: 'twas given while we were yet enemies, and before we had so much as repented. It was from the love of God that saw no excellency in us to attract it; and it was without expectation of ever being requited for it.

And 'tis from mere grace that the benefits of Christ are applied to such and such particular persons. Those that are called and sanctified are to attribute it alone to the good pleasure of God's goodness, by which they are distinguished. He is sovereign and hath mercy on whom he will have mercy, and whom he will he hardens.

Man hath now a greater dependence on the grace of God than he had before the fall. He depends on the free goodness of God for much more than he did then: then he depended on God's goodness for conferring the reward of perfect obedience; for God was not obliged to promise and bestow that reward: but now we are dependent on the grace of God for much more: we stand in need of grace, not only to bestow glory upon us, but to deliver us from hell and eternal wrath. Under the first covenant we depended on God's goodness to give us the reward of righteousness; and so we do now. And not only so, but we stand in need of God's free and sovereign grace to give us that righteousness; and not only so, but we stand in need of his grace to pardon our sin, and release us from the guilt and infinite demerit of it.

And as we are dependent on the goodness of God for more now than under the first covenant, so we are dependent on a much greater, more free and wonderful goodness. We are now more dependent on God's arbitrary and sovereign good pleasure. We were in our first estate dependent on God for holiness: we had our original righteousness from him; but then holiness was not bestowed in such a way of sovereign good pleasure as it is now. Man was created holy, for it became God to create holy all the reasonable creatures he created: it would have been a disparagement to the holiness of God's nature, if he had made an intelligent creature unholy. But now when man is made holy, it is from mere and arbitrary grace; God may forever deny holiness to the fallen creature if he pleases, without any disparagement to any of his perfections.

And we are not only indeed more dependent on the grace of God, but our dependence is much more conspicuous, because our own insufficiency and helplessness in ourselves is much more apparent, in our fallen and undone state, than it was before we were either sinful or miserable. We are more apparently dependent on God for holiness, because we are first sinful, and utterly polluted, and afterward holy: so the production of the effect is sensible, and its derivation from God more obvious. If man was ever holy and always was so, it would not be so apparent, that he had not holiness necessarily, as an inseparable qualification of human nature. So we are more apparently dependent on free grace for the favor of God, for we are first justly the objects of his displeasure, and afterwards are received into favor. We are more apparently dependent on God for happiness, being first miserable, and afterwards happy. 'Tis more apparently free and without merit in us, because we are actually without any kind of excellency to merit, if there could be any such thing as merit in creature-excellency. And we are not only without any true excellency, but are full of, and wholly defiled with, that which is infinitely odious. All our good is more apparently from God, because we are first naked and wholly without any good, and afterward enriched with all good.

2. We receive all of the *power* of God. Man's redemption is often spoken of as a work of wonderful power as well as grace. The great power of God appears in bringing a sinner from his low state, from the depths of sin and misery, to such an exalted state of holiness and happiness. Eph. 1:19. *And what is the exceeding greatness of his power to us-ward who believe, according to the working of his mighty power.*

We are dependent on God's power through every step of our redemption. We are dependent on the power of God to convert us, and give faith in Jesus Christ, and the new nature. 'Tis a work of creation: *If any man be in Christ, he is a new creature,* (2 Cor. 5:17). *We are created in Christ Jesus,* (Eph. 2:10.) The fallen creature can't attain to true holiness, but by being created again. Eph. 4: 24, *And that ye put on the new man, which after God is created in righteousness and true holiness.* 'Tis a raising from the dead. Cols. 2:12–13, *Wherein also ye are risen with him through the faith of the operation of God, who hath raised him from the dead.* Yea, 'tis a more glorious work of power than mere creation, or raising a dead body to life, in that the effect attained is greater and more excellent. That holy and happy being, and spiritual life which is reached in the work of conversion, is a far greater, and more glorious effect, than mere being and life. And the state from whence the change is made, of such a death in sin, and total corruption of nature, and depth of misery, is far more remote from the state attained, than mere death or non-entity.

'Tis by God's power also that we are preserved in a state of grace. 1 Pet. 1:5. *Who are kept by the power of God through faith unto salvation.* As grace is at first from God, so 'tis continually from him, and is maintained by him, as much as light in the atmosphere is all day long from the sun, as well as at first dawning, or at sun-rising.

Men are dependent on the power of God, for every exercise of grace, and for carrying on that work in the heart, for subduing of sin and corruption, and increasing holy principles, and enabling to bring forth fruit in good works, and at last bringing grace to its perfection, in making the soul completely amiable in Christ's glorious likeness, and filling of it with a satisfying joy and blessedness; and for the raising of the body to life, and to such a perfect state, that it shall be suitable for an habitation and organ for a soul so perfected and blessed. These are the most glorious effects of the power of God, that are seen in the series of God's acts with respect to the creatures.

Man was dependent on the power of God in his first estate, but he is more dependent on his power now; he needs God's power to do more things for him, and depends on a more wonderful exercise of his power. It was an effect of the power of God to make man holy at the first; but more remarkably so now, because there is a great deal of opposition and difficulty in the way. 'Tis a more glorious effect of power to make that holy that was so depraved and under the dominion of sin, than to confer holiness on that which before had nothing of the contrary. 'Tis a more glorious work of power to rescue a soul out of the hands of the devil, and from the powers of darkness, and to bring it into a state of salvation, than to confer holiness where there was no prepossession or opposition. Luke 11:21–22, *When a strong man armed keepeth his palace, his goods are in peace: but when a stronger than he shall come upon him, and overcome him, he taketh from him all his armor wherein he trusted, and divideth his spoils.* So 'tis a more glorious work of power to uphold a soul in a state of grace and holiness, and to carry it on till it is brought to glory, when there is so much sin remaining in the heart, resisting, and Satan with all his might opposing, than it would have been to have kept man from falling at first, when Satan had nothing in man.

Thus we have shown how the redeemed are dependent on God for all their good as they have all *of* him.

*Second.* They are also dependent on God for all, as they have all *through* him. 'Tis God that is the medium of it, as well as the author and fountain of it. All we have, wisdom, and the pardon of sin, deliverance from hell, acceptance into God's favor, grace and holiness, true comfort and happiness, eternal life and glory, we have from God by a mediator; and this mediator is God; which mediator we have an absolute dependence upon, as he *through* whom we receive all. So that here is another way wherein we have our dependence on God for all good. God not only gives us the mediator, and accepts his mediation, and of his power and grace bestows the things purchased by the mediator, but he the mediator.

Our blessings are what we have by purchase; and the purchase is made of God, the blessings are purchased of him, and God gives the purchaser; and not only so but God is the purchaser. Yea, God is both the purchaser and the price; for Christ, who is God, purchased these blessings for us, by offering up himself as the price of our salvation. He purchased eternal life by the sacrifice of himself. Heb. 7:27, *He offered up himself.* And 9:26, *He hath appeared to take away sin by the sacrifice of himself.* Indeed it was the human nature that was offered; but it was the same person with the divine, and therefore was an infinite price: it was looked upon as if God had been offered in sacrifice.

As we thus have our good *through* God, we have a dependence on God in a respect that man in his first estate had not. Man was to have eternal life then through his own righteousness; so that he had partly a dependence upon what was in himself; for we have a dependence upon that *through* which we have our good, as well as that *from* which we have it: and though man's righteousness that he then depended on was indeed from God, yet it was his own, it was inherent in himself; so that his dependence was not so immediately on God. But now the righteousness that we are dependent on is not in ourselves, but in God. We are saved through the righteousness of Christ: he is made unto us righteousness; and therefore is prophesied of, Jer. 23:6, under that name of *the Lord our righteousness.* In that the righteousness we are justified by is the righteousness of Christ, it is the righteousness of God. 2 Cor. 5:21, *That we might be made the righteousness of God in him.*

Thus in redemption, we han't only all things *of* God, but *by* and *through* him. 1 Cor. 8:6, *But to us there is but one God, the Father, of whom are all things, and we in him; and one Lord Jesus Christ, by whom are all things, and we by him.*

*Third.* The redeemed have all their good *in* God. We not only have it *of* him and *through* him, but it consists *in* him; he *is* all our good.

The good of the redeemed is either objective or inherent. By their objective good I mean, that extrinsic object, in the possession and enjoyment of which they are happy. Their inherent good is that excellency or pleasure which is in the soul itself. With respect to both of which the redeemed have all their good in God, or which is the same thing, God himself is all their good.

1. The redeemed have all their *objective* good in God. God himself is the great good which they are brought to the possession and enjoyment of by redemption. He is the highest good, and the sum of all that good which Christ purchased. God is the inheritance of the saints; he is the portion of their souls. God is their wealth and treasure, their food, their life, their dwelling place, their ornament and diadem, and their everlasting honor and glory. They have none in heaven but God; he is the great good which the redeemed are received to at death, and which they are to rise to at the end of the world. The Lord God, he is the light of the heavenly Jerusalem; and is the *river of the water of life* that runs, and the tree of life that grows, *in the midst of the paradise of God.* [Rev. 2:7] The glorious excellencies and beauty of God will be what will forever entertain the minds of the saints, and the love of God will be their everlasting feast. The redeemed will indeed enjoy other things; they will enjoy the angels, and will enjoy one another; but that which they shall enjoy in the angels, or each other, or in anything else whatsoever, that will yield them delight and happiness, will be what will be seen of God in them.

2. The redeemed have all their *inherent* good in God. Inherent good is

twofold; 'tis either *excellency* or *pleasure*. These the redeemed not only derive from God, as caused by him, but have them in him. They have spiritual excellency and joy by a kind of participation of God. They are made excellent by a communication of God's excellency: God puts his own beauty, i.e. his beautiful likeness upon their souls: they are made *partakers of the divine nature*, or moral image of God, (2 Pet. I. 4). They are holy by being made partakers of God's holiness, (Heb. 12. 10). The saints are beautiful and blessed by a communication of God's holiness and joy as the moon and planets are bright by the sun's light. The saint hath spiritual joy and pleasure by a kind of effusion of God on the soul. In these things the redeemed have communion with God; that is, they partake with him and of him.

The saints have both their spiritual excellency and blessedness by the gift of the Holy Ghost or Spirit of God, and his dwelling with them. They are not only caused by the Holy Ghost, but are the Holy Ghost as their principle. The Holy Spirit becoming an inhabitant, is a vital principle in the soul: he acting in, upon and with the soul, becomes a fountain of true holiness and joy, as a spring is of water, by the exertion and diffusion of itself. John 4:14, *But whosoever drinketh of the water that I shall give him, shall never thirst; but the water that I shall give him shall be in him a well of water springing up into everlasting life.* Compared with chap. 7:38–39, *He that believeth on me, as the scripture hath said, out of his belly shall flow rivers of living water.* But this spake he of the Spirit, which they that believe on him should receive. The sum of what Christ has purchased for us, is that spring of water spoken of in the former of those places, and those rivers of living water spoken of in the latter. And the sum of the blessings, which the redeemed shall receive in heaven, is that *river of water of life,* that proceeds from the throne of God and the Lamb. (Rev. 22:1) Which doubtless signifies the same with those rivers of living water, explained, John 7:38–39, which is elsewhere called the *river of God's pleasures.* Herein consists the fullness of good, which the saints receive of Christ. 'Tis by partaking of the Holy Spirit, that they have communion with Christ in his fullness. God hath given the Spirit, not by measure unto him; and they do receive of his fullness, and grace for grace. This is the sum of the saints' inheritance: and therefore that little of the Holy Ghost which believers have in this world, is said to be the earnest of their inheritance. 2 Cor. 1:22, *Who hath also sealed us, and given us the earnest of the spirit in our hearts.* And ch. 5:5, *Now he that hath wrought us for the self same thing is God, who also hath given unto us the earnest of the Spirit.* And Eph. 1:13–14, *Ye were sealed with that Holy Spirit of promise, which is the earnest of our inheritance, until the redemption of the purchased possession.*

The Holy Spirit and good things are spoken of in Scripture as the same; as if the Spirit of God communicated to the soul, comprised all good things. Matt. 7:11, *How much more shall your heavenly Father give good things to them that ask him?* In Luke it is, ch. 11: 13, *How much more shall your heavenly Father give the Holy spirit to them that ask him?* This is the sum of the blessings that Christ died to procure, and that are the subject of gospel promises. Gal. 3:13–14, *He was made a curse for us, that we might receive the promise of the Spirit through faith.* The Spirit of God is the great promise of the Father, Luke 24:49, *Behold, I send the promise of my father upon you.* The Spirit of God therefore is called *the Spirit of promise,* (Eph. 1:33). This promised thing Christ received, and had given into his hand, as soon as he had finished the work of our redemption, to bestow on all that he had redeemed. Acts 2:13, *Therefore being by the right hand of God exalted, and having received of the Father the promise of the Holy Ghost, he hath shed forth this, which ye both see and hear.* So that all the holiness and happiness of the redeemed is *in* God. 'Tis in the communications, indwelling and acting of the Spirit of God. Holiness and happiness is in the fruit, here and hereafter, because God dwells in them, and they in God.

Thus 'tis God has given us the Redeemer, and 'tis of him that our good is purchased: so 'tis God is the Redeemer, and the price: and 'tis God also that is the good purchased. So that all that we have is *of* God, and *through* him, and *in* him. Rom. 11: 36, *For of him, and through him, and to him* (or *in* him) *are all things:* the same in the Greek that is here rendered *to him,* is rendered in him. (1 Cor. 8:6)

II. God is glorified in the work of redemption by this means, viz. by there being so great and universal a dependence of the redeemed on him.

*First.* Man hath so much the greater occasion and obligation to notice and acknowledge God's perfections and all-sufficiency. The greater the creature's dependence is on God's perfections, and the greater concern he has with them, so much the greater occasion has he to take notice of them. So much the greater concern anyone has with and dependence upon the power and grace of God, so much the greater occasion has he to take notice of that power and grace. So much the greater and more immediate dependence there is on the divine holiness, so much the greater occasion to take notice of and acknowledge that. So much the greater and more absolute dependence we have on the divine perfections, as belonging to the several persons of the Trinity, so much the greater occasion have we to observe and own the divine glory of each of them. That which we are most concerned with, is surely most in the way of our observation and notice; and this kind of concern with anything, viz. dependence, does especially tend to commend and oblige the attention and observation. Those things that we are not much dependent upon, 'tis easy to neglect; but we can scarce do any other than mind that which we have a great dependence on. By reason of our so great dependence on God, and his perfections, and in so many respects; he and his glory are the more directly set in our view, which way soever we turn our eyes.

We have the greater occasion to take notice of God's all-sufficiency, when all our sufficiency is thus every way of him. We have the more occasion to contemplate him as an infinite good, and as the fountain of all good. Such a dependence on God *demonstrates* God's all-sufficiency. So much as the dependence of the creature is on God, so much the greater does the creature's emptiness in himself appear to be: and so much the greater the creature's emptiness, so much the greater must the fullness of the Being be, who supplies him. Our having all *of* God, shows the fullness of his power and grace: our having all *through* him, shows the fullness of his merit and worthiness; and our having all *in* him demonstrates his fullness of beauty, love, and happiness.

And the redeemed, by reason of the greatness of their dependence on God, han't only so much the greater occasion, but obligation to contemplate and acknowledge the glory and fullness of God. How unreasonable and ungrateful should we be, if we did not acknowledge that sufficiency and glory, that we do absolutely, immediately and universally depend upon?

*Second.* Hereby is demonstrated how great God's glory is considered comparatively, or as compared with the creature's. By the creature's being thus wholly and universally dependent on God, it appears that the creature is nothing, and that God is all. Hereby it appears that God is infinitely above us; that God's strength, and wisdom, and holiness are infinitely greater than ours. However great and glorious the creature apprehends God to be, yet if he be not sensible of the difference between God and him, so as to see that God's glory is great compared with his own, he will not be disposed to give God the glory due to his name. If the creature in any respects sets himself upon a level with God, or exalts himself to any competition with him, however he may apprehend that great honor and profound respect may belong to God from those that are more inferior, and at a greater distance, he will not be so sensible of its being due from him. So much the more men exalt themselves, so much the less will they surely be disposed to exalt God. 'Tis certainly a thing that the affair of God aims at in the disposition of things in redemption (if we allow the Scriptures to be a revelation of God's mind,) that God should appear full, and man in himself empty, that God should appear all, and man nothing. 'Tis God's declared design that others should not "glory in his presence," which implies that 'tis his design to advance his own comparative glory. So much the more man "glories in God's presence," so much the less glory is ascribed to God.

*Third.* By its being thus ordered, that the creature should have so absolute and universal a dependence on God, provision is made that God should have our whole souls, and should be the object of our undivided respect. If we had our dependence partly on God, and partly on something else, man's respect would be divided to those different things on which he had dependence. Thus it would be if we depended on God only for a part of our good, and on ourselves, or some other being, for another part; or if we had our good only *from* God, and *through* another that was not God, and *in* something else distinct from both, our hearts would be divided between the good itself, and him *from* whom, and him *through* whom we received it. But now there is no occasion for this, God being not only he *from* or *of* whom we have all good, but also *through* whom, and is that good itself, that we have from him one that, and through him. So that whatsoever there is to attract our respect, the tendency is still directly towards God, all unites in him as the center.

## USE

I. We may here observe the marvelous wisdom of God, in the work of redemption. God hath made man's emptiness and misery, his low, lost and ruined state into which he is sunk by the fall, an occasion of the greater advancement of his own glory, as in other ways so particularly in this, that there is now a much more universal and apparent dependence of man on God. Though God be pleased to lift man out of that dismal abyss of sin and woe into which he has fallen, and exceedingly to exalt him in excellency and honor, and to an high pitch of glory and blessedness, yet the creature hath nothing in any respect to glory of; all the glory evidently belongs to God, all is in a mere, and most absolute and divine dependence on the Father, Son, and Holy Ghost.

And each person of the Trinity is equally glorified in this work: there is an absolute dependence of the creature on every one for all: all is *of* the Father, all *through* the Son, and all *in* the Holy Ghost. Thus God appears in the work of redemption as "all in all." 'Tis fit that he that is, and there is none else, should be the Alpha and Omega, the first and the last, the all and the only, in this work.

II. Hence those doctrines and schemes of divinity that are in any respect opposite to such an absolute, and universal dependence on God, do derogate from God's glory, and thwart the design of the continuance for our redemption. Those schemes that put the creature in God's stead, in any of the mentioned respects, that exalt man into the place of either Father, Son, or Holy Ghost, in anything pertaining to our redemption; that however they may allow of a dependence of the redeemed on God, yet deny a dependence that is so absolute and universal; that own an entire dependence on God for some things, but not for others; that own that we depend on God for the gift and acceptance of a Redeemer, but deny so absolute a dependence on him for the obtaining of an interest in the Redeemer; that own an absolute dependence on the Father for giving his Son, and on the Son for working out redemption, but not so entire a dependence on the Holy Ghost for conversion, and a being in Christ, and so coming to a title to his benefits; that own a dependence on God for means of grace, but not absolutely for the benefit and success of those means; that own a partial dependence on the power of God, for the obtaining and exercising holiness, but not a mere dependence on the arbitrary and sovereign grace of God; that own a dependence on the free grace of God for a reception into his favor, so far that it is without any proper merit, but not as it is without being attracted, or moved with any excellency; that own a partial dependence on Christ, as he through whom we have life, as having purchased new terms of life, but still hold that the righteousness through which we have life is inherent in ourselves, as it was under the first covenant: and whatever other way any scheme is inconsistent with our entire dependence on God for all, and is each of those ways, and of having all *of* him, *through* him, and *in* him, it is repugnant to the design and tenor of the gospel, and robs it of that which God accounts its luster and glory.

III. Hence we may learn a reason why faith is that by which we come to have an interest in his redemption; for there is included in the nature of faith, a sensibleness, and acknowledgment of this absolute dependence on God in this affair. 'Tis very fit that it should be required of all, in order to their having the benefit of this redemption, that they should be sensible of, and acknowledge the dependence on God for it. 'Tis by this means that God hath contrived to glorify himself in redemption, and 'tis fit that God should at least have this glory of those that are the subjects of this redemption; and have the benefit of it.

Faith is a sensibleness of what is real in the work of redemption; and as we do really wholly depend on God, so the soul that believes doth entirely depend on God for all salvation, in its own sense, and act. Faith abases men, and exalts God; it gives all the glory of redemption to God alone. It is necessary in order to saving faith, that man should be emptied of himself, that he should be sensible that he is "wretched, and miserable, and poor, and blind, and naked." Humility is a great ingredient of true faith: he that truly receives redemption receives it "as a little child." Mark 10:15, *Whosoever shall not receive the kingdom of heaven as a little child, he shall not enter therein.* 'Tis the delight of a believing soul to abase itself and exalt God alone: that is the language of it. Ps. 115:1, *Not unto us, O Lord, not unto us, but to thy name give glory.*

IV. Let us be exhorted to exalt God alone, and ascribe to him all the glory of redemption. Let us endeavor to obtain, and increase in, a sensibleness of our great dependence on God, to have our eye to him alone, to mortify a self-dependent, and self-righteous disposition. Man is naturally exceeding prone to exalt himself, and depending on his own power or goodness; as though he were he from whom he must expect happiness, and to have respect to enjoyments alien from God and his Spirit, as those in which happiness is to be found.

And this doctrine should teach us to exalt God alone as by trust and reliance, so by praise. "Let him that glories, glory in the Lord." Hath any man hope that he is converted, and sanctified, and that his mind is endowed with true excellency and spiritual beauty, and his sins forgiven, and he received into God's favor, and exalted to the honor and blessedness of being his child, and an heir of eternal life; let him give God all the glory; who alone makes him to differ from the worst of men in this world, or the miserablest of the damned in hell. Hath any man much comfort and strong hope of enternal life, let not his hope lift him up, but dispose him the more to abase himself, and reflect on his own exceeding unworthiness of such a favor, and to exalt God alone. Is any man eminent in holiness, and abundant in good works, let him take nothing of the glory of it to himself, but ascribe it to him whose "workmanship we are, created in Christ Jesus unto good works."

# A DIVINE AND SUPERNATURAL LIGHT

(Boston, 1734)

Immediately imparted to the Soul by the Spirit of God,
Shown to be both a Scriptural, and Rational
Doctrine;

In a Sermon Preach'd at Northampton,
And Published at the Desire of some of the Hearers.

> Job 28. 20.—*Whence then cometh wisdom? and where is the place of understanding?*
> Prov. 2. 6. *The LORD giveth wisdom.*
> Isa. 42. 18. *Look ye blind that ye may see.*
> 2 Pet. 1. 19.—*Until the day dawn and the day-star arise in your hearts.*

## THE PREFACE.

I am sensible that my consenting that the following discourse of mine should be published, needs excuse; but yet don't think it worth the while for me, here, to excuse my self, by declaring how backward I was to it, and how much I was urged, and that I was prevail'd with to do it, more to gratify others, and from an aim at promoting the interest of religion, and the good of souls, than by any thought I had of any honour that I should get by it: for such things, I apprehend, ordinarily make less impresson upon the readers, to alter their thought of the author, and his design, than the authors generally think for. They at whose desire, and upon whose account chiefly, this sermon is printed, are already acquainted with the circumstances of the matter; and if any others should happen to see it, and should think it worth their while to read it, I shall only desire of them, that they would put as favourable a construction upon my herein appearing in print, as they can; and that they would read the following discourse with candour, and without prejudice against it, either from an idea of the author's forwardness and ostentation, or the unfashionableness of the subject. As to you, that are the people of the flock, of which Christ hath called me to the oversight, I have no reason to be jealous that you will have any prejudice against this discourse, upon either of those mention'd accounts, to stand in the way of your duly weighing, and considering, and suitably entertaining the things treated of in it. I have reason to bless God, that there is a more happy union between us, than that you should be prejudiced against any thing of mine, because 'tis mine; and however the subject is out of mode in the world, 'tis doubtless your peculiar happiness, that you have been so thoroughly instructed in such like doctrines, even from your beginning: and I rejoice in it, that Providence, in this day of corruption and confusion, has cast my lot where such doctrines, that I look upon so much the life and glory of the Gospel, are not only own'd, but where there are so many, in whom the truth of them is so apparently manifest, in their experience, that any one who has had the opportunity of acquaintance with them in such matters, that I have had, must be very unreasonable to doubt of it. It is pleasant to me to read discourses on such subjects, and to see such doctrines well treated of in books, but much more pleasant, to see them clearly exemplified. If what is here offered to you, shall be a means further to establish you in such truths, and to make those among you, that yet remain in spiritual darkness and blindness, sensible of their misery, and stir them up earnestly to seek after this spiritual and divine illumination; and shall be for the comfort and edification of those that have experienced it, I shall have great reason to rejoice, and be thankful: and I desire your earnest and continual prayers for me, that I may be the instrument of much such good to you, and glory to God therein.

J.E.

## THE REALITY OF SPIRITUAL LIGHT

MATTHEW 16. 17.

*And Jesus answered and said unto him, blessed art thou* Simon
Barjona: *for flesh and blood hath not revealed it unto thee, but
my Father which is in heaven.*

CHRIST says these words to Peter, upon occasion of his professing his
faith in him as the Son of God. Our Lord was enquiring of his disciples,
who men said he was; not that he needed to be informed, but only to
introduce and give occasion to what follows. They answer, that some said
he was John the Baptist, and some Elias, and others Jeremias or one of
the Prophets. When they had thus given an account, who others said he
was, Christ asks them, who they said he was. Simon Peter, whom we find
always zealous and forward, was the first to answer; he readily replied to
the question, *Thou art Christ, the Son of the living God.*

Upon this occasion Christ says as he does to him and of him in the
text: in which we may observe,

1. That Peter is pronounced blessed on this account. *Blessed art thou*—
"Thou art a happy man, that thou art not ignorant of this, that I am
Christ the Son of the living God. Thou art distinguishingly happy.
Others are blinded, and have dark and deluded apprehensions, as you
have now given an account, some thinking that I am Elias, and some that
I am Jeremias, and some one thing, and some another; but none of them
thinking right, all of them misled. Happy art thou, that art so
distinguished as to know the truth in this matter."

2. The evidence of this his happiness declared; *viz.* that God and he
only had revealed it to him. This is an evidence of his being blessed.

First, as it shows how peculiarly favoured he was of God, above others.
*q. d.* "How highly favored art thou, that others, that are wise and great men,
the scribes, Pharisees, and rulers, and the nation in general, are left in
darkness, to follow their own misguided apprehensions, and that thou
should'st be singled out, as it were by name, that my heavenly father should
thus set his love on thee Simon Bar-jona. This argues thee blessed, that thou
should'st thus be the object of God's distinguishing love."

Secondly, it evidences his blessedness also, as it intimates that this
knowledge is above any that flesh and blood can reveal. "This is such
knowledge as my Father which is in heaven only can give: it is too high
and excellent to be communicated by such means as other knowledge is.
Thou art blessed, that thou knowest that which God alone can teach thee."

The original of this knowledge is here declared; both negatively and
positively. Positively, as God is here declared the author of it. Negatively,
as 'tis declared that flesh and blood had not revealed it. God is the author

of all knowledge and understanding whatsoever: He is the author of the knowledge, that is obtained by human learning: He is the author of all moral prudence, and of the knowledge and skill that men have in their secular business. Thus it is said of all in Israel that were wise-hearted, and skill'd in embroidering, that God had fill'd them with the spirit of Wisdom. Exod. 28. 3.

God is the author of such knowledge; but yet not so but that flesh and blood reveals it. Mortal men are capable of imparting the knowledge of human arts and sciences, and skill in temporal affairs. God is the author of such knowledge by those means: flesh and blood is made use of by God as the mediate or second cause of it; he conveys it by the power and influence of natural means. But this spiritual knowledge, spoken of in the text, is what God is the author of, and none else: he reveals it and flesh and blood reveals it not. He imparts this knowledge immediately, not making use of any intermediate natural causes, as he does in other knowledge.

What had passed in the preceeding discourse, naturally occasioned Christ to observe this; because the disciples had been telling how others did not know him, but were generally mistaken about him, and divided and confounded in their opinions of him: but Peter had declared his assured faith that he was the Son of God. Now it was natural to observe, how it was not flesh and blood, that had revealed it to him, but God; for if this knowledge were dependent on natural causes or means, how came it to pass that they, a company of poor fishermen, illiterate men, and persons of low education, attain'd to the knowledge of the truth; while the scribes and Pharisees, men of vastly higher advantages, and greater knowledge and sagacity in other matters, remain'd in ignorance? This could be owing only to the gracious distinguishing influence and revelation of the Spirit of God. Hence, what I would make the subject of my present discourse from these words, is this

## DOCTRINE, VIZ.

*That there is such a thing, as a spiritual and divine light, immediately imparted to the soul by God, of a different nature from any that is obtain'd by natural means.*

In what I say on this subject at this time, I would

I. Show what this divine light is.

II. How it is given immediately by God, and not obtain'd by natural means.

III. Show the truth of the doctrine.

And then conclude with a brief improvement.

I. I would show what this spiritual and divine light is. And in order to it would shew,

First, in a few things what it is not. And here,

1. Those convictions that natural men may have of their sin and misery is not this spiritual and divine light. Men in a natural condition may have convictions of the guilt that lies upon them, and of the anger of God, and their danger of divine vengeance. Such convictions are from light or sensibleness of truth: that some sinners have a greater conviction of their guilt and misery than others, is because some have more light, or more of an apprehension of truth, than others. And this light and conviction may be from the spirit of God; the spirit convinces men of sin: but yet nature is much more concern'd in it than in the communication of that spiritual and divine light, that is spoken of in the doctrine; 'tis from the spirit of God only as assisting natural principles, and not as infusing any new principles. Common grace differs from special, in that it influences only by assisting of nature; and not by imparting grace, or bestowing any thing above nature. The light that is obtain'd, is wholly natural, or of no superior kind to what meer nature attains to; tho' more of that kind be obtained. than would be obtained if men were left wholly to themselves. or in other words, common grace only assists the faculties of the soul to do that more fully, which they do by nature, as natural conscience, or reason, will by meer nature make a man sensible of guilt, and will accuse and condemn him when he has done amiss. Conscience is a principle natural to men; and the work that it doth naturally, or of it self, is to give an apprehension of right and wrong; and to suggest to the mind the relation that there is between right and wrong and a retribution. The Spirit of God, in those convictions which unregenerate men sometimes have, assists conscience to do this work in a further degree, than it would do if they were left to themselves: He helps it against those things that tend to stupify it, and obstruct its exercise. But in the renewing and sanctifying work of the Holy Ghost, those things are wrought in the soul that are above nature; and of which there is nothing of the like kind in the soul by nature; and they are caused to exist in the soul habitually, & according to such a stated constitution or law, that lays such a foundation for exercises in a continued course as is called a principle of nature. Not only are remaining principles assisted to do their work more freely and fully, but those principles are restored that were utterly destroyed by the fall; and the mind thenceforward habitually exerts those acts that the dominion of sin had made it as wholly destitute of, as a dead body is of vital acts.

The Spirit of God acts in a very different manner in the one case, from what he doth in the other. He may indeed act upon the mind of a natural man; but he acts in the mind of a saint as an indwelling vital principle. He acts upon the mind of an unregenerate person as an extrinsick occasional agent; for in acting upon them, he doth not unite himself to them; for notwithstanding all his influences that they may be the subjects of, they are still sensual having not the spirit. Jude 19. But he unites himself with the mind of a saint, takes him for his temple, actuates and influences him as a new, supernatural principle of life and action. There is this difference; that the Spirit of God in acting in the soul of a godly man, exerts and communicates himself there in his own proper nature. Holiness is the proper nature of the Spirit of God. The HOLY SPIRIT operates in the minds of the godly, by uniting himself to them, and living in them, and exerting his own nature in the exercise of their faculties. The Spirit of God may act upon a creature, and yet not, in acting communicate himself. The Spirit of God may act upon inanimate creatures; as the spirit moved upon the face of the waters, in the beginning of the creation: So the spirit of God may act upon the minds of men, many ways, and communicate himself no more than when he acts upon an inanimate creature. For instance: he may excite thoughts in them, may assist their natural reason and understanding, or may assist other natural principles, and this without any union with the soul, but may act, as it were, as upon an external object. But as he acts in his holy influences, and spiritual operations, he acts in a way of peculiar communication of himself; so that the subject is thence denominated spiritual.

2. This spiritual and divine light doth consist in any impression made upon the imagination. 'Tis no impression upon the mind, as tho' one saw any thing with the bodily eyes: 'tis is no imagination or idea of an outward light or glory, or any beauty of form or countenance, or a visible lustre or brightness of any object. The imagination may be strongly impress'd with such things; but this is not spiritual light. Indeed when the mind has a lively discovery of spiritual things, and is greatly affected by the power of divine light, it may, and probably very commonly doth, much affect the imagination; so that impressions of an outward beauty or brightness, may accompany those spiritual discoveries. But spiritual light is not that impression upon the imagination, but an exceeding different thing from it. Natural men may have lively impressions on their imaginations; and we can't determine but that the devil, who transforms himself into an angel of light, may cause imaginations of an outward beauty, or visible glory, and of sounds and speeches, and other such things; but these are things of a vastly inferior nature to spiritual light.

3. This spiritual light is not the suggesting of any new truths, or propositions not contain'd in the word of God. This suggesting of new

truths or doctrines to the mind, independent of any antecedent revelation of those propositions, either in word or writing, is inspiration; such as the Prophets and Apostles had, and such as some enthusiasts pretend to. But this spiritual light that I am speaking of, is quite a different thing from inspiration: It reveals no new doctrine, it suggests no new proposition to the mind, it teaches no new thing of God, or Christ, or another world, not taught in the Bible; but only gives a due apprehension of those things that are taught in the word of God.

4. 'Tis not every affecting view that men have of the things of religion, that is this spiritual and divine light. Men by meer principles of nature are capable of being affected with things that have a special relation to religion, as well as other things. A person by meer nature, for instance, may be liable to be affected with the story of JESUS Christ, and the sufferings he underwent, as well as by any other tragical story: He may be the more affected with it from the interest he conceives mankind to have in it: Yea he may be affected with it without believing it; as well as a man may be affected with what he reads in a romance, or see's acted in a stag-play. He may be affected with a lively and eloquent description of many pleasant things that attend the state of the blessed in heaven; as well as his imagination be entertain'd by romantick description of the pleasantness of fairy land, or the like. And that common belief of the truth of the things of religion, that persons may have from education, or otherwise, may help forward their affection. We read in Scripture of many that were greatly affected with things of a religious nature, who yet are there represented as wholly graceless, and many of them very ill men. A person therefore may have affecting views of the things of religion, and yet be very destitute of spiritual light. Flesh and blood may be the author of this: one man may give another an affecting view of divine things with but common assistance; but God alone can give a spiritual discovery of them.

But I proceed to show,

Secondly, positively what this spiritual and divine light is.

And it may be thus described, a true sense of the divine excellency of the things revealed in the word of God, and a conviction of the truth and reality of them, thence arising.

This spiritual light primarily consists in the former of these, viz. a real sense and apprehension of the divine excellency of things revealed in the Word of God. A spiritual and saving conviction of the truth and reality of these things, arises from such a sight of their divine excellency and glory; so that this conviction of their truth is an effect and natural consequence of this sight of their divine glory. There is therefore in this spiritual light,

1. A true sense of the divine and superlative excellency of the things of

religion; a real sense of the excellency of God, and Jesus Christ, and of the work of redemption, and the ways and works of God revealed in the Gospel. There is a divine and superlative glory in these things; an excellency that is of a vastly higher kind, and more sublime nature, than in other things; a glory greatly distinguishing them from all that is earthly and temporal. He that is spiritually enlightened truly apprehends and sees it, or has a sense of it. He don't meerly rationally believe that God is glorious, but he has a sense of the gloriousness of God in his heart. There is not only a rational belief that God is holy, and that holiness is a good thing; but there is a sense of the loveliness of God's holiness. There is not only a speculatively judging that God is gracious, but a sense how amiable God is upon that account; or a sense of the beauty of this divine attribute.

There is a twofold understanding or knowledge of good, that God has made the mind of man capable of. The first, that which is meerly speculative or notional; as when a person only speculatively judged, that any thing is, which by the agreement of mankind, is called good or excellent, viz. that which is most to general advantage, and between which and a reward there is a suitableness; and the like. And the other is that which consists in the sense of the heart: as when there is a sense of the beauty, amiableness, or sweetness of a thing; so that the heart is sensible of pleasure and delight in the presence of the idea of it. In the former is exercised meerly the speculative faculty, or the understanding strictly so called, or as spoken of, in distinction from the will or disposition of the soul. In the latter will, or inclination, or heart, are mainly concern'd.

Thus there is a difference between having an opinion that God is holy and gracious, and having a sense of the loveliness and beauty of that holiness and grace. There is a difference between having a rational judgment that honey is sweet, and having a sense of its sweetness. A man may have the former, that knows not how honey tasts; but a man can't have the latter, unless he has an idea of the tast of honey in his mind. So there is a difference between believing that a person is beautiful, and having a sense of his beauty. The former may be obtain'd by hear-say, but the latter only by seeing the countenance. There is a wide difference between meer speculative, rational judging any thing to be excellent, and having a sense of its sweetness, and beauty. The former rests only in the head, speculation only is concern'd in it; but the heart is concern'd in the latter. When the heart is sensible of the beauty and amiableness of a thing, it necessarily feels pleasure in the apprehension. It is implied in a persons being heartily sensible of the loveliness of a thing, that the idea of it is sweet and pleasant to his soul; which is a far different thing from having a rational opinion that it is excellent.

2. There arises from this sense of the divine excellency of things contain'd in the word of God, a conviction of the truth and reality of them: and that either indirectly, or directly.

First, indirectly, and that two ways.

1. As the prejudices that are in the heart, against the truth of divine things, are hereby removed; so that the mind becomes susceptive of the due force of rational arguments for their truth. The mind of man is naturally full of prejudices against the truth of divine things. It is full of enmity against the doctrines of the Gospel; which is a disadvantage to those arguments that prove their truth, and causes them to lose their force upon the mind. But when a person has discovered to him the divine excellency of Christian doctrines, this destroys the enmity, removes those prejudices, sanctifys the reason, and causes it to lie open to the force of arguments for their truth.

Hence was the different effect that Christ's miracles had to convince the disciples, from what they had to convince the scribes and Pharisees. Not that they had a stronger reason, or had their reason more improved; but their reason was sanctified, and those blinding prejudices, that the scribes and Pharisees were under, were removed by the sense they had of the excellency of Christ, and his doctrine.

2. It not only removes the hindrances of reason, but positively helps reason. It makes even the speculative notions the more lively. It engages the attention of the mind, with the more fixedness and intenseness to that kind of objects; which causes it to have a clearer view of them, and enables it more clearly to see their mutual relations, and occasions it to take more notice of them. The ideas themselves that otherwise are dim, and obscure, are by this means impress'd with the greater strength, and have a light cast upon them; so that the mind can better judge of them. As he that beholds the objects on the face of the earth, when the light of the sun is cast upon them, is under greater advantage to discern them in their true forms and mutual relations, than he that sees them in a dim star-light or twilight.

The mind having a sensibleness of the excellency of divine objects, dwells upon them with delight; and the powers of the soul are more awaken'd and enliven'd to employ themselves in the contemplation of them, and exert themselves more fully and much more to purpose. The beauty and sweetness of the objects draws on the faculties, and draws forth their exercises: so that reason it self is under far greater advantages for its proper and free exercises, and to attain its proper end, free of darkness and delusion. But,

Secondly, a true sense of the divine excellency of the things of God's word doth more directly and immediately convince of the truth of them; and that because the excellency of these things is so superlative. There is a beauty in them that is so divine and Godlike, that is greatly and evidently distinguishing of them from things meerly human, or that men are the inventors and authors of a glory so high and great, that when clearly seen, commands assent to their divine reality. When there is an actual and lively discovery of this beauty and excellency, it won't allow of any such thought as that it is a human work, or the fruit of mens invention. This evidence, that they, that are spiritually enlightened, have of the truth of the things of religion, is a kind of intuitive and immediate evidence. They believe the doctrines of God's word to be divine, because they see a divine, and transcendent, and most evidently distinguishing glory in them; such a glory as, if clearly seen, does not leave room to doubt of their being of God, and not of men.

Such a conviction of the truths of religion as this, arising, these ways, from a sense of the divine excellency of them, is that true spiritual conviction, that there is in saving faith. And this original of it, is that by which it is most essentially distinguished from that common assent, which unregenerate men are capable of.

II. I proceed now to the second thing proposed, viz. to show how this light is immediately given by God, and not obtained by natural means. And here,

1. 'Tis not intended that the natural faculties are not made use of in it. The natural faculties are the subject of this light; and they are the subject in such a manner, that they are not meerly passive, but active in it; the acts and exercises of man's understanding are concern'd and made use of in it. God in letting in this light into the soul, deals with man according to his nature, or as a rational creature; and makes use of his human faculties. But yet this light is not the less immediately from God for that; tho' the faculties are made use of, 'tis as the subject and not as the cause; and that acting of the faculties in it, is not the cause, but is either implied in the thing it self (in the light that is imparted) or is the consequence of it. As the use that we make of our eyes in beholding various objects, when the sun arises, is not the cause of the light that discovers those objects to us.

2. 'Tis not intended that outward means have no concern in this affair. As I have obsearved already, 'tis not in this affair, as it is in inspiration, where new truths are suggested: for here is by this light only given a due apprehension of the same truths that are revealed in the word of God; and therefore it is not given without the word. The Gospel is made use of in this affair: This light is the *light of the glorious Gospel of Christ* 2 Cor. 4. 4. The Gospel is as a glass, by which this light is conveyed to us. 1 Cor. 13. 12. *Now we see through a glass.*—But,

3. When it is said that this light is given immediately by God, and not obtained by natural means, hereby is intended, that 'tis given by God

without making use of any means that operate by their own power, or a natural force. God makes use of means; but 'tis not as mediate causes to produce this effect. There are not truly any second causes of it; but it is produced by God immediately. The Word of God is no proper cause of this effect: It don't operate by any natural force in it. The Word of God is only made use of to convey to the mind the subject matter of this saving instruction: and this indeed it doth convey to us by natural force or influence. It conveys to our minds these and those doctrines; it is the cause of the notion of them in our heads, but not of the sense of the divine excellency of them in our hearts. Indeed a person can't have spiritual light without the Word. But that does not argue, that the Word properly causes that light. The mind can't see the excellency of any doctrine, unless that doctrine be first in the mind; but the seeing the excellency of the doctrine may be immediately from the spirit of God; tho' the conveying of the doctrine or proposition it self may be by the word. So that the notions that are the subject-matter of this light, are conveyed to the mind by the Word of God; but that due sense of the heart, wherein this light formally consists, is immediately by the spirit of God. As for instance, that notion that there is a Christ, and that Christ is holy and gracious, is conveyed to the mind by the Word of God: but the sense of the excellency of Christ by reason of that holiness and grace, is nevertheless immediately the work of the Holy spirit.

I come now,

III. To show the truth of the doctrine; that is to show that there is such a thing as that spiritual light that has been described, thus immediately let into the mind by God. And here I would show briefly, that this doctrine is both scriptural, and rational.

First, 'tis scriptural. My text is not only full to the purpose, but 'tis a doctrine that the Scripture abounds in. We are there abundantly taught, that the saints differ from the ungodly in this, that they have the knowledge of God, and a sight of God, and of Jesus Christ. I shall mention but few texts of many: 1 John 3. 6. *Whosoever sinneth hath not seen him, nor known him.* 3 John 11. *He that doth good, is of God: but he that doth evil, hath not seen God.* John 14. 19. *The world seeth me no more; but ye see me.* John 17. 3. *And this is eternal life, that they might know thee, the only true God, and Jesus Christ whom thou hast sent.* This knowlege, or sight of God and Christ, can't be a meer speculative knowlege; because it is spoken of as a seeing and knowing, wherein they differ from the ungodly. And by these Scriptures it must not only be a different knowledge in degree and circumstances, and different in its effects; but it must be entirely different in nature and kind.

And this light and knowlege is always spoken of as immediately given of God: Mat. 11. 25, 26, 27. At that time Jesus answered and said,

*I thank thee, oh Father, Lord of heaven and earth, because thou hast hid these things from the wise and prudent, and hast revealed them unto babes; even so, father, for so it seemed good in thy sight. All things are delivered unto me of my Father: and no man knoweth the Father, save the Son, and he to whomsoever the Son will reveal him.* Here this effect is ascribed alone to the arbitrary operation, and gift of God, bestowing this knowlege on whom he will, and distinguishing those with it, that have the least natural advantage or means for knowlege, even babes, when it is denied to the wise and prudent. And the imparting the knowlege of God is here appropriated to the Son of God, as his sole prerogative. And again, 2 Cor. 4. 6. *For God who commanded the light to shine out of darkness, hath shined in our hearts, to give the light of the knowlege of the glory of God, in the face of Jesus Christ.* This plainly shows, that there is such a thing as a discovery of the divine superlative glory and excellency of God and Christ; and that peculiar to the saints; and also, that 'tis as immediately from God, as light from the sun: and that 'tis the immediate effect of his power and will; for 'tis compared to God's creating the light by his powerful word in the beginning of the creation; and is said to be by the Spirit of the Lord, in the eighteenth verse of the preceeding chapter. God is spoken of as giving the knowlege of Christ in conversion, as of what before was hidden and unseen in that, Gal. 1. 15, 16. *But when it pleased God, who separated me from my mother's womb, and called me by his grace, to reveal his Son in me.*—The Scripture also speaks plainly of such a knowledge of the word of God, as has been described, as the immediate gift of God; Ps. 119. 18. *Open thou mine eyes, that I may behold wondrous things out of thy law.* What could the Psalmist mean, when he begged of God to open his eyes? Was he ever blind? Might he not have resort to the Law and see every word and sentence in it when he pleased? And what could he mean by those wondrous things? Was it the wonderful stories of the creation, and deluge, and Israel's passing thro' the Red Sea, and the like? Were not his eyes open to read these strange things when he would? Doubtless by wondrous things in God's law, he had respect to those distinguishing and wonderful excellencies, and marvellous manifestations of the divine perfections, and glory, that there was in the commands and doctrines of the word, and those works and counsels of God that were there revealed. So the Scripture speaks of a knowlege of God's dispensation, and covenant of mercy, and way of grace towards his people, as peculiar to the saints, and given only by God, Ps. 25. 14. *The secret of the Lord is with them that fear him; and he will shew them his covenant.*

And that a true and saving belief of the truth of religion is that which arises from such a discovery, is also what the Scripture teaches. As John 6. 40. *And this is the will of him that sent me, that every one that seeth the Son, and believeth on him, may have everlasting life.* Where it is plain that a true faith is what arises from a spiritual sight of Christ. And, John 17. 6, 7, 8. *I have manifested thy name unto the men which thou gavest me out of the world.—Now they have known that all things whatsoever thou has given me, are of thee; for I have given unto them the words which thou gavest me, and they have received them, and known surely that I came out from thee, and they have believed that thou didst send me.* Where Christ's manifesting God's name to the disciples, or giving them the knowledge of God, was that whereby they knew that Christ's doctrine was of God, and that Christ himself was of him, proceeded from him, and was sent by him. Again John 12. 44, 45, 46, *Jesus cried and said, he that believeth on me, believeth not on me, but on him that sent me; and he that seeth me, seeth him that sent me. I am come a light into the world, that whosoever believeth on me should not abide in darkness.* There believing in Christ and spiritually seeing him, are spoken of as running parallel.

Christ condemns the Jews, that they did not know that he was the Messiah, and that his doctrine was true, from an inward distinguishing tast and relish of what was divine, in Luke 12. 56, 57. He having there blamed the Jews, that though they could discern the face of the sky and of the earth, and signs of the weather, that they could not discern those times; or as 'tis expressed in Matthew, the signs of those times; he adds, *yea, and why even of your own selves, judge ye not what is right?* i.e. without extrinsick signs. "Why have ye not that sense of true excellency, whereby ye may distinguish that which is holy and divine? Why have ye not that savour of the things of God, by which you may see the distinguishing glory, and evident divinity of me and my doctrine?"

The Apostle Peter mentions it as what gave them (the Apostles,) and his companions good and well-grounded assurance of the truth of the Gospel, that they had seen the divine glory of Christ. 2 Pet. 1. 16. *For we have not followed cunningly devised fables, when we made known unto you, the power and coming of our Lord Jesus Christ, but were eye-witnesses of his majesty.* The Apostle has respect to that visible glory of Christ which they saw in his transfiguration: That glory was so divine having such an ineffable appearance and semblance of divine holiness, majesty, and grace, that it evidently denoted him to be a divine person. But if a sight of Christ's outward glory might give a rational assurance of his divinity, why may not an apprehension of his spiritual glory do so too. Doubtless Christ's spiritual glory is in itself as distinguishing, and as plainly shewing his divinity, as his outward glory, and a great deal more: for his spiritual glory is that wherein his divinity consists; and the outward glory of his transfiguration shew'd him to be divine, only as it was a remarkable image or representation of that spiritual glory. Doubtless therefore he that has had a clear sight of the spiritual glory of Christ, may say, I have not followed cunningly devised fables, but have been an eye-witness of his majesty, upon as good grounds as the Apostle, when he had respect to the outward glory of Christ, that he had seen. But this brings me to what was proposed next, viz. to show that,

Secondly, this doctrine is rational.

1. 'Tis rational to suppose that there is really such an excellency in divine things, that is so transcendent and exceedingly different from what is in other things, that if it were seen, would most evidently distinguish them. We can't rationally doubt but that things that are divine, that appertain to the supreme Being, are vastly different from things that are human; that there is that Godlike, high, and glorious excellency in them, that does most remarkably difference them from the things that are of men; insomuch that if the difference were but seen, it would have a convincing, satisfying influence upon any one, that they are which they are, viz. *divine*. What reason can be offered against it? Unless we would argue that God is not remarkably distinguished in glory from men.

If Christ should now appear to any one, as he did on the Mount at his Transfiguration; or if he should appear to the world in the glory that he now appears in in heaven, as he will do at the day of judgment; without doubt, the glory and majesty that he would appear in, would be such as would satisfy every one, that he was a divine person, and that religion was true: and it would be a most reasonable, and well grounded conviction too. And why may there not be that stamp of divinity, or divine glory, on the word of God, on the scheme and doctrine of the Gospel, that may be in like manner distinguishing and as rationally convincing, provided it be but seen? 'Tis rational to suppose, that when God speaks to the world, there should be something in his Word or speech vastly different from men's word. Supposing that God never had spoken to the world, but we had notice that he was about to do it; that he was about to reveal himself from heaven, and speak to us immediately himself, in divine speeches or discourses, as it were from his own mouth, or that he should give us a book of his own inditing; after what manner should we expect that he would speak? Would it not be rational to suppose, that his speech would be exceeding different from men's speech, that he should speak like a God; that is, that there should be such an excellency and sublimity in his speech or word, such a stamp of wisdom, holiness, majesty, and other divine perfections, that the word of men, yea of the wisest of men, should appear mean and base in comparison of it? Doubtless it would be thought rational to expect this, and unreasonable to think otherwise. When a wise man speaks in the exercise of his wisdom, there is something in every thing he says, that is very distinguishable from the talk of a little child. So, without doubt, and much more, is the speech of God, if there be any such thing as the speech of God, to be distinguished from that of the wisest of men; agreeable to Jer. 23. 28, 29. God having there been reproving the false Prophets that prophesied in his name, and pretended that what they spake was his word, when indeed it was their own word, says, *The Prophet that hath a dream, let him tell a dream; and he that hath my word, let him speak my word faithfully: What is the chaff to the wheat? saith the Lord. Is not my word like as a fire, saith the Lord, and like a hammer that breaketh the rock in pieces?*

2. If there be such a distinguishing excellency in divine things; 'tis rational to suppose that there may be such a thing as seeing it. What should hinder but that it may be seen? 'Tis no argument, that there is no such thing as such a distinguishing excellency, or that, if there be, it can't be seen, that some don't see it, tho' they may be discerning men in temporal matters. It is not rational to suppose, if there be any such excellency in divine things, that wicked men should see it. 'Tis not rational to suppose, that those whose minds are full of spiritual pollution, and under the power of filthy lusts, should have any relish or sense of divine beauty, or excellency; or that their minds should be susceptive of that light that is in its own nature so pure and heavenly. It need not seem at all strange, that sin should so blind the mind, seeing that mens particular natural tempers and dispositions will so much blind them in secular matters; as when mens natural temper is melancholly, jealous, fearful, proud, or the like.

3. 'Tis rational to suppose that this knowledge should be given immediately by God, and not be obtain'd by natural means. Upon what account should it seem unreasonable, that there should be any immediate communication between God and the creature? 'Tis strange that men should make any matter of difficulty of it. Why should not he that made all things, still have something immediately to do with the things that he has made? Where lies the great difficulty, if we own the being of a God, and that he created all things out of nothing, of allowing some immediate influence of God on the creation still. And if it be reasonable to suppose it with respect to any part of the creation, 'tis especially so with respect to reasonable intelligent creatures; who are next to God in the gradation of the different orders of beings, and whose business is most immediately with God; who were made on purpose for those exercises that do respect God, and wherein they have nextly to do with God: for reason teaches that man was made to serve and glorify his Creator. And if it be rational to suppose that God immediately communicates himself to man in any affair, it is in this. 'Tis rational to suppose that God would reserve that knowledge and

wisdom, that is of such a divine and excellent nature, to be bestowed immediately by himself, and that it should not be left in the power of second causes. Spiritual wisdom and grace is the highest and most excellent gift that ever God bestows on any creature: in this the highest excellency and perfection of a rational creature consists. 'Tis also immensely the most important of all divine gifts: 'tis that wherein man's happiness consists, and on which his everlasting welfare depends. How rational is it to suppose that God, however he has left meaner goods and lower gifts to second causes, and in some sort in their power, yet should reserve this most excellent, divine, and important of all divine communications, in his own hands, to be bestowed immediately by himself, as a thing too great for second causes to be concern'd in? 'Tis rational to suppose that this blessing should be immediately from God; for there is no gift or benefit that is in itself so nearly related to the divine nature, there is nothing that the creature receives that is so much of God, of his Nature, so much a participation of the Deity: 'tis a kind of emanation of God's beauty, and is related to God as the light is to the sun. 'Tis therefore congruous and fit, that when it is given of God, it should be nextly from himself, and by himself, according to his own sovereign will.

'Tis rational to suppose, that it should be beyond man's power to obtain this knowledge, and light, by the meer strength of natural reason; for 'tis not a thing that belongs to reason, to see the beauty and loveliness of spiritual things; it is not a speculative thing, but depends on the sense of the heart. Reason indeed is necessary in order to it, as 'tis by reason only that we are become the subjects of the means of it; which means I have already shown to be necessary in order to it, though they have no proper causal influence in the affair. 'Tis by reason, that we become possessed of a notion of those doctrines that are the subject matter of this divine light; or knowledge; and reason may many ways be indirectly, and remotely an advantage to it. And reason has also to do in the acts that are immediately consequent on this discovery: far seeing the truth of religion from hence, is by reason; though it be but by one step, and the inference be immediate. So reason has to do in that accepting of, and trusting in Christ, that is consequent on it. But if we take reason strictly, not for the faculty of mental perception in general, but for ratiocination, or a power of inferring by arguments; I say if we take Reason thus, the perceiving of spiritual beauty and excellency no more belongs to reason, that it belongs to the sense of feeling to perceive colours, or to the power of seeing to perceive the sweetness of food. It is out of reason's province to perceive the beauty or loveliness of any thing: such a perception don't belong to that faculty. Reason's work is to perceive truth and not excellency. 'Tis not ratiociation that gives men the perception of the beauty and amiableness of a countenance; tho' it may be many ways indirectly an advantage to it; yet 'tis is no more reason that immediately perceives it, than it is reason that perceives the sweetness of honey: it depends on the sense of the heart. Reason may determine that a countenance is beautiful to others, it may determine that honey is sweet to others; but it will never give me a perception of its sweetness.

I will conclude with a very brief improvement of what has been said.

First. This doctrine may lead us to reflect on the goodness of God, that has so ordered it, that a saving evidence of the truth of the Gospel is such, as it is attainable by persons of mean capacities, and advantages, as well as those that are of the greatest parts and learning. If the evidence of the Gospel depended only on history, and such reasonings as learned men only are capable of, it would be above the reach of far the greatest part of mankind. But persons, with but an ordinary degree of knowlege, are capable without a long and subtil train of reasoning, to see the divine excellency of the things of religion: they are capable of being taught by the spirit of God, as well as learned men. The evidence that is this way obtained, is vastly better and more satisfying, than all that can be obtain'd by the arguings of those that are most learned, and greatest masters of reason. And babes are as capable of knowing these things, as the wise and prudent; and they are often hid from these, when they are revealed to those. 1 Cor. 1. 26, 27. *For ye see your calling brethren, how that not many wise men after the flesh, not many mighty, not many noble are called. But God hath chosen the foolish things of the world—.*

Secondly. This doctrine may well put us upon examining our selves, whether we have ever had this divine light, that has been desribed, let into our souls. If there be such a thing indeed, and it ben't only a notion, or whimsy of persons of weak and distempered brains, then, doubtless 'tis a thing of great importance, whether we have thus been taught by the spirit of God; whether the light of the glorious Gospel of Christ, who is the image of God hath shined unto us, giving us the light of the knowledge of the glory of God, in the face of Jesus Christ; whether we have seen the Son, and believed on him, or have that faith of Gospel doctrines that arises from a spiritual sight of Christ.

Thirdly. All may hence be exhorted, earnestly to seek this spiritual light. To influence and move to it, the following things may be consider'd.

1. This is the most *excellent and divine* wisdom, that any creature is capable of. 'Tis more excellent than any human learning.; 'tis far more

excellent than all the knowlege of the greatest philosophers, or statesmen. Yea the least glimpse of the glory of God in the face of Christ doth more exalt and enoble the soul, than all the knowlege of those that have the greatest speculative understanding in divinity, without grace. This knowlege has the most noble object that is, or can be, viz. the divine glory, and excellency of God, and Christ. The knowlege of these objects is that wherein consists the most excellent knowledge of the angels, yea, of God himself.

2. This knowlege is that which is above all others sweet and joyful. Men have a great deal of pleasure in human knowlege, in studies of natural things; but this is nothing to that joy which arises from this divine light shining into the soul. This light gives a view of those things that are immensely the most exquisitely beautiful, and capable of delighting the eye of the understanding. This spiritual light is the dawning of the light of glory in the heart. There is nothing so powerful as this to support persons in affliction, and to give the mind peace and brightness, in this stormy and dark world.

3. This light is such as effectually influences the inclination, and changes the nature of the soul. In assimilates the nature to the divine nature, and changes the soul into an image of the same glory that is beheld. 2 Cor. 3. 18. *But we all with open face beholding as in a glass the glory of the Lord, are changed into the same image, from glory to glory, even as by the spirit of the Lord.* This knowlege will wean from the world, and raise the inclination to heavenly things. It will turn the heart to God as the fountain of good, and to choose him for the only portion. This light, and this only, will bring the soul to a saving close with Christ. It conforms the heart to the Gospel, mortifies its enmity and opposition against the scheme of salvation therein revealed: it causes the heart to embrace the joyful tidings, and entirely to adhere to, and acquiesce in the revelation of Christ as our Saviour: it causes the whole soul to accord and symphonize with it, admitting it with entire credit and respect, cleaving to it with full inclination and affection. And it effectually disposes the soul to give up it-self entirely to Christ.

4. This light and this only has its fruit in an universal holiness of life. No meerly notional or speculative understanding of the doctrines of religion will ever bring to this. But this light as it reaches the bottom of the heart, and changes the nature, so it will effectually dispose to an universal obedience. It shews God's worthiness to be obeyed and served. It draws forth the heart in a sincere love to God, which is the only principle of a true, gracious and universal obedience. And it convinces of the reality of those glorious rewards that God has promised to them that obey him.

# SINNERS IN THE HANDS OF AN ANGRY GOD

A sermon preached at Enfield, July 8th 1741.
At a time of great awakenings; and attended with
remarkable impressions on many of the hearers.

Amos 9. 2, 3. *Though they dig into Hell, thence shall mine Hand take them; though they climb up to Heaven, thence will I bring them down. And though they hide themselves in the top of Carmel, I will search and take them out thence; and though they be hid from my sight in the bottom of the sea, thence I will command the serpent, and he shall bite them.*

---

DEUT. 32. 35
*—Their foot shall slide in due time.—*

IN THIS verse is threat'ned the vengeance of God on the wicked unbelieving Israelites, were God's visible people, and lived under that means of grace; and that, notwithstanding all God's wonderful works that he had wrought towards that people, yet remained, as is expressed, ver. 28. void of counsel, having no understanding in them; and that, under all the cultivations of heaven, brought forth bitter and poisonous fruit; as in the two verses next preceeding the text.

The expression that I have chosen for my text, *Their foot shall slide in due time;* seems to imply the following things, relating to the punishment and destruction that these wicked Israelites were exposed to.

1. That they were *always* exposed to destruction, as one that stands or walks in slippery places is always exposed to fall. This is implied in the manner of their destruction's coming upon them, being represented by their foot sliding. The same is express'd, Psal. 73. 18. *Surely thou didst set them in slippery places; thou castedst them down into destruction.*

2. It implies that they were always exposed to sudden unexpected destruction. As he that walks in slippery places is every moment liable to fall; he can't foresee one moment whether he shall stand or fall the next; and when he does fall, he falls at once, without warning. Which is also expressed in that, Psal. 73. 18, 19. *Surely thou didst set them in slippery places; thou castedst them down into destruction. How are they brought into desolation as in a moment?*

3. Another thing implied is that they are liable to fall of themselves, without being thrown down by the hand of another. As he that stands or walks on slippery ground, needs nothing but his own weight to throw him down.

4. That the reason why they are not fallen already, and don't fall now, is only that God's appointed time is not come. For it is said, that when that due time, or appointed time comes, their foot shall slide. Then they shall be left to fall as they are inclined by their own weight. God won't hold them up in these slippery places any longer, but will let them go; and then, at that very instant, they shall fall into destruction; as he that stands in such slippery declining ground on the edge of a pit that he can't stand alone, when he is let go he immediately falls and is lost.

The observation from the words that I would now insist upon is this,

> *There is nothing that keeps wicked men, at any one*
> *moment, out of hell, but the meer pleasure of God.*

By the meer pleasure of God, I mean his sovereign pleasure, his arbitrary will, restrained by no obligation, hinder'd by no manner of difficulty, any more than if nothing else but God's meer will had in the least degree, or in any respect whatsoever, any hand in the preservation of wicked men one moment.

The truth of this observation may appear by the following considerations.

1. There is no want of power in God to cast wicked men into hell at any moment. Mens hands can't be strong when God rises up: The strongest have no power to resist him, nor can any deliver out of his hands.

He is not only able to cast wicked men into hell, but he can most easily do it. Sometimes an earthly prince meets with a great deal of difficulty to subdue a rebel, that has found means to fortify himself, and has made himself strong by the numbers of his followers. But it is not so with God. There is no fortress that is any defence from the power of God. Tho' hand join in hand, and vast multitudes of God's enemies combine and associate themselves, they are easily broken in pieces: They are as great heaps of light chaff before the whirlwind; or large quantities of dry stubble before devouring flames. We find it easy to tread on and crush a worm that we see crawling on the earth; so 'tis easy for us to cut or singe a slender thread that any thing hangs by; thus easy is it for God when he pleases to cast his enemies down to hell. What are we, that we should think to stand before him, at whose rebuke the earth trembles, and before whom the rocks are thrown down?

2. They deserve to be cast into hell; so that divine justice never stands in the way, it makes no objection against God's using his power at any moment to destroy them. Yea, on the contrary, justice calls aloud for an infinite punishment of their sins. Divine justice says of the tree that brings forth such grapes of Sodom, *Cut it down, why cumbreth it the ground,*

Luke 13:7. The sword of divine justice is every moment brandished over their heads, and 'tis nothing but the hand of arbitrary mercy, and God's meer will, that holds it back.

3. They are already under a sentence of condemnation to hell. They don't only justly deserve to be cast down thither; but the sentence of the law of God, that eternal and immutable rule of righteousness that God has fixed between him and mankind, is gone out against them, and stands against them; so that they are bound over already to hell. Joh. 3:18. *He that believeth not is condemned already.* So that every unconverted man properly belongs to hell; that is his place; from thence he is. Joh. 8:23. *Ye are from beneath.* And thither he is bound; 'tis the place that justice, and God's word, and the sentence of his unchangeable law assigns to him.

4. They are now the objects of that very same anger & wrath of God that is expressed in the torments of hell: and the reason why they don't go down to hell at each moment, is not because God, in whose power they are, is not then very angry with them; as angry as he is with many of those miserable creatures that he is now tormenting in hell, and do there feel and bear the fierceness of his wrath. Yea God is a great deal more angry with great numbers that are now on earth, yea doubtless, with many that are now in this congregation, that it may be are at ease and quiet, than he is with many of those that are now in the flames of hell.

So that it is not because God is unmindful of their wickedness, and don't resent it, that he don't let loose his hand and cut them off. God is not altogether such an one as themselves, tho' they may imagine him to be so. The wrath of God burns against them, their damnation don't slumber, the pit is prepared, the fire is made ready, the furnace is now hot, ready to receive them, the flames do now rage and glow. The glittering sword is whet, and held over them, and the pit hath opened her mouth under them.

5. The Devil stands ready to fall upon them, and seize them as his own, at what moment God shall permit him. They belong to him; he has their souls in his possession, and under his dominion. The Scripture represents them as his goods, Luk. 11. 21. The Devils watch them; they are ever by them, at their right hand; they stand waiting for them, like greedy hungry lions that see their prey, and expect to have it, but are for the present kept back; if God should withdraw his hand, by which they are restrained, they would in one moment fly upon their poor souls. The old serpent is gaping for them; hell opens its mouth wide to receive them; and if God should permit it, they would be hastily swallowed up and lost.

6. There are in the souls of wicked men those hellish principles reigning, that would presently kindle and flame out into hell fire, if it were not for God's restraints. There is laid in the very nature of carnal men, a foundation for the torments of hell: There are those corrupt

principles, in reigning power in them, and in full possession of them, that are seeds of hell fire. These principles are active and powerful, exceeding violent in their nature, and if it were not for the restraining hand of God upon them, they would soon break out, they would flame out after the same manner as the same corruptions, the same enmity does in the hearts of damned souls, and would beget the same torments in 'em as they do in them. The souls of the wicked are in Scripture compared to the troubled sea, Isia. 57. 20. For the present God restrains their wickedness by his mighty power, as he does the raging waves of the troubled sea, saying, *Hitherto shalt thou come, and no further*; but if God should withdraw that restraining power, it would soon carry all afore it. Sin is the ruin and misery of the soul; it is destructive in it's nature; and if God should leave it without restraint, there would need nothing else to make the soul perfectly miserable. The corruption of the heart of man is a thing that is immoderate and boundless in its fury; and while wicked men live here, it is like fire pent up by God's restraints, when as if it were let loose it would set on fire the course of nature; and as the heart is now a sink of sin, so, if sin was not restrain'd, it would immediately turn the soul into a fiery oven, or a furnace of fire and brimstone.

7. It is no security to wicked men for one moment, that there are no visible means of death at hand. 'Tis no security to a natural man, that he is now in health, and that he don't see which way he should now immediately go out of the world by any accident, and that there is no visible danger in any respect in his circumstances. The manifold and continual experience of the world in all ages, shews that this is no evidence, that a man is not on the very brink of eternity, and that the next step won't be into another world. The unseen, unthought-of ways and means of persons going suddenly out of the world are innumerable and inconceivable. Unconverted men walk over the pit of hell on a rotten covering, and there are innumerable places in this covering so weak that they won't bear their weight, and these places are not seen. The arrows of death fly unseen at noon-day; the sharpest sight can't discern them. God has so many different unsearchable ways of taking wicked men out of the world and sending 'em to hell, that there is nothing to make it appear that God had need to be at the expence of a miracle, or go out of the ordinary course of his providence, to destroy any wicked man, at any moment. All the means that there are of sinners going out of the world, are so in God's hands, and so universally absolutely subject to his power and determination, that it don't depend at all less on the meer will of God, whether sinners shall at any moment go to hell, than if means were never made use of, or at all concerned in the case.

8. Natural men's prudence and care to preserve their own lives, or the

care of others to preserve them, don't secure 'em a moment. This divine providence and universal experience does also bear testimony to. There is this clear evidence that men's own wisdom is no security to them from death; that if it were otherwise we should see some difference between the wise and politick men of the world, and others, with regard to their liableness to early and unexpected death: but how is it in fact? Eccles. 2. 16. *How dieth the wise man? as the fool.*

9. All wicked men's pains and contrivance which they use to escape hell, while they continue to reject Christ, and so remain wicked men, don't serve them from hell one moment. Almost every natural man that hears of hell, flatters himself that he shall escape it; he depends upon himself for his own security; he flatters himself in what he has done, in what he is now doing, or what he intends to do; every one lays out matters in his own mind how he shall avoid damnation, and flatters himself that he contrives well for himself, and that his schemes won't fail. They hear indeed that there are but few saved, and that the bigger part of men that have died heretofore are gone to hell; but each one imagines that he lays out matters better for his own escape than others have done: He don't intend to come to that place of torment; he says within himself, that he intends to take care that shall be effectual, and to order matters so for himself as not to fail.

But the foolish children of men miserably delude themselves in their own schemes, and in their confidence in their own strength and wisdom; they trust to nothing but a shadow. The bigger part of those that heretofore have lived under the same means of grace, and are now dead, are undoubtedly gone to hell: and it was not because they were not as wise as those that are now alive: it was not because they did not lay out matters as well for themselves to secure their own escape. If it were so, that we could come to speak with them, and could inquire of them, one by one, whether they expected when alive, and when they used to hear about hell, ever to be the subjects of that misery, we doubtless should hear one and another reply, "No, I never intended to come here; I had laid out matters otherwise in my mind; I thought I should contrive well for my self; I thought my scheme good; I intended to take effectual care; but it came upon me unexpected; I did not look for it at that time, and in that manner; it came as a thief; death outwitted me; God's wrath was too quick for me; Oh my cursed foolishness! I was flattering my self, and pleasing my self with vain dreams of what I would do hereafter, and when I was saying peace and safety, then sudden destruction came upon me."

10. God has laid himself under no obligation, by any promise to keep any natural man out of hell one moment. God certainly has made no promises either of eternal life, or of any deliverance or preservation from eternal death, but what are contained in the covenant of grace, the

promises that are given in Christ, in whom all the promises are Yea and Amen. But surely they have no interest in the promises of the covenant of grace that are not the children of the covenant, and that don't believe in any of the promises of the covenant, and have no interest in the Mediator of the covenant.

So that whatever some have imagined and pretended about promises made to natural men's earnest seeking and knocking, 'tis plain and manifest that whatever pains a natural man takes in religion, whatever prayers he makes, till he believes in Christ, God is under no manner of obligation to keep him a moment from eternal destruction.

So that, thus it is, that natural men are held in the hand of God over the pit of Hell; they have deserved the fiery pit, and are already sentenced to it; and God is dreadfully provoked, his anger is as great towards them as to those that are actually suffering the executions of the fierceness of his wrath in hell, and they have done nothing in the least to appease or abate that anger, neither is God in the least bound by any promise to hold them up one moment; the Devil is waiting for them, Hell is gaping for them, the flames gather and flash about them, and would fain lay hold on 'em, and swallow them up; the fire pent up in their own hearts is struggling to break out: and they have no interest in any Mediator, there are no means within reach that can be any security to them. In short, they have no refuge, nothing to take hold of, all that preserves them every moment is the meer arbitrary will, and uncovenanted unobliged forbearance of an incensed God.

## APPLICATION

The use may be of awakening to unconverted persons in this congregation. This that you have heard is the case of every one of you that are out of Christ. That world of misery, that lake of burning brimstone is extended abroad under you. There is the dreadful pit of the glowing flames of the wrath of God; there is hell's wide gaping mouth open; and you have nothing to stand upon, nor any thing to take hold of; there is nothing between you and Hell but the air; 'tis only the power and meer pleasure of God that holds you up.

You probably are not sensible of this; you find you are kept out of Hell, but don't see the hand of God in it, but look at other things, as the good state of your bodily constitution, your care of your own life, and the means you use for your own preservation. But indeed these things are nothing; if God should withdraw his hand, they would avail no more to keep you from falling, than the thin air to hold up a person that is suspended in it.

Your wickedness makes you as it were heavy as lead, and to tend downwards with great weight and pressure towards Hell; and if God should let you go, you would immediately sink and swiftly descend & plunge into the bottomless gulf, and your healthy constitution, and your own care and prudence, and best contrivance, and all your righteousness, would have no more influence to uphold you and keep you out of hell, than a spider's web would have to stop a falling rock. Were it not that so is the sovereign pleasure of God, the earth would not bear you one moment; for you are a burden to it; the creation groans with you; the creature is made subject to the bondage of your corruption, not willingly; the sun don't willingly shine upon you to give you light to serve sin and Satan; the earth don't willingly yield her increase to satisfy your lusts; nor is it willingly a stage for your wickedness to be acted upon; the air don't willingly serve you for breath to maintain the flame of life in your vitals, while you spend your life in the service of God's enemies. God's creatures are good, and were made for men to serve God with, and don't willingly subserve to any other purpose, and groan when they are abused to purposes so directly contrary to their nature and end. And the world would spew you out, were it not for the sovereign hand of him who hath subjected it in hope. There are the black clouds of God's wrath now hanging directly over your heads, full of the dreadful storm, and big with thunder; and were it not for the restraining hand of God it would immediately burst forth upon you. The sovereign pleasure of God for the present, stays his rough wind; otherwise it would come with fury, and your destruction would come like a whirlwind, and you would be like the chaff of the summer threshing floor.

The wrath of God is like great waters that are dammed for the present; they increase more and more, & rise higher and higher, till an outlet is given, and the longer the stream is stop'd, the more rapid and mighty is it's course, when once it is let loose. 'Tis that judgment against your evil works has not been executed hitherto; the floods of God's vengeance have been withheld; but your guilt in the mean time is constantly increasing, and you are every day treasuring up more wrath; the waters are continually rising and waxing more and more mighty; and there is nothing but the meer pleasure of God that holds the waters back that are unwilling to be stopped, and press hard to go forward; if God should only withdraw his hand from the flood-gate, it would immediately fly open, and the fiery floods of the fierceness and wrath of God would rush forth with inconceivable fury, and would come upon you with omnipotent power; and if your strength were ten thousand times greater than it is, yea, ten thousand times greater than the strength of the stoutest, sturdiest Devil in Hell, it would be nothing to withstand or endure it.

The bow of God's wrath is bent, and the arrow made ready on the string, and justice bends the arrow at your heart, and strains the bow, and it is nothing but the meer pleasure of God, and that of an angry God, without any promise or obligation at all, that keeps the arrow one moment from being made drunk with your blood.

Thus are all you that never passed under a great change of heart, by the mighty power of the Spirit of GOD upon your souls; all that were never born again, and made new creatures, and raised from being dead in sin, to a state of new, and before altogether unexperienced light and life, (however you may have reformed your life in many things, and may have had religious affections, and may keep up a form of religion in your families and closets, and in the house of God, and may be strict in it,) you are thus in the hands of an angry God; 'tis nothing but his meer pleasure that keeps you from being this moment swallowed up in everlasting destruction.

However unconvinced you may now be of the truth of what you hear, by & by you will be fully convinced of it. Those that are gone from being in the like circumstances with you, see that it was so with them; for destruction came suddenly upon most of them, when they expected nothing of it, and while they were saying, peace and safety: now they see, that those things that they depended on for peace and safety, were nothing but thin air and empty shadows.

The God that holds you over the pit of Hell, much as one holds a spider, or some loathsome insect, over the fire, abhors you, and is dreadfully provoked; his wrath towards you burns like fire; he looks upon you as worthy of nothing else, but to be cast into the fire; he is of purer eyes than to bear to have you in his sight; you are ten thousand times so abominable in his eyes as the most hateful venomous serpent is in ours. You have offended him infinitely more than ever a stubborn rebel did his prince: and yet 'tis nothing but his hand that holds you from falling into the fire every moment: 'Tis is to be ascribed to nothing else, that you did not go to Hell the last night; that you was suffer'd to awake again in this world, after you closed your eyes to sleep: and there is no other reason to be given why you have not dropped into Hell since you arose in the morning, but that God's hand has held you up: There is no other reason to be given why you han't gone to Hell since you have sat here in the house of God, provoking his pure eyes by your sinful wicked manner of attending his solemn worship: Yea, there is nothing else that is to be given as a reason why you don't this very moment drop down into Hell.

O sinner! Consider the fearful danger you are in: 'tis a great furrnace of wrath, a wide and bottomless pit, full of the fire of wrath, that you are held over in the hand of that God, whose wrath is provoked and incensed as much against you as against many of the damned in Hell. You hang by a slender thread, with the flames of divine wrath flashing about it, and ready every moment to singe it, and burn it asunder; and you have no interest in any Mediator, and nothing to lay hold of to save yourself, nothing to keep off the flames of wrath, nothing of your own, nothing that you ever have done, nothing that you can do, to induce God to spare you one moment.

And consider here more particularly several things concerning that wrath that you are in such danger of.

1. Whose wrath it is: it is the wrath of the infinite God. If it were only the wrath of man, tho' it were of the most potent prince, it would be comparatively little to be regarded. The wrath of kings is very much dreaded, especially of absolute monarchs, that have the possessions and lives of their subjects wholly in their power, to be disposed of at their meer will. Prov. 20. 2. *The fear of a king is as the roaring of a lion: whoso provoketh him to anger, sinneth against his own soul.* The subject that very much enrages an arbitrary prince, is liable to suffer the most extream torments, that human art can invent or human power can inflict. But the greatest earthly potentates, in their greatest majesty and strength, and when clothed in their greatest terrors, are but feeble despicable worms of the dust, in comparison of the great and almighty Creator and King of Heaven and Earth: It is but little that they can do, when most enraged, and when they have exerted the utmost of their fury. All the kings of the earth before God are as grasshoppers, they are nothing and less than nothing: both their love and their hatred is to be despised. The wrath of the great King of Kings is as much more terrible than their's, as his majesty is greater. Luke 12. 4, 5. *And I say unto you, my friends, be not afraid of them that kill the body, and after that have no more that they can do: But I will forewarn you whom ye shall fear; fear him, which after he hath killed, hath power to cast into Hell; yea I say unto you, fear him.*

2. 'Tis the fierceness of his wrath that you are exposed to. We often read of the fury of God; as in Isai. 59:18. *According to their deeds, accordingly he will repay fury to his adversaries.* So Isai. 66. 15. *For behold, the Lord will come with fire, and with chariots like a whirlwind, to render his anger with fury, and his rebukes with flames of fire.* And so in many other places. So we read of God's fierceness Rev. 19:15 we read of the wine press of the fierceness and wrath of almighty God. The words are exceeding terrible. There 'tis not only said so, but if it had only been said, *the wrath of God,* the words would have implied that which is infinitely dreadful: but 'tis the fierceness and wrath of God: the fury of God! the fierceness of Jehovah! Oh how dreadful that must be! Who can utter or conceive what such expressions carry in them! But it is not only said so, but the fierceness and wrath of almighty God. As tho' there would be a very great manifestation of his almighty power, in what the fierceness of his wrath should inflict, as tho' omnipotence should be as it were enraged, and excited, as men are wont

to exert their strength in the fierceness of their wrath. Oh! then what will be the consequence! What will become of the poor worm that shall suffer it! Whose hands can be strong? And whose heart can endure? To what a dreadful, inexpressible, inconceivable depth of misery must the poor creature be sunk, who shall be the subject of this!

Consider this, you that are here present, that yet remain in an unregenerate state. That God will execute the fierceness of his anger, implies that he will inflict wrath without any pity: when God beholds the ineffable extremity of your case, and sees your torment to be so vastly disproportion'd to your strength, and sees how your poor soul is crushed and sinks down, as it were into an infinite gloom, he will have no compassion upon you, he will not forbear the executions of his wrath, or in the least lighten his hand; there shall be no moderation or mercy, nor will God then at all stay his rough wind; he will have no regard to your welfare, nor be at all careful lest you should suffer too much, in any other sense than only that you shall not suffer beyond what strict justice requires: nothing shall be with held, because it's so hard for you to bear. Ezek. 8. 18. *Therefore will I also deal in fury; mine eye shall not spare, neither will I have pity; and tho' they cry in mine ears with a loud voice, yet I will not hear them.* Now God stands ready to pity you; this is a day of mercy; you may cry now with some encouragement of obtaining mercy, but when once the day of mercy is past, your most lamentable and dolorous cries and shrieks will be in vain; you will be wholly lost and thrown away of God as to any regard to your welfare; God will have no other use to put you to but only to suffer misery; you shall be continued in being to no other end; for you will be a vessel of wrath fitted to destruction; and there will be no other use of this vessel but only to be filled full of wrath: God will be so far from pitying you when you cry to him, that 'tis said he will only *laugh and mock,* Prov. 1. 25, 26, &c.

How awful are those words, Isai. 63:3, which are the words of the great God, *I will tread them in mine anger, and will trample them in my fury, and their blood shall be sprinkled upon my garments, and I will stain all my raiment.* 'Tis perhaps impossible to conceive of words that carry in them greater manifestations of these three things, viz. contempt, and hatred, and fierceness of indignation. If you cry to God to pity you, he will be so far from pitying you in your doleful case, or shewing you the least regard or favour, that instead of that, he'll only tread you under foot: And tho' he will know that you can't bear the weight of omnipotence treading upon you, yet he won't regard that, but he will crush you under his feet without mercy; he'll crush out your blood, and make it fly, and it shall be sprinkled on his garments, so as to stain all his raiment. He will not only hate you, but he will have you in the utmost contempt; no place shall be thought fit for you, but under his feet, to be trodden down as the mire of the streets.

3. The misery you are exposed to is that which God will inflict to that end, that he might shew what that wrath of Jehovah is. God hath had it on his heart to shew to angels and men, both how excellent his love is, and also how terrible his wrath is. Sometimes earthly kings have a mind to shew how terrible their wrath is, by the extream punishments they would execute on those that provoke 'em. Nebuchadnezzar, that mighty and haughty monarch of the Chaldean empire, was willing to shew his wrath, when enraged with Shadrach, Meshach, and Abednego; and accordingly gave order that the burning fiery furnace should be het seven times hotter than it was before; doubtless it was raised to the utmost degree of fierceness that humane art could raise it: But the great God is also willing to shew his wrath, and magnify his awful majesty and mighty power in the extream sufferings of his enemies. Rom. 9:22. *What if God willing to show his wrath, and to make his power known, endured with much long-suffering the vessels of wrath fitted to destruction?* And seeing this is his design, and what he has determined, to shew how terrible the unmixed, unrestrained wrath, the fury and fierceness of Jehovah is, he will do it to effect. There will be something accomplished and brought to pass, that will be dreadful with a witness. When the great and angry God hath risen up and executed his awful vengeance on the poor sinner, and the wretch is actually suffering the infinite weight and power of his indignation, then will God call upon the whole universe to behold that awful majesty, and mighty power that is to be seen in it. Isai. 33. 12, 13, 14. *And the people shall be as the burning of lime, as thorns cut up shall they be burnt in the fire. Hear ye that are far off what I have done; and ye that are near acknowledge my might. The sinners in Zion are afraid, fearfulness hath surprized the hypocrites, &c.*

Thus it will be with you that are in an unconverted state, if you continue in it; the infinite might, and majesty and terribleness of the OMNIPOTENT GOD shall be magnified upon you, in the ineffable strength of your torments: You shall be tormented in the presence of the holy angels, and in the presence of the Lamb; and when you shall be in this state of suffering, the glorious inhabitants of heaven shall go forth and look on the awful spectacle, that they may see what the wrath and fierceness of the Almighty is, and when they have seen it, they will fall down and adore that great power and majesty. Isai. 66. 23, 24. *And it shall come to pass, that from one new moon to another, and from one sabbath to another, shall all flesh come to worship before me, saith the Lord; and they shall go forth and look upon the carcasses of the men that have transgressed against me; for their worm shall not die, neither shall their fire be quenched, and they shall be an abhorring unto all flesh.*

4. 'Tis everlasting wrath. It would be dreadful to suffer this fierceness and wrath of Almighty God one moment; but you must suffer it to all

eternity: there will be no end to this exquisite horrible misery: When you look forward, you shall see a long forever, a boundless duration before you, which will swallow up your thoughts, and amaze your soul; and you will absolutely despair of ever having any deliverance, any end, any mitigation, any rest at all; you will know certainly that you must wear out long ages, millions of millions of ages, in wrestling and conflicting with this almighty merciless vengeance; and then when you have so done, when so many ages have actually been spent by you in this manner, you will know that all is but a point to what remains. So that your punishment will indeed be infinite. Oh who can express what the state of a soul in such circumstances is! All that we can possibly say about it, gives but a very feeble, faint representation of it; 'tis inexpressible and inconceivable: for who knows the power of God's anger?

How dreadful is the state of those that are daily and hourly in danger of this great wrath, and infinite misery! But this is the dismal case of every soul in this congregation, that has not been born again, however moral and strict, sober and religious, they may otherwise be. Oh that you would consider it, whether you be young or old. There is reason to think, that there are many in this congregation now hearing this discourse, that will actually be the subjects of this very misery to all eternity. We know not who they are, or in what seats they sit, or what thoughts they now have: it may be they are now at ease, and hear all these things without much disturbance, and are now flattering themselves that they are not the persons, promising themselves that they shall escape. If we knew that there was one person, and but one, in the whole congregation, that was to be the subject of this misery, what an awful thing would it be to think of! If we knew who it was, what an awful sight would it be to see such a person! How might all the rest of the congregation lift up a lamentable and bitter cry over him! But, alass! instead of one, how many is it likely will remember this discourse in Hell? And it would be a wonder if some that are now present, should not be in Hell in a very short time, before this year is out. And it would be no wonder if some person that now sits here in some seat of this meeting-house in health, and quiet & secure, should be there before tomorrow morning. Those of you that finally continue in a natural condition, that shall keep out of Hell longest, will be there in a little time! your damnation don't slumber; it will come swiftly, and, in all probability very suddenly upon many of you. You have reason to wonder, that you are not already in Hell. 'Tis doubtless the case of some that heretofore you have seen and known, that never deserved Hell more than you, and that heretofore appeared as likely to have been now alive as you: Their case is past all hope; they are crying in extream misery and perfect despair; but here you are in the land of the living, and in the house of

God, and have an opportunity to obtain salvation. What would not those poor damned, hopeless souls give for one day's such opportunity as you now enjoy!

And now you have an extraordinary opportunity, a day wherein Christ has flung the door of mercy wide open, and stands in the door calling and crying with a loud voice to poor sinners; a day wherein many are flocking to him, and pressing into the kingdom of God; many are daily coming from the East, West, North and South; many that were very lately in the same miserable condition that you are in, are now in an happy state, with their hearts filled with love to him that has loved them and washed them from their sins in his own blood, and rejoicing in hope of the glory of God. How awful is it to be left behind at such a day! To see so many others feasting, while you are pining and perishing! To see so many rejoycing and singing for joy of heart, while you have cause to mourn for sorrow of heart, and howl for vexation of spirit! How can you rest one moment in such a condition? Are not your souls as precious as the souls of the people at Suffield, where they are flocking from day to day to Christ?

Are there not many here that have lived long in the world, that are not to this day born again, and so are aliens from the common-wealth of Israel, and have done nothing ever since they have lived, but treasure up wrath against the day of wrath? Oh sirs, your case in an especial manner is extreamly dangerous; your guilt and hardness of heart is extreamly great. Don't you see how generally persons of your years are pass'd over and left, in the present remarkable & wonderful dispensation of God's mercy? You had need to consider your selves, and wake throughly out of sleep; you cannot bear the fierceness and wrath of the infinite God.

And you that are young men, and young women, will you neglect this precious season that you now enjoy, when so many others of your age are renouncing all youthful vanities, and flocking to CHRIST? You especially have now an extraordinary opportunity; but if you neglect it, it will soon be with you as it is with those persons that spent away all the precious days of youth in sin, and are now come to such a dreadful pass in blindness and hardness.

And you children that are unconverted, don't you know that you are going down to Hell, to bear the dreadful wrath of that God that is now angry with you every day, and every night? Will you be content to be the children of the Devil, when so many other children in the land are converted, and are become the holy and happy children of the King of Kings?

And let every one that is yet out of Christ, and hanging over the pit of Hell, whether they be old men and women, or middle aged, or young people, or little children, now hearken to the loud calls of God's word and providence. This acceptable year of the LORD, that is a day of such great favour to some, will doubtless be a day of as remarkable vengeance to others. Men's hearts harden, and their guilt increases apace at such a day as this, if they neglect their souls: and never was there so great danger of such persons being given up to hardness of heart, and blindness of mind. God seems now to be hastily gathering in his elect in all parts of the land; and probably the bigger part of adult persons that ever shall be saved, will be brought in now in a little time, and that it will be as it was on the great out-pouring of the Spirit upon the Jews in the Apostles days, the election will obtain, and the rest will be blinded. If this should be the case with you, you will eternally curse this day, and will curse the day that ever you was born, to see such a season of the pouring out of God's spirit; and will wish that you had died and gone to Hell before you had seen it. Now undoubtedly it is, as it was in the days of John the Baptist, the axe is in an extraordinary manner laid at the root of the trees, that every tree that brings not forth good fruit, may be hewen down, and cast into the fire.

Therefore let every one that is out of CHRIST, now awake and fly from the wrath to come. The wrath of Almighty God is now undoubtedly hanging over great part of this congregation: Let every one fly out of Sodom: *Haste and escape for your lives, look not behind you, escape to the mountain, least you be consumed.*

# CHARLES CHAUNCY
## (1705–1787)

## MAN'S LIFE CONSIDERED UNDER THE SIMILITUDE OF A VAPOUR, THAT APPEARETH FOR A LITTLE TIME, AND THEN VANISHETH AWAY

### (Boston, 1731)

A Sermon on the Death of that Honourable & Vertuous
Gentlewoman Mrs. Sarah Byfield,
The amiable Consort of the Honorable
Nathanael Byfield, Esq;
Who died Decemb. 21st. 1730.
In the 58th of her Age.

1 Chron. 29. 15. *Our days on earth are as a shadow, and there is none abiding.*

Psal. 39. 4. *LORD, make me to know mine end, and the measure of my days what it is: that I may know how frail I am.*

TO THE HONOURABLE NATHANAEL BYFIELD ESQ;

*Honoured SIR,*

*When I had fallen in with your desire to print this sermon, I could not prevail with my self to let it go to the press, without first paying public regards to so good a friend: whom, I have reason to love & reverence as a father.*

*The sermon was preach'd on the lamented death of your dear & amiable consort. I tho't it proper to take special notice of such a Providence: and as I endeavour'd to improve it for the benefit of all my hearers; so for your's in particular. In the character I have given Madam Byfield, I have not affected niceness & accuracy; yet have had a strict regard to truth & uprightness. And I doubt not, but all that were*

185

*acquainted with her, will judge, that her memory is worthy to be transmitted to posterity, with more honour, than I have been able to do it.*

*I heartily joyn with you, sir, in rendring thanks to a good God, who directed you to a person, every way so agreeable: and that he continued her, so long a blessing and comfort to you; the pleasant companion of your age; your crown & ornament. 'Tis the same most wise & merciful God, that has taken her away from you. And 'tis for your good, he has thus afflicted you. This correction of your heavenly father, was necessary in that chain of events, by which, he had ordained to bring you to glory: which is the highest motive to patience & submission.*

*May this, and all other divine dispensations be sanctify'd to you! and bless'd as a means to make you still more meet for that world, where there is no sin nor sorrow; where all tears shall be wip'd from your eyes, and you shall be compleatly happy in the sight and fruition of the blessed God. And may your children, (already propagated to the fourth generation, and) throughout all generations, follow you into the heavenly state, and be an eternal spring of joy to you!*

So Prays,

Your much oblig'd and
Affectionate Servant in Christ,
Charles Chauncy.

## Man's Life Consider'd Under the Similitude of a Vapour

### JAMES 4. 14.

*For what is your Life? It is even a Vapour, that
appeareth for a little time, and then vanisheth away.*

I HAVE made choice of this text, to lead you into some proper meditations on humane frailty: a subject never unsuitable for dying men to employ their tho'ts upon; and particularly seasonable, after any fresh, affecting instance of mortality.

We are here presented with a very instructive description of life. It's consider'd under the similitude of a vapour, that appeareth for a little time, and then vanisheth away. A true and lively representation of the state, of man's life upon earth! which is of but short continuance, inconstant and uncertain: the effect whereof shou'd be, our living after the best and wisest manner; to the purposes of another world, & so as to secure to our selves, an interest in that future & eternal life, which the Gospel has reveal'd, and promises to them, who, by patient continuance in well doing, seek for glory, honour and immortality.

And that we may be excited and quicken'd, in making such an improvement of the present life, I shall beg your attention, while I am discoursing to you, upon the two following important points; agreeable to the scope of the Apostle in the words, I have sed to you.

I. I shall consider the representation that is here given us of man's life.

II. I shall show, what influence, such a representation, ought, in all reason, to have upon us.

I. I am to consider the representation, that is here made of man's life. It is even a vapour, that appeareth for a little time, and then vanisheth away.

I have no Design to pursue this metaphor, in all the little resemblances, which one's imagination might easily suggest: but shall confine my self to a few particulars; which lie open to common view, and were, no doubt, the things intended by the Apostle. And they are such as these. 1. That man's life, upon earth, is short. 2. Uncertain. 3. Inconstant. 4. Irrecoverable, when once gone.

I. Man's life may be represented by a vapour, to signifie the exceeding shortness of it. A vapour is of but short continuance. It may for a while "wander upon the surface of the earth or water;" but is soon driven away by the wind: or spends it self, and vanishes away. Just the same thing may be said of the life of man: which, whatever it is, and however active and buisie it may for a while appear, is yet soon extinguished: or of it self languishes and expires. The Scriptures are full of affecting illustrations to this purpose. They sometimes comprehend man's life, within the narrow compass of an hand-breadth; which is one of the most inconsiderable measures. Psal. 39. 5. *Behold, thou hast made my days as an hand-breadth.* Sometimes they limit it to the time a man takes in telling a story; which soon passes away, and is gone. Psal. 90. 9. *For all our days are passed away in thy wrath:* we spend our days as a tale that is told. At other times, they measure life, by some of the swiftest motions; to signify how soon it arrives at it's determin'd period. Our days are said to be swifter than a weaver's shuttle, which is no sooner thrown in at one side of the web, but it is out at the other; to pass away as the swift ships, which with a brisk gale, are quickly carried out of sight; to be swifter than a post, who hurries along, with all possible speed: and the eagle that maketh towards her prey, does not fly more swiftly, than the life of man passes away: as these things are elegantly express'd, Job. 9. 25, 26. *Now my days are swifter than a post: they flee away:—they are passed away as the swift ships: as the eagle that hasteth to her prey.*

And there is a certain justness and propriety in these Scripture representations of man's life; tho' borrow'd from things, some of which are but of few days, and others of but few moments continuance: and that, if at the same time, we should suppose it to each the utmost bounds of it's appointed duration. For what are threescore or fourscore years? As the Psalmist's expression is, they are soon cut off, and we fly away. Indeed, when we look forward from youth or childhood, to old age; it appears at a vast distance: and as tho' we should scarce ever arrive at it. But by only changing the scituation of our selves, how different will the prospect appear! Let a person look back from age to youth, and it will seem but a very small space: those thirty or forty years, which were judged by him in his childhood unattainable, how short do they seem, now he has passed thro' them! So true is that observation, that a day to come shews longer to us than a year that is gone. And it is the universal sense of all that are grown into years concerning it. They are even surpriz'd, when they look back to find, how insensibly their days are rolled away. If they extend their view forty, fifty, or threescore years backwards; they can scarce believe they have liv'd so long, it appears such a moment of time. And generally speaking, the longer persons live, the shorter their past days and years seem to them: and when they are in a serious turn of tho't, they more thoroughly realize, what a small part of duration, the term of humane life contains.

And if the life of man appears thus short even to men themselves, when set in a due light: how much more inconsiderable must it seem in God's eye! with whom there is no beginning of days, nor end of years; and in whose sight a thousand years are but as one day. Surely in this view of life, it must sink into the smallest point of time. Yea, as the Psalmist phrases it, our age is as nothing before God. Nay, if our lives, like Methusalah's, were protracted to near a thousand years; in God's account, and in compare with his eternal duration, they would seem but as a single moment. And yet, how many of our ages go to make up a thousand years! and yet further, how few live to what we call the full age of a man! Perhaps the greatest part of mankind die within the space of the first seven years. And where one arrives at the general period affix'd to humane life, a thousand die in youth or middle age. Such a justness and propriety is there in these Scripture representations of man's life: like a vapour, it appears but for a little time, and then vanishes away.

If any shou'd now feel themselves uneasie at this representation of life, and be tempted to think hardly of God, for making the limits of it so exceeding narrow; it will at once satisfy all their obections, to consider life in the true and proper notion of it: as a probation season for eternity.

The God that gave us our beings, design'd them for an end worthy of himself, and those noble powers, he has endow'd us with. But this end is not to be obtain'd in this world. There is nothing here, that can satisfy the desires of our souls, or be a commensurate happiness for them. We must look beyond the grave for this, to the unseen unutterable glories of the heavenly state. And if we take a view of the present life, as referring to this state, and a tryal for our entrance into it, it will sufficiently justify, both the wisdom and goodness of God in the shortness of it.

Especially, if we go on and consider, that the time of life is a space full long enough for the business we were sent into the world upon; viz. to make preparation for eternity. For thro' the Lord Jesus Christ, who has obey'd the law, and suffer'd the penalty of it, for us and in our stead; the terms of salvation are bro't down to our present fallen state: and nothing more is absolutely requir'd of us, but faith in Jesus Christ, as the Son of the living God, including in it the seeds & principles of sincere repentance, and a true Gospel obedience. And no sooner is such a faith wrought in our souls, but our main work is done, and the great design of life answered. And persons not only may, but often are, even in the beginning of life, thus endow'd with faith. And a little time, if it be well improv'd, in the diligent use of proper means, will serve for this purpose. And all that is afterwards necessary, will be only to give proof of our good estate; to continue in the faith of Christ; to grow in grace; to shine in the world by our good examples; and in a word, to glorify God by our holy carriage of our selves under whatever condition he shall please to order out unto us. And when our lives come to be thus employ'd, the shorter they are the better; inasmuch as we shall hereby the sooner obtain the end of our faith, the salvation of our souls. And this is the tho't of all that are truly wise. They would not willingly have the term of life set at a further distance, least the tryal of their graces should be too heavy and tedious; and the full reward of their faith and good works too long detain'd from them.

And on the other hand, when persons do pervert the grand design of life; neglecting their souls, and taking no care to prepare themselves for the future state; 'tis unreasonable to expect their lives should be protracted, beyond what the lives of men ordinarily are, that so they might have a longer space of tryal, before their condition is unalterably determined. For if they should live over the present life, as bounded by God, tho'tless of eternity, and unconcern'd to make preparation for it; and instead hereof, should spend their days in vanity, or the gratification of their fleshly lusts, there would be but little hope of their amendment and returning to a better mind, if their time should be lengthend out to the longest period: but on the contrary, great reason to fear, that they would only grow more bold and obstinate in wickedness, and get still at a further distance from God and Happiness. Besides, the ordinary duration of man's life, is full long enough for such persons to be continued plagues to mankind, by their evil practices and bad examples. And 'tis in mercy to the world in general, that the time of their life is limited to threescore or fourscore years.

But I must not enlarge here. To proceed,

II. By the metaphor in the text, we have represented to us, the utter uncertainty of humane life. What more uncertain than the appearance of a vapour? It sometimes continues a longer, and sometimes a shorter time: is sometimes suddenly extinguished, and sometimes slowly and by degrees. Alike uncertain is the life of man. 'Tis certain indeed, that all men shall once die. And there is no man living but knows that he shall die. We know likewise, that we are surrounded with an infinite variety of distempers, and every moment lie expos'd to innumerable accidents, which may put a period to our days. So that there is no point of time, in which we are free from danger, and may be sure of not falling by the stroke of death. Yet, the precise time when, and particular means and manner how, remain, as to us, absolute uncertainties. Man knoweth not his time. This is the sole prerogative of the most high God. Nothing, to him, is either contingent or uncertain. And in a very particular manner, he is the Supream Lord of Life and Death. And as such, he hath appointed the day and hour; nay, the very moment, when every son and daughter of Adam, shall undergo the change of death. Job seems to have put this matter beyond dispute, Job. 7. 1. *Is there not an appointed time to man upon earth? Are not his days also like the days of an hireling? An hireling, we all know, hath his fix'd time of service: and when this is expired, he is discharg'd from his labour.* The same thing may be said of man: he has his determin'd time of duration; and whenever this comes, in a moment he expires. This matter is further illustrated, Chap. 14. 5. *Man's days are determined, the number of his months are with thee: thou hast appointed his bounds, that he cannot pass.* So that, let our character be what it will; if we are never so desirable, or never so useful: or let our state be what it will; be we prepar'd or unprepar'd, we must at such a particular point of time, which God from eternity, has pitch'd upon, be dismis'd from the body. And he will so order it in his active providence, that all necessary natural causes shall unitedly concur, to put a period to our life, not only at the very time, but after the same manner, that he has decreed.

God has not indeed alotted to all men the same number of months and years: nor determin'd to accomplish his decree upon them, by the same means and after the same manner; but has variously fix'd the periods of life in different persons, and uses as great a variety in the means and manner of their death. And upon this account it is, that both the time and means & manner of our going out of the world, are, as to us, matters of the greatest uncertainty.

We know not when we shall die: whether in infancy or childhood, while our natures are weak and tender; before we are instructed in the worth of life, or are capable of exerting ourselves to any valuable purposes? Or in youth, our constitutions being strong & healthy; our powers active and sprightly, and in the best capacity of serving the ends of life? Or whether we shall continue, till the evil days come, and the years draw nigh, when we shall say, we have no pleasure in them?

We know not the manner in which we shall die: whether on a sudden, or by slow & leisurely steps? in the height of prosperity, or depth of adversity? in a throng of worldly business, or free from outward cares and incumberances? Death will most certainly seize upon us: but where will it be? In the closet, or the street? in the shop, or the field? at sea, or on dry land?—these things are secrets in the breast of God alone—.

In fine, we are absolutely ignorant by what means God will take us out of the world: whether by disease, or accident? according to nature, or by force & violence? He will doubtless make use of natural causes: but what will they be? A fever, or a frenzy? the teeth of an insect, or a blast of wind? a morsel of meat, or a hair from our heads? a fall from a horse, or the hand of malice? Or will he suffer us to live, till nature is spent, & we die of ourselves?—

Thus uncertain a thing is the life of man.—and it is an argument of great wisdom and goodness in God, that 'tis so. For if we knew the determinate space of life, or that it would surely expire at such a particular term, it would have a very unhappy influence upon us. For, on the one hand, if it was at a considerable distance, we should be in utmost hazard of allowing our selves liberty, to live according to the course of this world; fulfilling the desires of the flesh & mind. And this we shou'd be apt to do, till we came within the near prospect of our dissolution: and then having so habituated ourselves to sin as to be harden'd in it; it would be almost a miracle, if we were ever prevail'd upon, to break off our sins by righteousness, and our iniquities by turning to God. For as the Prophet argues, Jer. 13. 23. *Can the Ethiopian change his skin, or the leopard his spots? Then may ye also do good, that are accustom'd to do evil.* And on the other hand, if the time of life was short, and to be terminated in the space of a few years: tho' it might awaken our consideration, & put us on endeavours to make our peace with God, and secure an interest in Christ; yet how melancholy & uncomfortable, would it be like to make our abode upon earth? We should enjoy no pleasure in the world: neither in friends, nor relatives; nor any of the good things, God has provided for our present happiness. Such would be our concern & fear; such our dark and gloomy apprehensions, as would not only unfit us to converse with one another; but even to live in such a world, as God has made this to be.

But now that the time remains uncertain, both these inconveniences are avoided. Instead of being encourag'd in a course of sin for the present, we have one of the strongest arguments to engage us in an immediate care, about the business of religion, and our soul's salvation; and at the same time, there is room left for the exercise of hope, which layes a foundation for the enjoyment of ourselves and the comforts of life.

We shou'd therefore thankfully acknowledge and admire the wisdom & goodness of God, in keeping us ignorant of the time & circumstances of our death: the knowledge of which, could not be of any real service to us; but very hurtful upon many accounts. We shou'd be content to be in the dark, as to these futurities, and improve our ignorance as a motive to zeal and industry in working out our own salvation with fear and trembling.

III. The metaphor in the text signifies to us, the inconstant, unsettled state of the present life. A vapour is an inconstant variable meteor. One while it extends it self far & wide, anon it dwindles away into nothing. Now it appears thick & dense, presently it becomes so thin & rarify'd as not to fall within reach of observation. Just such an inconstant variable thing is the life of man.

We seldom continue long in the same state; but are constantly passing under innumerable changes. This moment we are well and in health; the next we are seiz'd with some fatal distemper. Now we abound in riches and plenty; on a sudden we are reduced to poverty and penury. In the morning we are in honour and dignity; before night, we wear the character of men of low degree. To day we are respected and well spoken of; by to morrow, we are hated, despis'd and evil spoken against. This week we are surrounded with friends and acquaintance; the next we have reason to make that complaint, Psal. 88. 18. *Lover and friend, thou hast put far from me, and mine acquaintance into darkness.* And so whatever our present state is, we quickly pass out of it into another; that is sometimes better, and sometimes worse.

And it is in a sort necessary, the present state of man's life should be thus variable. For so perverse & depraved are our tempers, since our fall from God, that it would be scarce possible for us, to carry it suitably, under any one invariable condition of life.

If, on the other Hand, we were bless'd with a constant run of prosperity; for a long time together enjoying our health & friends, and all the comforts and good things of life: ten to one, but it would be the means of our being ruined for ever. We could not bear such an uninterrupted series of worldly happiness. We should be apt to grow proud & insolent; forgetful of God & our own souls: & instead of being the more strongly engaged in his love & service, it would be likely we should kick against him; contemn his law, slight his goodness, and by our hard & impenitent heart, treasure up to ourselves wrath against the day of wrath. And on the other hand, if we were frown'd upon in Providence, and kept under poor, difficult and afflictive circumstances; and this was to be our condition invariably; it would sink our spirits, discourage our endeavours, and unfit us for every thing. We shou'd have no heart to engage in any affair, neither respecting our souls nor bodies: or if we had, we shou'd not be able to pursue it, with zeal and resolution.

It is therefore a wise disposal of Providence, that our present state is variable, that we are sometimes in one condition & sometimes in another; sometimes in adversity & sometimes in prosperity. Such a mixt inconstant state is best suited to the present frame of our minds; and no doubt was design'd by God as a Kindness to the world in general; as being a means wisely adapted, to serve the end of life, which is the glory of God, in such a temper & behaviour of ourselves, as he has made necessary, in order to our future & eternal well being.

IV. The metaphor in the text represents to us, the irrecoverableness of man's life, when once gone. A vapour when once vanish'd away, is irrecoverably gone. The same must be said of life: when once expir'd, it can never be recall'd. The extinction of life is therefore described, Psal. 39. ult. *As agoing hence, & being here no more.* And Job speaking of man's death, expresses himself in such language as that, Job 14. 12. *Man lieth down, and riseth not till the heavens be no more: they shall not awake, nor rise out of their sleep.* And in the 14. v. *If a man die, shall he live again?* The question does not infer a doubt, whether such as die, shall return back to live their lives over again: but is the strongest negation. They shall not live again. They shall never return back to any of the employments or enjoyments of the present life. When death hath once passed upon men, their probation season is over, and state made unalterable for eternity. Eccl. 11. 3.—*If the tree fall towards the south, or towards the north: in the place where the tree falleth, there shall it be.* An awful consideration! It should surely affect us to think, that as death leaves us, so judgment will find us; that as soon as ever this frail life of our's is ended, our condition from that moment is for ever determined; our place of abode so fix'd, as that if we have misimprov'd the present season, we can never amend or correct our mistake. O how shou'd our attention be awaken'd at this! and our hearts animated with zeal & resolution in doing the work, we were sent into the world upon! beloved, seeing things are thus, what manner of persons ought we to be in all holy conversation & godliness? With what diligence should we labour, that we may be found of our judge, in peace, without spot and blameless. Which brings me to our next general head of discourse, viz.

II. To show what influence, the representation, the text gives of life, ought, in all reason to have upon us. And here that I might not exceed the limits of my hour, I must confine my self to only a few general hints. As,

1. It shou'd put us upon weaning our affections from the world, and moderating our endeavours after it. And are there any, whose hearts are too much set upon the world, & that employ too much pains in the pursuit of it? It shou'd seem incredible, that men, whom God has endow'd with reason & understanding, shou'd be so little govern'd, by a sense of their own frailty, the exceeding shortness & uncertainty of the present life. And yet alas! so it is. Yea, and the generality of persons are so strangely

fond of the world as to think, they can never love it too well, nor endeavour too much after it. They will rise up early, and sit up late; go thro' difficulties and hardships; expose themselves to hazards; run all risques; submit to any thing, and do any thing, for the obtaining only of a a few scraps or portions of it. If we were to judge by the temper & behaviour of some men, we must suppose they imagin'd, that both themselves and their houses would continue for ever, and their dwelling-places to all generations: when alas! their life, like a vapour, appeareth but for a little time, and then vanisheth away. How shou'd this tho't beat down the price of the world in our esteem, and check our endeavours after it? For if at the longest we must quickly leave the world; and may in a moment, at any time, be snatch'd away from all the enjoyments of it: why shou'd our hearts be wedded to it, and our whole time and souls employ'd about it! Is it not far more reasonable to loosen our affections from the earth? to set light by the good things of it? and spend no more pains in the pursuit of them, than is realy necessary for our present comfort?

Perhaps we look upon the world, as our only place of happiness: and entertain in our minds such exalted apprehensions of the value of outward enjoyments, as to desire & aim at nothing higher. But O! let us remember, we shan't always have such Tho'ts of the world. We are hastening apace to the grave. It won't be long, however far we may put from us the evil day, before we shall find ourselves in the agonies of death. And when this comes to be our case; what think we, will our apprehensions about the world be? As we shall view it in a different light, so will it certainly appear in quite different colours. It will seem altogether vanity. We shall see nothing desirable in it: but shall be amaz'd at our former folly, in a setting so high a price on it, and making it the chief object of our sollicitous concern. And at such a time as this: of what great advantage will it be to us, if we have gain'd even as much of this world, as we could possibly desire? Has our highest ambition been gratified, in being honour'd and preferr'd among men?—our honour must now be laid in the dust; all our marks of distinction drop'd at the mouth of the grave: and when we appear in the other world, it will be upon a level with the most ignoble slave.—Or have we indulg'd our selves in ease & pleasure? taking all the carnal delight we could wish for, or are capable of enjoying?—it is now all over and gone. And what remains, but cutting reflections; restless fears and convulsions of soul?—or have we heap'd up riches; joyning house to house, and field to field, till we are placed alone in the midst of the earth?—yet let us consider, that riches are not for ever; and that, "of all our possessions, we shall now need no more than will but suffice to bury us. Silver & gold are too heavy laden, to be carried into another world. And what is it to a dying man, whether his chamber be richly furnish'd or not; whether he breath out his soul in a palace, or a cottage." In an hour of death, "We shall not take pleasure in summing up our estates, and counting how much we shall die worth, and how many hundreds or thousands we shall leave behind us." Alas! the concerns of dying persons are usually of a quite different nature. The necessities of our souls will now crowd themselves upon us. An accusing conscience, and a fearful expectation of approaching torments, will shake out of our minds all Tho'ts of the world, and fill us with the greatest sollicitude to obtain the favour of God, the pardon of sin, peace of conscience, and an interest in the great saviour of sinners. And of what service will the world be to us, in these respects? What suitableness is there in it to supply these wants of our souls? "Food may satisfy hunger, and raiment fence off the injuries of the weather": there is a suitableness in them to do so. But what will all worldly enjoyments avail towards appeasing God's anger, or giving us a comfortable hope of future blessedness? What suitableness is there in a bag "of gold, or a sumptuous building, to satisfy a man's mind, when perplex'd with fears of wrath & hell? You may as well seek to cure a wound in the body, by applying a plaister to the garment, as seek to ease a wounded spirit, by all the treasures, pleasures & enjoyments of this world." *Riches profit not in the day of wrath.* There is no aptness in them to bring any true solace to the soul. O let us not then suffer the world to engross our affections, and take off our tho'ts & care from things of infinitely more weight & importance: but remembring, that we are dying creatures, and that our life, like a vapour, will appear but for a little time; let us make no other use of the world, nor put a higher value upon it, than is reasonable for such kind of creatures. The Apostle directs us, after what manner to use this world; with whose words, I shall finish this head. *But this, I say brethren, the time is short. It remaineth, that both they that have wives, be as tho' they had none; and they that weep, as tho' they wept not; and they that rejoyce, as tho' they rejoyced not; and they that buy, as tho' they possess'd not; and they that use this world, as not abusing it: for the fashion of this world passeth away,* 1 Cor. 7. 29–31.

2. The account, we have had of life, should reconcile our tho'ts to whatever condition, it shall please God to order out to us in the world; it is not a matter of much concernment, what our outward circumstances are: provided, we make use of them, as a means, to our better preparation for eternity. For whatever our condition is, if we are contented with it, and make it our care to glorify God under it, it will be no hindrance to our future & everlasting well-being. And in order to this, we should meditate upon the present life, under the representation, our text gives of it. And the influence of such meditations, shou'd be to compose our minds, and make us perfectly calm and resign'd to the will of heaven.

Has it pleased God to allow us but a small portion of this world's Goods. Why, a little shou'd content us for a little while: and tis but for a

short time, we shall have our abode here. Or are our circumstances strait
& difficult? Are we hard put to it, and often suffering for want? It cannot
last long. Our lives will soon come to their appointed period. And this is
a consideration, that shou'd restrain discontent, check all misgivings of
heart, & silence our murmurings. Or does God call us to undergo great
tryals & afflictions? It shou'd make us easy, to think they shall shortly have
an end: when, if we have behav'd suitably under them, our reward will be
great, far beyond the proportion of our sufferings. In a word, however
undesirable our present circumstances are, & what ever troubles &
inconveniences we may meet with, we shou'd solace our selves with this,
that if we despise not these chastenings of the Lord, nor faint when
rebuked of him: but are patient, humble and submissive; it won't be long,
before we shall be deliver'd out of all our difficulties, and translated to a
world that is free from all kind of evil; where we shall be compleatly
happy, without interruption for ever.

3. The representation we have had of life, should make us good
husbands of our time, and put us upon improving it to the wisest
purposes. For since, like a vapour, it is so exceeding short and uncertain:
we ought in all reason to redeem our time, and improve the whole of it
to the best advantage; in mortifying our lusts, restraining our appetites,
governing our passions, rectifying our tempers; and in a word,
accomplishing the great work, for which our life is designed. We should
improve all opportunities of doing and getting as much good as we can;
and should avoid all occasions, either of doing hurt to others, or receiving
any of our selves. We should always employ ourselves about something;
and something that shall some how or other turn to a good account. We
should beware of squandering away our time in idleness; unprofitable
chat; too frequent diversions & visits: than which nothing more tends to
wear off that serious temper of mind, that becomes such dying creatures.
In a word, we should labour that our life may be filled up with work, and
that it be such, both as to matter and manner, as shall subserve the interest
of our souls and their eternal salvation: and as that we may have peace in
our latter end. And indeed what more comfortable in an hour of death,
than to be able to look back into a well spent life; carefully employ'd to
the honour of God, the true service of ourselves, and the benefit of our
fellow creatures? As on the contrary, what more cutting and stinging, than
to be forced to reflect upon a useless and unprofitable life? spent to no
purpose at all: or worse than none, in the service of sin and Satan? These
considerations, if there were no other, make it highly worth men's while,
to husband their time well and so improve it to the best advantage.

4. The consideration of life as a vapour, that appeareth but for a little
time, and then vanishes away, should put us upon frequent examination
into our state. Serious self-examination can never be an unsuitable

exercise for such frail short liv'd creatures as we are. And we should be often calling ourselves to an account; looking into our hearts and lives, and inquiring what would become of us, if we should die within a few days, and be called to give up our account. Suppose our case to be like Hezekiah's, who received such a message as that from God, *Thus saith the Lord, set thine house in order, for thou shalt die, and not live.* Or suppose God should say to us, as He did to the rich fool in the Gospel, *This night, shall thy soul be required of thee.* What provision have we made for an amazing eternity? Are we secure of the friendship of God? Are we interested in the merits of the great Redeemer? Is our account ready for our Lord and Judge? Or is God our enemy, and Christ our enemy? Are we wholly unprepared to die? and unmeet for an appearance before the Son of man? These are very serious and solemn inquiries. And whatever the loose and unthinking part of the world, may imagine; they are very proper and seasonable inquiries, for such to make, whose lives, like a vapour, are exceeding short and uncertain. And the consideration that they are so, should put us upon frequent questioning with our selves, after some such manner as this: what if my life should expire within a few months, or days? Yea, what if I should be seiz'd with death, this very day or hour? Where would my poor soul take up its everlasting abode? in heaven or in hell? O let none of us rest satisfy'd, till ye know what our condition is with respect to the eternal world, & how it would fare with us forever, if God should speedily & suddenly call us hence! Can we with ease lie down to sleep, & not know but we may awake in everlasting burnings! Surely we must be dreadfully stupify'd and harden'd, if we can live in quiet, while uncertain what our eternal state is!—

5ly & finally, the representation that has been given of life, should put us upon particular and immediate endeavours to prepare for the time of its expiration. And this is the best improvement, we can make of it. And tis not a matter of indifferency, whether we will make this use of it, yea or no: but of the nearest concern; yea, of absolute necessity. Our well being forever depends upon it. For the present is the only state, wherein we can make provision for eternity. And if we are negligent in an affair of such infinite importance, and leave it undone, we shall perish without any remedy.

And the sooner we set about this great work the better; because when we have in any good measure accomlish'd it, we shall at once have freed ourselves, from that spirit of bondage, which otherwise we might, all our days, have been subject to, by reason of continual fears of death. Besides, the sooner we begin upon this work, the more fit we shall be to engage in it, the better dispos'd to it, and the easier we shall find it. But above all, the utter uncertainty of life discovers the wisdom of a speedy preparation for death.

O let us not then procrastinate in a work of such infinite and everlasting moment! but immediately set about it, and in God's strength pursue it with the utmost vigour & resolution; giving ourselves no rest, till we are in a fair way of going thro' with it.

But perhaps we imagine death to be afar off, and that tis time eno'uh hereafter to think of dying, & in earnest to set about getting ready for it. Multitudes have tho't thus, and have acted under the power of such a vain imagination, to their eternal undoing. God grant this may not be the case of any of us! There is infinite danger of it, while while we put off the tho'ts of death. And yet alas! how apt are we all to do so! We can; but few of us, bear the prospect of dying; and because we are inclin'd to live a great while; we hope we shall; and so live and act, as tho' we certainly should. What madness is this! At what a dreadful hazard, do we put our soul's salvation! Is it not altogether uncertain, how long we shall live? Are we sure of living another day? Yea, can any particular person say, that he shall go alive out of this assembly? And shall we then run ventures in a case, where our everlasting well being is dependant! Is not this infinite & amazing folly! Do we manage thus in the common affairs of life? Should we not be condemned for fools and madmen if we did? And shall we act after this manner, only in that case, wherein if we are surpriz'd in our folly by death, it will be too late to repent of it for ever! Surely we an't appriz'd of the desperate folly we bewray! If we were duly sensible of it, we could not be easy with ourselves; but should, being filled with agony of soul, immediately betake ourselves to God, & peirce even heaven it self with ardent cries for pardoning mercy—.

Or it may be we think a few of our latest days are enough, to be employ'd about the work of preparing ourselves for another world! and that, if we have time, upon a death-bed, to cry to God for mercy, it will be sufficient for our admission into heaven.

To expose the folly of this pretence, I dare not say, as some have done, that a death-bed repentance is impossible; and that, if persons ever obtain salvation in such a case, it must be thro' the unconvenanted mercy of God. Such an opinion as this; as it seems contrary to the tenure of the Bible, so it very much lessens the riches and glory of free grace—.

There is no truly humble penitent, but is a qualify'd object of pardoning mercy; and shall, according to the Gospel convenant, certainly obtain it. And tho' a person, who has been no ways concern'd about his soul, till he comes to lie upon a death-bed, is very unfit for the work of salvation, and has but little reason, comparatively speaking, to expect the aids of divine grace: yet, who can say, but God may dissolve such a sinner into grief & shame; give him a true sight and sense of his sins, and cause him to repent in dust & ashes: and so pluck him, as a fire-brand out of the fire.

This is what the most merciful God may do, if he should so please. Yea, and he has encouraged to hope, this is what he will do; if we have not out sinned the day of his grace, and we are not wanting to our selves. And no sinner, tho' he may have rolled away his days in vanity, and is now just dropping into eternity, has reason to despair of divine mercy. The case of the penitent thief on the cross, seems to have been recorded as an encouragement to such sinners—. And it must be constantly affirmed, that the grace of God, is not confin'd to any particular age or time of life. He may bestow his grace, as upon whomsoever, so whensoever he pleases. And tis past doubt, many have experienced the loving-kindness of God in Christ, in some of their last moments; and instead of going away into everlasting punishment, have inherited eternal life.

But let no sinner encourage himself from the mercy of God, to continue his evil courses, and put off the business of religion, till a dying hour. What can be more base & disingenuous than this? to live in sin all our days, dishonouring and offending God, because he is so merciful and compassionate, as to accept even our latest repentance, rather than we should perish forever; wherein could we discover a more vile ungenerous temper of mind! Surely this goodness of God should work upon our ingenuity, lead us to repentance, & immediately engage us in the divine love & service. This ought to be the influence of such wonderful grace and & mercy: nor unless it is, shall we be able to free ourselves from the charge of the greatest baseness, the blackest ingratitude.

Or if there was nothing of disingenuity in such a proceedure: yet how infinitely unreasonable is it: "What strange tho'ts must men have of God & heaven, & what extravagant conceits of the little evil of sin, and the great easiness of repentance, that can impose upon themselves at this rate?" And how shall we be able to apply our selves to God now, when we have scarce ever had a serious tho't of him all our lives? "Can we have the face to bespeak him in this manner? Lord, now the world and my lusts have left me, and I feel my self ready to sink into eternal perdition, I lay hold upon thy mercy to deliver my soul from going down into the pit. I have heard strange things of thy goodness, and that thou art merciful even to a miracle. This is that which I always trusted to, that after a long life of sin & vanity thou wouldest at last be satisfy'd with a few penitent words & sighs at the hour of death. Let me not, I pray thee, be disappointed of this hope, and put to confusion. Is this an address fit to be made to a wise man, much less to the all-wise and just judge of the world? and yet this seems to be the plain interpretation of the late & forced application of a great & habitual sinner to Almighty God in his last extremity, and when he is just giving up the ghost & going to appear before his dreadful tribunal."

Besides, is a time of sickness and death the most fit season, in which to make preparation for eternity, that we put it off till then? Certainly, if we have had occasion to visit sick chambers, and have taken a view of the circumstances of dying persons, we can never imagine thus! they have now enough to graple with their illness. The whole strength of their nature is laid out in sustaining the infirmities of it. And they have little or no heart to think of their souls, or make provision for their future happiness. Or if they have, they are less fit for this now, than they ever were before. For either their senses are stupify'd, their tho'ts confused and shatter'd, their frame discompos'd: or else their pains are so extream, or their bodies so very weak and faint, as to incapacitate them for the work of getting ready to go out of the world. And O! how many, when upon a death-bed, have, with tears in their eyes, most bitterly lamented their folly, in deferring to make their peace with God till then; they have now found so many difficulties & inconveniences in the way, beyond what they would have done, if they had engaged in this business sooner, and in a more proper time of life.

Furthermore, there is nothing more precarious than a death-bed preparation for another world. Sinners indeed, at such a time, are often in great consternation of mind; their cries for mercy serious &ᵃ affecting, & their vows & promises particular and solemn.—Yet, tis to be fear'd their concern about their state most frequently arises, only from an awaken'd sense of what a fearful thing it is to fall into the hands of the living God. They can't bear to think of going away, to dwell with devouring fire, and to inhabit everlasting burnings. And because they are in distress & agony of soul, they themselves, and perhaps their friends too, are ready to hope for the best, and willing to believe that their sorrows are the sorrows of a repentance unto life: when alas! it may be, they are no ways troubled, that they have offended God and rejected Christ and acted all their days unworthy of themselves, and below the glory of their natures; but are fill'd with horrour at the prospect, of what is like to be the consequence of their evil doings. Many while under apprehensions of death approaching, have been as much terrify'd and as heartily troubled; and have made as fair pretences & as solemn promises: and yet, when God has ransom'd their lives from destruction, they have forgot the anguish of spirit they were in, and return'd to their former folly & wickedness: yea, they have made themselves seven-fold more the children of the devil: whereby they have evidently discovered it to the world, that their repentance was not sincere; and that if they had died, they would have perish'd forever. And no doubt, this is the case of many, whose lives were not spared to them. If they had been raised up again, their repentance would have prov'd it self to have been, nothing more than the terrours of a guilty conscience. In a word, tis a matter of the greatest niceness and difficulty, to determine concerning any death-bed repentance in particular, whether it be sincere and such as God will accept: and after all that can be said, it must & will remain very precarious and uncertain.

Moreover, when we come to lie upon a sick bed, we shan't find the business of getting ready for death and judgment such an easie thing, as at present we may imagine it to be. I doubt not, but most sinners have slight tho'ts of the work of repentance & salvation. They suppose it is but confessing their sins with external signs of sorrow, and putting up a few prayers to God for mercy, and so an entrance shall be ministered unto them abundantly into the everlasting Kingdom of our Lord and Saviour Jesus Christ: and they imagine they can do this as well, just at the point of death, as at any time, and so put it off till then. But O! what amazing folly is this! and how dreadfully do we impose upon ourselves in a matter of the highest moment! Is the work of salvation such an easie one, and so dependant on our own pleasure, that we may thus dally with it? Alas! if God ever give us a true sight and sense of things, we shall have quite different tho'ts of it, and find that we were miserably mistaken. Heaven is not so easily obtained. Tis a great and difficult work to prepare ourselves for it, and we shall certainly find it to be so. And to convince us of this truth, I tho't now to have gone on to tell you, what is included in that preparation for death, that I have been thus long urging upon you. But I see the time will allow me only to observe in general,

That there is a two fold preparation for death, the one habitual, the other actual. The ingredients that constitute the former, are true faith in Christ, an inward rooted aversion to all sin, & a prevailing disposition to universal holiness: in order to which, generally speaking, it is necessary, that we take a great deal of pains in the use of prayer, meditation, reading & hearing God's word, &c. which are the ways, in which he ordinarily makes known the exceeding greatness of his power, in putting persons into a state of salvation. But besides this, there is an actual preparation; which, tho' not of absolute necessity, yet is highly requisite, as tending to a peaceful & comfortable death. And the best way in order to our obtaining this, is to familiarize to ourselves the tho'ts of death; to keep a constant sense of our own frailty upon our minds; to mortify our affections to the world, and place them upon those things that are above: and in a word, to look upon every day of our lives, as not knowing but tit may be our last; and to live & act every day, as tho' we were certain, before the next, our eternal state would be determin'd.

I have now done with my text: and shall only add a few words on the mournful occasion of my discoursing to you upon such a subject at this time, viz. the lamented death of that honourable and vertuous gentlewoman, Mrs. Sarah Byfield, whom, last week, we follow'd to the grave.

For her character, I think my self, in justice to her memory, oblig'd to say,—that as she was honoured by her birth; being daughter to a renowned father of this country, who, for several years, with universal love and reverence, sat in the first chair of government over it; so that her temper & conduct were every way worthy of such distinguished parentage.

She had naturally a weak & tender body; but a strong & noble soul: which, being cultivated & enrich'd by a good education and great industry, render'd her truly amiable & desirable; and fitted her to be a blessing in the station Providence had assign'd her.

Her temper was lively & chearful; yet far from light & vain: being well ballast by a singular discretion. In her most pleasant hours, she was never unfit to enter upon a serious subject, and always treated it with a becoming gravity and reverence.

She had a good taste in conversation, and was excellently well turn'd for it: having a ready wit; a sprightly genius; an easy smooth way of expressing herself; and being able, without stiffness or ostentation, to be both entertaining and profitable.

She was a person of great sincerity & plainheartedness; meek & humble; patient & resign'd: which she had frequent opportunities of discovering, by reason of those many indispositions, that were inseparable from so brittle a constitution.

In a word, she was an honour to her sex, in her exemplary deportment under all the various characters & relations of life: as a neighbour, kind & pitiful: as a friend, true & hearty; without disguise & abhorrent to flattery and deceit: as a wife, tender & dutiful; engaging in her carriage; reverent & respectful: as mistress in a family, discreet in her management; a lover of good order; neat & cleanly; tho'tful of all under her care; indulgent & compassionate to her servants: especially concern'd about their souls, and frequent in teaching them the good knowledge of the Lord; in her treatment of strangers, hospitable; courteous, pleasant, obliging & edifying to those that came to visit her.

But her chief excellency, & what most recommended to all that knew her, was her undissembled piety. She had an habitual prevailing awe and reverence of God upon her heart: which early discovered it self, and all along thro' the course of her life, not only in an utter abhorrence of every thing that savour'd of prophanness & irreverence; but in a due treatment of those things, wherein the divine honour is nearly concern'd. She lov'd the house, & sanctify'd the day of God; gave her constant devout attendance on the publick worship, and all Gospel ordinances; paid a singular regard to the Holy Scriptures; valued the ministers of religion; and had an universal regard to all good men. But above all, Christ was the object of her love, her faith, her hope. It was in her account a faithful saying, and the esteem'd it worthy of all acceptation, that Christ Jesus was come into the world to save sinners. Him therefore she embrac'd as the alone redeemer of souls; Him she trusted with the great affair of her eternal salvation; Him she lov'd with her whole heart; Him she made it her care to please in all things; His image she was adorn'd with; & the graces of His spirit she liv'd in the daily exercise of: and we charitably believe she is gone to be with Christ, which is best of all.

I doubt not, but the mourning friends & relatives have often refresh'd their souls, by looking back to her past conversation in Christ; and then by turning their view forward to those unutterable glories, she is now possess'd of, in the place of God has ordain'd for the spirits of believers, in their separate state. And while by faith, they are beholding her, as in the bosome of Jesus, I may well suppose, they grieve not for her; but rather rejoyce, that she is got beyond the reach of sorrow, the power of temptation and the possibility of sinning; and that she is entred upon the reward of righteousness, which is joy & peace, quietness & assurance for ever: yet upon their own accounts, they may have reason to mourn, and stand in need of consolation.

We heartily wish, for all the relatives, divine support under this tryal of their faith; the comforting presence of the Holy Ghost; and the sanctifying influences of supernatural grace, whereby they may be enabled, so to behave themselves, as that God may be honour'd their own holiness increased, and their future & eternal weight of glory inhanced.

And particularly, we would sympathize with that aged & honourable servant of God, who was most nearly related to the person deceased. You little tho't to appear in mourning for one, you expected and desir'd shou'd follow you to the grave. Yet so the sovereign God has order'd it! He has taken from you the pleasant companion of your age, who might have been the helper of it's griefs, and render'd it far more easie and desirable to you! But be dumb with silence;—meekly bear this chastening of the Lord;—take a realizing view of it, as coming from your covenant God and Father, who never afflicts willingly, nor grieves his children:—adore the sovereignty, the wisdom, the righteousness and holiness of this providence.—Let it be your chief care so to carry your self under it, as to give a bright example of subjection to the father of spirits; of humility, patience, resignation—and may it serve to make you a partaker of the divine nature in still greater measures, and so advance you yet further in your preparedness for that eternal happy state, you hope and long for, and are arrived at the confines of!—we heartily pray God to be the staff of your age, your joy and comfort thro' the remaining part of your life; your guide thro' death, and when your flesh and heart faileth, the strength of your heart and your God forever.

To conclude: the death even of women of so distinguish'd a character is a publick loss: and we shou'd resent it as such;—and be importunate in our cries to the God of all Grace, that as he removes them away by death, so that he would raise up others of the same excellent spirit to supply their place, and make good their ground—we should all lay the deaths of such persons to heart—particularly our women shou'd do so, and labour to imitate them in those things that were vertuous and praise-worthy. And it is to be wish'd for all our women, that they may be well reported of for good works being in behaviour as becometh Godliness; not false accusers; not given to much wine: teachers of good things; sober, lovers of their husbands; lovers of their children; discreet; chast; keepers at home; good; obedient to their own husbands, that the word of God be not blasphemed. In like manner also, that they adorn themselves in modest apparel, with shame-facedness & sobriety;—and (which becometh women professing godliness) with good works. Amen.

# JONATHAN MAYHEW
## (1720-1766)

# A DISCOURSE CONCERNING
# UNLIMITED SUBMISSION
### (Boston, 1750)

IF WE calmly consider the nature of the thing itself, nothing can well be imagined more directly contrary to common sense, than to suppose that millions of people should be subjected to the arbitrary, precarious pleasure of one single man; (who has naturally no superiority over them in point of authority) so that their estates, and every thing that is valuable in life, and even their lives also, shall be absolutely at his disposal, if he happens to be wanton and capricious enough to demand them. What unprejudiced man can think, that God made all to be thus subservient to the lawless pleasure and phrenzy of one, so that it shall always be a sin to resist him! Nothing but the most plain and express revelation from heaven could make a sober impartial man believe such a monstrous, unaccountable doctrine, and, indeed, the thing itself, appears so shocking—so out of all proportion, that it may be questioned, whether all the miracles that ever were wrought, could make it credible, that this doctrine really came from God. At present, there is not the least syllable in Scripture which gives any countenance to it. The hereditary, indefeasible, divine right of kings, and the doctrine of non-resistance, which is built upon the supposition of such a right, are altogether as fabulous and chimerical, as transubstantiation; or any of the most absurd reveries of ancient or modern visionaries. These notions are fetched neither from divine revelation, nor human reason; and if they are derived from neither of those sources, it is not much matter from whence they come, or whither they go. Only it is a pity that such doctrines should be propagated in society, to raise factions and rebellions, as we see they have, in fact, been both in the last, and in the present, reign.

But then, if unlimited submission and passive obedience to the higher powers, in all possible cases, be not a duty, it will be asked, "How far are we obliged to submit? If we may innocently disobey and resist in some cases, why not in all? Where shall we stop? What is the measure of our duty? This doctrine tends to the total dissolution of civil government; and to introduce such scenes of wild anarchy and confusion, as are more fatal to society than the worst of tyranny."

After this manner, some men object; and, indeed, this is the most plausible thing that can be said in favor of such an absolute submission as they plead for. But the worst (or rather the best) of it, is, that there is very little strength or solidity in it. For similar difficulties may be raised with respect to almost every duty of natural and revealed religion.—To instance only in two, both of which are near akin, and indeed exactly parallel, to the case before us. It is unquestionably the duty of children to submit to their parents; and of servants, to their masters. But no one asserts, that it is their duty to obey, and submit to them, in all supposeable cases; or universally a sin to resist them. Now does this tend to subvert the just authority of parents and masters? Or to introduce confusion and anarchy into private families? No. How then does the same principle tend to unhinge the government of that larger family, the body politic? We know, in general, that children and servants are obliged to obey their parents and masters respectively. We know also, with equal certainty, that they are not obliged to submit to them in all things, without exception; but may, in some cases, reasonably, and therefore innocently, resist them. These principles are acknowledged upon all hands, whatever difficulty there may be in fixing the exact limits of submission. Now there is at least as much difficulty in stating the measure of duty in these two cases, as in the case of rulers and subjects. So that this is really no objection, at least no reasonable one, against resistance to the higher powers: Or, if it is one, it will hold equally against resistance in the other cases mentioned.—It is indeed true, that turbulent, vicious-minded men, may take occasion from this principle, that their rulers may, in some cases, be lawfully resisted, to raise factions and disturbances in the state; and to make resistance where resistance is needless, and therefore, sinful. But is it not equally true, that children and servants of turbulent, vicious minds, may take occasion from this principle, that parents and masters may, in some cases be lawfully resisted, to resist when resistance is unnecessary, and therefore, criminal? Is the principle in either case false in itself, merely because it may be abused; and applied to legitimate disobedience and resistance in those instances, to which it ought not to be applied? According to this way of arguing, there will be no true principles in the world; for there are none but what may be wrested and perverted to serve bad purposes, either through the weakness or wickedness of men.*

A people, really oppressed to a great degree by their sovereign, cannot well be insensible when they are so oppressed. And such a people (if I may allude to an ancient fable) have, like the hesperian fruit, a dragon for their protector and guardian: Nor would they have any reason to mourn, if some Hercules should appear to dispatch him—For a nation thus abused to arise unanimously, and to resist their prince, even to the dethroning him, is not criminal; but a reasonable way of vindicating their liberties and just rights; it is making use of the means, and the only means, which God has put into their power, for mutual and self-defence. And it would be highly criminal in them, not to make use of this means. It would be stupid tameness, and unaccountable folly, for whole nations to suffer one unreasonable, ambitious and cruel man, to wanton and riot in their misery. And in such a case it would, of the two, be more rational to suppose, that they that did not resist, than that they who did, would receive to themselves damnation.

---

*We may very safely assert these two things in general, without undermining government: one is, That no civil rulers are to be obeyed when they enjoin things that are inconsistent with the commands of God: all such disobedience is lawful and glorious; particularly, if persons refuse to comply with any legal establishment of religion, because it is a gross perversion and corruption (as to doctrine, worship and discipline) of a pure and divine religion, brought from heaven to earth by the Son of God, (the only king and head of the Christian church) and propagated through the world by his inspired Apostles. All commands running counter to the declared will of the supreme legislator of heaven and earth, are null and void: and therefore disobedience to them is a duty, not a crime. . . . Another thing that may be asserted with equal truth and safety, is, that no government is to be submitted to, at the expence of that which is the sole end of all government,—the common good and safety of society. Because, to submit in this case, if it should ever happen, would evidently be to set up the means as more valuable, and above, the end: than which there cannot be a greater solecism and contradiction. The only reason of the institution of civil government; and the only rational ground of submission to it, is the common safety and utility. If therefore, in any case, the common safety and utility would not be promoted by submission to government, but the contrary, there is no ground or motive for obedience and submission, but, for the contrary.

Whoever considers the nature of civil government must, indeed, be sensible that a great degree of implicit confidence, must unavoidably be placed in those that bear rule: this is implied in the very notion of authority's being originally a trust, committed by the people, to those who are vested with it, as all just and righteous authority is; all besides, is mere lawless force and usurpation; neither God nor nature, having given any man a right of dominion over any society, independently of that society's approbation, and consent to be governed by him—now as all men are fallible, it cannot be supposed that the public affairs of any state, should be always administered in the best manner possible, even by persons of the greatest wisdom and integrity. Nor is it sufficient to legitimate disobedience to the higher powers that they are not so administered; or that they are, in some instances, very ill-managed; for upon this principle, it is scarcely supposeable that any government at all could be supported, or subsist. Such a principle manifestly tends to the dissolution of government; and to throw all things into confusion and anarchy.—But it is equally evident, upon the other hand, that those in authority may abuse their trust and power to such a degree, that neither the law of reason, nor of religion, requires, that any obedience or submission should be paid to them; but, on the contrary, that they should be totally discarded; and the authority which they were before vested with, transferred to others, who may exercise it more to those good purposes for which it is given.—Nor is this principle, that resistance to the higher powers, is, in some extraordinary cases, justifiable, so liable to abuse, as many persons seem to apprehend it. For although there will be always some petulant, querulous men, in every state—men of factious, turbulent and carping dispositions,—glad to lay hold of any trifle to justify and legitimate their caballing against their rulers, and other seditious practices; yet there are, comparatively speaking, but few men of this contemptible character: It does not appear but that mankind, in general, have a disposition to be as submissive and passive and tame under government as they ought to be.—Witness a great, if not the greatest, part of the known world, who are now groaning, but not murmuring, under the heavy yoke of tyranny! While those who govern; do it with any tolerable degree of moderation and justice, and, in any good measure act up to their office and character, by being public benefactors; the people will generally be easy and peaceable; and be rather inclined to flatter and adore, than to insult and resist, them. Nor was there ever any general complaint against any administration, which lasted long, but what there was good reason for. Till people find themselves greatly abused and oppressed by their governors, they are not apt to complain; and whenever they do, in fact, find themselves thus abused and oppressed, they must be stupid not to complain. To say that subjects in general are not proper judges when their governors oppress them, and play the tyrant; and when they defend their rights, administer justice impartially, and promote the public welfare, is as great treason as ever man uttered;—'tis treason,—not against one single man, but the state—against the whole body politic;—'tis treason against mankind;—'tis treason against common sense;—'tis treason against God. And this impious principle lays the foundation for justifying all the tyranny and oppression that ever any prince was guilty of. The people know for what end they set up, and maintain, their governors; and they are the proper judges when they execute their trust as they ought to do it;—when their prince exercises an equitable and paternal authority over them;—when from a prince and common father, he exalts himself into a tyrant—when from subjects and children, he degrades them into the class of slaves;—plunders them, makes them his prey, and unnaturally sports himself with their lives and fortunes—